Human Rights

Second Edition

Key Concepts series

HUMAN RIGHTS
An Interdisciplinary Approach

Second Edition

Michael Freeman

polity

First published in 2011 by Polity Press
Reprinted 2011, 2012

Polity Press
65 Bridge Street
Cambridge CB2 1UR, UK

Polity Press
350 Main Street
Malden, MA 02148, USA

ISBN-13: 978-0-7456-3965-9
ISBN-13: 978-0-7456-3966-6 (pb)

A catalogue record for this book is available from the British Library.

Typeset in 10.5 on 12 pt Sabon
by Toppan Best-set Premedia Limited
Printed and bound in Great Britain by the MPG Books Group

The publisher has used its best endeavours to ensure that the URLs for external websites referred to in this book are correct and active at the time of going to press. However, the publisher has no responsibility for the websites and can make no guarantee that a site will remain live or that the content is or will remain appropriate.

Every effort has been made to trace all copyright holders, but if any have been inadvertently overlooked the publisher will be pleased to include any necessary credits in any subsequent reprint or edition.

For further information on Polity, visit our website: www.politybooks.com

Contents

Preface to the Second Edition

The first edition of this book was completed late in 2001. Although the attack on the USA on September 11, 2001 ('9/11') had taken place, I was unable at the time to see its implications for human rights. This second edition therefore includes a discussion of terrorism and the 'global war on terror', and the implications of the election of President Barack Obama.

The event that did cast a shadow over the first edition was NATO's war against Serbia-Montenegro over Kosovo. This posed complex questions for human rights (and divided human-rights supporters) because: 1) it was almost certainly illegal; 2) it had a very plausible humanitarian and/or human-rights justification; 3) it undermined the dictatorship of Slobodan Milošević; 4) it was a *war*, and wars at best raise difficult questions for human-rights supporters. Since 9/11, the USA and its allies have invaded Afghanistan and Iraq. Both countries had experienced gross human-rights violations under the regimes of the Taliban and Saddam Hussein respectively, but both military actions were very controversial, especially that in Iraq. The international community had been severely criticized for *not* intervening to prevent the genocide in Rwanda in 1994, and, while the intervention in Iraq attracted much criticism, the failure to intervene in Darfur, Sudan, where hundreds of thousands of people were being killed, and millions displaced, was also deplored. The question of humanitarian intervention, which had a long history in thought about international law and international relations, had become a leading issue for the theory and practice of human rights. Discussion of this topic, too, is included in this edition.

Another change that has taken place since the first edition is less dramatic, but may be as important. Two global phenomena appear to be occurring, may be interrelated, and will probably have a massive impact on human rights. These are now commonly captured by the terms 'globalization' and 'climate change'. Human rights have traditionally been conceived, in both international law and political theory, as claims by, or protections for, individuals against states or governments. There is now a concern that some non-state organizations, such as multinational corporations, or transnational *processes*, such as international trade negotiations, may themselves be causes of human-rights violations. The workings of the global economy are immensely complex, technical and controversial. Nevertheless, human-rights activists are beginning to come to grips with their implications for human rights. Although climate change is now much in the news, its possible consequences for human rights are rarely mentioned. This is another technical and controversial topic, but it may be that climate change will kill more people than do many dictators. Determining what the problem is, and what the best solutions are, presents mind-boggling challenges which inevitably raise questions about the adequacy of traditional models of human rights.

The field of human rights was once populated mainly by male adults: male-dominated governments persecuted mainly male dissidents. More recently, however, the question of women's rights has become an increasingly prominent part of the human-rights agenda. Likewise, while children were once regarded as victims of human-rights violations indirectly, as the result of the persecution of their parents, nowadays issues such as child labour and child soldiers have received much attention. The human rights of women and children raise a wide range of issues – from inheritance laws to domestic violence, and including infant and maternal mortality – but one issue in particular has emerged to demand attention: the fate of women and children in war. It has been widely observed that, in recent years, war between states has decreased, while armed conflict is increasingly dominated by civil wars. Modern hi-tech warfare has for some time made civilians into victims of war, but it is becoming clear that women and children are as likely, and in some cases more likely, to become victims, compared with men. As I claimed in the first edition of this book, the highlighting of women's rights has been 'one of the most significant shifts in the interpretation of human rights in international politics since the end of the Cold War'.

A final development that has taken place since the first edition has been the growth of interdisciplinary approaches to human rights. Many research institutes and degree schemes at Master's level have been established recently that, in different ways, take an interdisciplinary approach. The dominance of legal analyses of human rights has to some extent been challenged, and the long sleep of the social science of human rights is beginning to come to an end. Nevertheless, the field of human rights is still predominantly legalistic. It might be argued that human rights are *conceptually* legal: to have a right is to have a legal claim, whether that claim be grounded in natural and/or in positive law. This is more plausible in languages other than English. The word *droit* in French, for example, can be translated either as 'right' or 'law'. Alternatively, it might be said that human rights are effective only if embodied in legal systems. But even if this is true, some of the most important questions about human rights cannot be answered by legal analysis. What, for example, do the texts of human-rights law *mean*? Are they (ethically, rationally) justifiable? How can we best explain the variable extent of compliance with international human-rights law? What difference (if any) does human-rights law make to the lives of ordinary people? How do human-rights claims relate to the 'tough choices' that governments have to make among priorities in situations of scarce resources? Can human rights conflict with each other? If so, how should we resolve such conflicts? It is questions such as these that philosophy and the social sciences are better suited than legal analysis to answer.

Although there has been some progress in the social science of human rights since the publication of the first edition, it has been slight compared with the challenges that science now faces. It is one task of this second edition to record, and to evaluate, this progress, in the hope of pointing the way to future research that may prove theoretically and practically useful.

I am reluctant to add to the acknowledgements included in the first edition, not because I have not since become indebted to numerous other scholars, but because it is likely that I will omit some that I should not. I will, however, take that risk in order to thank in particular Richard Claude, Stan Cohen, Richard Wilson, Wiktor Osyatinksi, Saladin Meckled-Garcia and Basak Çali.

Michael Freeman
University of Essex
September 2010

Acknowledgements

One evening in the autumn of 1977, Nick Bunnin, then teaching in the Department of Philosophy at the University of Essex, invited me to accompany him to a meeting of Amnesty International in Colchester. I agreed, reluctantly (for no reason other than laziness), but ended that evening as Chairperson of the newly formed Colchester Group of Amnesty International. This book would never have been written were it not for Nick Bunnin and my colleagues – local, national and international – at Amnesty. I would like to remember particularly the late Peter Duffy, whose moral commitment and intellectual rigour made him an exemplary human-rights activist.

I hesitate to list those to whom this book owes an intellectual debt, for fear of omitting many unfairly. I would, nevertheless, like to thank Onora O'Neill, Sheldon Leader, Nigel Rodley, Françoise Hampson, Geoff Gilbert, Brian Barry, Alan Ryan, Albert Weale, Tom Sorell, the late Deborah Fitzmaurice, Matthew Clayton, Marcus Roberts, Andrew Fagan, David Beetham, Peter Jones, Simon Caney, Hillel Steiner, Bhikhu Parekh, Brenda Almond, Paul Gilbert, Peter Baehr, David Forsythe, Jack Donnelly, Rhoda Howard-Hassmann, Joseph Chan, Julia Tao, Will Kymlicka, Barry Clarke, Hugh Ward, John Gray and David Robertson.

I have learned a great deal from students in the Department of Government and the Human Rights Centre at the

University of Essex, far too numerous to mention. I have been invited to teach and learn about human rights in many countries, from China to Brazil, and cannot emphasize too much how important the ensuing cross-cultural dialogue has been.

None of the above is, of course, responsible for the errors in this book, which I have managed on my own. The book is dedicated to June, Saul and Esther with love and admiration. Without them, especially, it would not have been possible.

Michael Freeman
University of Essex
February 2002

1
Introduction
Thinking about Human Rights

Realities

On a visit to Darfur, a region of western Sudan, Nicholas Kristof, a journalist on the *New York Times*, arrived at an oasis where tens of thousands of people were sheltering under trees after having been driven from their villages by *Janjaweed* militia, supported by the government of Sudan. He describes what he saw there:

> Under the first tree, I found a man who had been shot in the neck and the jaw; his brother, shot only in the foot, had carried him for forty-nine days to get to this oasis. Under the next tree was a widow whose parents had been killed and stuffed in the village well to poison the local water supply; then the Janjaweed had tracked down the rest of her family and killed her husband. Under the third tree was a four-year-old orphan girl carrying her one-year-old baby sister on her back; their parents had been killed. Under the fourth tree was a woman whose husband and children had been killed in front of her, and then she was gang-raped and left naked and mutilated in the desert. (Kristof 2006: 14)

This report will arouse various emotions in those who can bear to read it: horror, sympathy, outrage. We may struggle to find words adequate to express our emotions. These are 'atrocities', we may say, or 'crimes against humanity'. We may demand that someone should stop them, although we may well not be clear who should do what to bring this about. We may ask why such things happen.

These terrible events are the product of complex historical, political and economic processes. Darfur is composed of many ethnic groups, all Muslim. It has suffered from economic and social neglect since colonial times. Nevertheless, it was relatively stable until recently, even though a long and brutal civil war had been waged between the government of Sudan and the Muslim north of the country against the mainly Christian south. The peace of Darfur was unsettled by a number of different factors: increased competition between farmers and nomads for land resources that were diminishing as a result of desertification; the emergence of a racist ideology in Sudan distinguishing supposedly superior Arabs from supposedly inferior Africans; the expansionist policies of Libya's Colonel Gaddafi in neighbouring Chad that destabilized the Sudan–Chad border with movements of insurgents and refugees; and the intrusion of southern Sudanese rebels. Darfurian self-defence organizations developed into a number of rebel forces. The Sudanese government sought to repress these rebellions by a savage counter-insurgency, employing Arab militias known as the *Janjaweed* ('evil horsemen'). A peace agreement was signed on 5 May 2006 by the Sudanese government and the largest rebel group, but not by other rebels. It has been estimated that at least 200,000 people were killed in the period 2003–6, more than two million were displaced, and more than four million have suffered deprivation on both sides of the Darfur–Chad border (Reeves 2006). (The population of Darfur is approximately six million).

Many people in many countries have been victims of state violence in recent times. Government forces massacred more than half a million civilians in Indonesia in the mid-1960s in an attempt to suppress Communism. Estimates of the number of people killed by the Khmer Rouge regime of Pol Pot in Cambodia are as high as 2.2 million, or between one-quarter and one-third of the entire population. More than 9,000 people 'disappeared' under the military government in Argentina in the late 1970s. During the rule of Idi Amin in

Uganda from 1972 to 1978 more than 250,000 people were killed. Hundreds of thousands of civilians were murdered by security forces in Iraq during the 1980s. Between 1980 and 1992 almost two per cent of the population of El Salvador is estimated to have died as the result of 'disappearances' and political killings during the civil war (Amnesty International 1993: 2). In 1994 between 500,000 and 1,000,000 people were killed in the government-directed genocide in Rwanda (Glover 1999: 120). This list is far from complete. It does not include Bosnia, Chechnya, Kosovo, East Timor, Iraq since the invasion of 2003, and many other places.

The concept of human rights provides a way of thinking about such events. As you read these words, there will probably be reports in the newspapers, and on radio, television, the internet and other 'new media', of similar cruelties and injustices elsewhere. These are stories about the violation of human rights. These events are all too real, but 'human rights' is a *concept*. It is a device for thinking about the real, and for expressing our thoughts. If we are to understand the discourse of human rights, we must analyse this concept. It is, however, easier to respond with sympathetic emotion to stories like those of the Darfurians than to analyse our concepts so that they are clear, precise and coherent. The understanding of concepts is the goal of the philosophical discipline of *conceptual analysis*. The concept of 'human rights', however, presents a challenge to this discipline. Concepts are abstract, and conceptual analysis is an abstract discipline. It can seem remote from the experiences of human beings. The analysis of the concept of human rights, therefore, must be combined with a sympathetic understanding of the human experiences to which the concept refers.

If conceptual analysis is both necessary and problematic for understanding human rights, so is statistical analysis. R. J. Rummel has calculated that governments murdered at least 169,202,000 persons in the twentieth century. According to his estimates, more than 45,000,000 political murders occurred between 1945 and the early 1990s (Rummel 1994: chapters 1–2). These statistics are important, but they can easily numb our sense of the human suffering involved. Human-rights violations are facts that can sometimes be best expressed in terms of numbers, but there is an uneasy relationship between our knowledge of the numbers and our understanding of what they mean.

We do not need the concept of 'human rights' to know and to say that these things are wrong. We do, however, need a *reason* to oppose them. If reality violates human rights, why should we take the side of human rights, and not that of reality? How do we know that there are any human rights? Such questions were posed, to challenge us, by the philosopher, Jean Améry, who survived the Nazi extermination camp at Auschwitz. Perhaps, he considered, the Nazis were right because they were the stronger. Perhaps people had no rights. Perhaps all moral concepts were mere fashions. Was this not the reality of history? After all, classical Greek civilization was based on slavery and massacre. Was Nazi Germany any different (Glover 1999: 40)?

Glover has suggested that, for most people, most of the time, the virtues that matter are personal and narrow in scope. In everyday life, ordinary kindness is more important than human rights (Glover 1999: 41). Ordinary people, however, are sometimes not permitted such an everyday life. Instead, they may get terror, massacres, mass rapes and 'ethnic cleansing'. The concept of human rights becomes relevant to ordinary people when the relative security of everyday life is absent or snatched away. It has been said that human rights are most needed when they are most violated. Where they are generally well respected, we tend to take them for granted, and may consequently underestimate their importance.

The concept of human rights is, to a considerable extent, though not wholly *legal*. It first appeared on the international agenda when the United Nations Charter declared in 1945 that the UN was determined 'to reaffirm faith in fundamental human rights, in the dignity and worth of the human person, in the equal rights of men and women and of nations large and small'. The fountain-head of human-rights law is the Universal Declaration of Human Rights, which was adopted by the UN General Assembly on 10 December 1948. This Declaration has, according to Morsink, 'profoundly changed the international landscape, scattering it with human rights protocols, conventions, treaties, and derivative declarations of all kinds'. There is now 'not a single nation, culture or people that is not in one way or another enmeshed in human rights regimes' (Morsink 1999: x). The Declaration was adopted in the aftermath of the victorious war against Fascism, and in a spirit of idealism. It was proclaimed to be 'a common standard of achievement for all peoples and all nations'. All human beings, Article 1 affirms, 'are born free and equal in dignity and rights'. Everyone, Article 2 states, 'is entitled to all the rights and freedoms set forth in this Declaration without discrimination of any kind, such as race, colour, sex, language, religion, political or other opinion, national or social origin, property, birth or other status'.

There is obviously a wide gap between the promises of the 1948 Declaration and the real world of human-rights violations. In so far as we sympathize with the victims, we may criticize the UN and its member governments for failing to keep their promises. However, we cannot understand the gap between human-rights ideals and the real world of human-rights violations by sympathy or by legal analysis. Rather, it requires investigation by the various social sciences of the causes of social conflict and political oppression, and of the interaction between national and international politics. The UN introduced the concept of human rights into international law and politics. The field of international politics is, however, dominated by states and other powerful actors (such as multinational corporations) that have priorities other than human rights. It is a leading feature of the human-rights field that the governments of the world proclaim human rights but have a highly variable record of implementing them. We must understand why this is so.

Concepts

The concept of human rights raises further difficulties because it stretches well beyond cases of extreme cruelty and injustice. Article 1 of the Universal Declaration, for example, states that all human beings are equal in rights. Article 18 says that everyone has the right to freedom of religion. How should we define the right to freedom of religion of those whose religion denies that all human beings are equal in rights? How can we make sense of human rights if the implementation of some human rights requires the violation of others? Here the problem of implementing human-rights ideals derives not from lack of political will or conflicts of political interests, but from the fact that human rights may not be 'compossible', that is, the implementation of one human right may require the violation of another, or the protection of a human right of one person may require the violation of the *same* human right of another. If a religious group, for example, forbids its members, on the basis of its religious beliefs, to change their religion, then the religious freedom of the group will conflict with that of any members who wish to change their religion. If we support human rights that are not compossible, our thinking must surely be confused.

The problem of compossibility has been aggravated by what has been called 'rights inflation', that is, the extension of the concept of human rights to an ill-defined number of causes. There are controversial human rights even in the Universal Declaration, such as the right to 'periodic holidays with pay'. If the concept of human rights is to be useful, we must distinguish human rights from other social demands. Courts may decide rather precisely the legal rights of those who appear before them. Human rights are rather vaguely worded, and their meaning is not always settled in courts of law. The determination of the meaning of human rights is a continuing *social* process that involves not only legal professionals (such as judges, UN experts and academic lawyers) but also various 'stakeholders' (such as governments, intergovernmental organizations, non-governmental organizations, non-legal academics and citizens). If the concept of human rights is to be useful, we must distinguish *human* rights from the *legal* rights of particular societies, and from other desirable social objectives.

What are 'rights', and how do 'human rights' differ from other kinds of rights? The concept of 'rights' is closely connected to that of 'right'. Something is 'right' if it conforms with a standard of rightness. All societies have such standards, but it is often said that many cultures have no conception of people 'having rights'. The idea of everyone having 'human rights' is said to be especially alien to most cultures. MacIntyre has argued that human rights do not exist. Belief in human rights is like belief in witches and unicorns; it is superstition (MacIntyre 1981: 67).

MacIntyre's mistake is to think of 'human rights' as 'things' that we could 'have' as we have arms and legs. This mistake is admittedly embedded in the language of rights, for we do speak of our 'having' rights. Rights are, however, not mysterious *things* that have the puzzling quality of not existing, but *just claims* or *entitlements* that derive from moral and/or legal rules. This conception of rights defeats MacIntyre's objection because it is not 'superstitious' to believe that human beings ought to be entitled to a certain kind of respect. The justification of human rights requires a *theory* of human rights. The problem of *validating* the concept of human rights lies partly in the general problem of validating beliefs, and does not arise only from supposed defects in the concept of human rights.

The social sciences

Until quite recently, social scientists had largely neglected the concept of human rights. The aspiration to be 'scientific' marginalized the legal and moral conceptions of human rights. However, the increasing importance of the concept in national and international politics has stimulated the interest of some social scientists. The explanation of variations in respect for human rights in different societies has been accepted as a proper object of social-scientific investigation. It is sometimes said that gross human-rights violations – such as genocide – are 'irrational' and beyond scientific explanation. There is, however, a body of knowledge about state behaviour, ethnic diversity, repression, rebellion and social conflict that may explain a great deal about such actions. While there is much controversy about theories and methodology in the social sciences, there is no reason why behaviour that either violates or respects human rights should be intrinsically less explicable than any other complex social phenomena.

The academic study of human rights has been dominated by lawyers. This may be explained by the fact that the concept has been developed to a large extent through national and international law. The field of human rights has become a technical, legal discourse, and lawyers dominate it because they are the technical experts. Law appears to provide 'objective' standards that 'protect' the concept of human rights from moral and political controversy. This appearance is, however, illusory, for the meaning and application of human-rights standards is legally and politically very controversial. International human-rights law is made by governments that act from political motives. The extent to which they implement human-rights law is influenced by political factors. Non-governmental organizations (NGOs) – which have come to play an increasingly important role in the making of human-rights law, monitoring its implementation and campaigning for improved human-rights performance by governments – are political actors, even if they appeal to legal standards. Major human-rights changes, such as those which took place in the Communist societies of central and eastern Europe, in Latin America, South Africa and elsewhere towards the end of the twentieth century, were primarily political events.

The study of international politics has been dominated by the theory of Realism, which is primarily concerned with the interests and power of states rather than with such ethical issues as those of human rights. The academic discipline of International Relations has recently shown some interest in human rights (Forsythe 2006), but the topic remains marginal. Some International Relations scholars challenge the Realist school by emphasizing the role of ideas in general, and of human-rights ideas in particular, in international politics (Risse, Ropp and Sikkink 1999). The study of human rights in international politics has, however, with a few notable exceptions, fallen between international law, which is not systematically empirical, and International Relations, which has neglected human rights for the supposed 'realities' of state power.

The neglect of human rights by the social sciences and the domination of human-rights studies by lawyers distort the concept of human rights. In the classic theory of 'natural rights' developed by John Locke in the seventeenth century, every human being had certain rights that derived from their nature, and not from their government or its laws, and the legitimacy of government rested on the respect that it accorded to these rights (Locke [1689] 1970). The modern concept of human rights is a reformulation of this idea, and refers primarily to the relations between governments and their citizens. Political theory is the discipline that explains and evaluates these relations. Political science is the discipline that describes and explains the variations in the degree to which governments respect their citizens' rights. The contribution of political science to the study of human rights has, however, been limited. The study of human-rights issues has sometimes been carried out with the use of related concepts such as 'dictatorship', 'totalitarianism', 'authoritarianism', 'repression', 'state terror' and 'genocide'. There is also much work in political science on democracy that is relevant to understanding the current state of human rights. The desire of political scientists to be 'scientific', however, has led them to neglect a concept that appears at worst moralistic, and at best legalistic. Slowly, this neglect is being overcome (Landman 2005b).

The Western tradition of political theory has produced many formidable critics of such rights. This presents a strong challenge to the political science of human rights, especially since the classical critics are echoed by contemporary theorists. Underlying any social sciences of human rights, therefore, are a number of controversial philosophical assumptions. This does not, however, distinguish the social science of human rights from other branches of social science, such as the politics of democracy or the sociology of inequality. Nevertheless, it requires the social scientist of human rights to be aware of these philosophical controversies.

Sociologists and anthropologists have recently begun to contribute to human-rights studies (Wilson and Mitchell 2003; Woodiwiss 2005). The impact of the global economy on the protection of human rights has increasingly become a subject of study (Dine and Fagan 2006). This has been accompanied by an interest in 'the human-rights movement' as a transnational social movement (Risse, Ropp and Sikkink 1999). There are, then, signs that the social science of human rights is beginning to wake up.

Beyond human-rights law

International law was traditionally concerned with regulating the relations among states with the primary aim of maintaining international peace. The leading concept of this project was that of *state sovereignty*, which forbade states from interfering in each other's internal affairs. The UN introduced the concept of human rights into international law without altering the concept of sovereignty. This legal framework is, however, subject to intense political pressures, as states and other actors seek to realize their interests and their principles in the international arena. The implementation of human rights by the UN is, therefore, highly politicized, and this leads to selective attention to human-rights problems, political bargaining and delays. The UN is not a utopian realm above politics, and the political character of human-rights implementation is unavoidable. The politics of human rights is not, however, always harmful to human rights, for governments may raise genuine human-rights issues from political motives, and, when such motives lead to a narrow and selective concern for human rights, appeals are sometimes made to human-rights principles that can be applied more widely.

The implementation of the UN's human-rights principles was seriously delayed and distorted for many years by the politics of the Cold War. The UN proclaimed human rights, but did little to implement them. The cost of proclaiming human rights is low, and many governments, in the conditions of the Cold War, thought that they had much to lose by respecting the human rights of their sometimes highly discontented citizens. In this context, what is at first sight surprising was the development, albeit slow, of international human-rights law, and of a movement of non-governmental organizations to campaign for its implementation. This situation placed the UN in an ambiguous position. It was, on the one hand, the author and guardian of international human-rights standards, while, on the other hand, it was an association of governments that were often serious human-rights violators. As a consequence, the UN has been the central institution where international human-rights law and politics have met, and often clashed, and where the gap between human-rights ideals and realities is especially apparent.

The political character of human rights has philosophical implications. The lawyers who dominate human-rights studies sometimes rely, explicitly or implicitly, on the philosophy of *legal positivism*, which says that human rights are what human-rights law says they are. Human rights are, however, made and interpreted by a political process. The provisions of the Universal Declaration were the subject of intense debates, and the final text was produced after a long series of votes (Morsink 1999). It is *politically* important that human rights have been codified in international and national law. It is a mistake, however, to believe that the legalization of human rights takes the concept out of politics.

The legal-positivist approach to human rights not only misrepresents their character but also has dangerous implications. The *point* of human rights has historically been to criticize legal authorities and laws that violate human rights. Legal positivists sometimes say that the only rights are those that are legally *enforceable*. However, while it may be desirable that human rights should be legally enforceable, it is not necessary that they should be so, and the concept of human rights implies that often they are not. If human rights were legally enforceable, one could, and normally would, appeal to one's *legal* rights, and would not need to appeal to one's human rights. One appeals to human rights precisely when legal institutions fail to recognize and enforce them. If legal positivism were true, an important basis for criticizing unjust legal systems would be eliminated.

The principal philosophical problem of human rights is to show how they can be justified if they derive neither from law nor superstitious beliefs. There is an historical reason at the root of this problem about the 'source' of human rights. The first systematic human-rights theory, presented by John Locke, assumed that God was the 'source' in question. Locke could assume agreement with and among his readers that this provided the ultimate validation of such rights: God was the source both of what exists and of value. The problem faced by the United Nations in proclaiming its Universal Declaration of Human Rights was that, precisely because it claimed that these rights were universal, it could not base them on any particular religious belief. The justificatory basis of human rights had to be *abstracted* from particular religious and ideological beliefs, but the character of that abstraction was not clear. The Declaration says little about the source of these rights, apart from some large and unsubstantiated claims in the preamble that recognition of human rights is 'the foundation of freedom, justice and peace in the world', and that disregard for human rights has resulted in 'barbarous acts which have outraged the conscience of mankind'. These claims may contain important truths, but they do not give a clear account of the source of human rights.

The very idea of such a 'source' contains an important and confusing ambiguity. It can refer to the *social origins* or to the *ethical justification* of human rights. Social scientists have studied the social origins of rights in, for example, popular political protest, and, important though such studies may be for an historical understanding of the discourse of rights, we must be careful not to confuse social origins with ethical justifications, since there are social origins of evil as well as of good. The social-scientific approach to rights, with its preference for avoiding ethical questions, sometimes falls into this confusion. There are, therefore, two distinct questions about the 'sources' of human rights that we need to answer: Why *do* we have human rights? Why *ought* we to have human rights?

Another set of philosophical questions concerns the relations between human rights and other values. Do human rights occupy the whole space of moral and political theory, or are there other important values? If there are other important values, how are human rights related to them? The Universal Declaration claims that human rights are the foundation of freedom, justice and peace, but does not say how these values are related, conceptually or empirically. It is important to determine as clearly as possible the *limits* as well as the *value* of human rights. It is common to say that human rights establish *minimum standards* of good government. Claiming too much for human rights may make it harder to defend them against their critics, and thereby weaken their appeal and effects. We need to be clear, therefore, whether the concept of human rights supports a *comprehensive* or a *minimum-standards* political philosophy.

There is a huge gap between the experiences of the Darfurians and the world of the United Nations. This gap has been filled to a large extent by law and legal studies, and these studies are certainly important. The gap is, however, also filled by politics, and by social, cultural and economic forces. These may in fact be more important, but they have been relatively neglected in academic discourse. The aim of this book is to make a contribution to rectifying this neglect.

Conclusion

The study and, to a considerable extent, the practice of human rights have been dominated by lawyers. The cause of human rights owes a great debt to them. There is a danger, however, that excessive attention to human-rights law distorts our understanding of human rights. This book seeks to put law in its place by adopting an interdisciplinary approach. The concept of human rights has a history marked by philosophical controversies. Knowing that history and understanding those controversies will illuminate the state of human rights today. In the past half-century, the concept has been incorporated into a large body of international and national law, but it has also been at the heart of political conflicts. The law is important, but understanding human rights requires us also to understand its politics. Furthermore, law and politics do not themselves exhaust the human-rights field. The other social sciences – such as sociology, anthropology and economics – are essential to our appreciation of human-rights problems and their possible solutions. In short, human rights is an interdisciplinary concept *par excellence*.

We begin this inquiry by tracing, in chapter two, the historical emergence of human rights. The story continues in chapter three by examining the gradual acceptance of human rights by the international community. Chapter four investigates the principal theoretical justifications of, and debates about, the concept. The distinctive contribution of the social sciences is then surveyed in chapter five. In chapter six, much-debated questions about the supposed universality of human rights and its relation to actual human differences are addressed, with particular emphasis on cultural minorities, indigenous peoples, and the rights of women, children and sexual minorities. In chapter seven the place of human rights in national and international politics is analysed, and the respective roles of international institutions, governments and non-governmental organizations evaluated. The political economy of human rights forms the subject of chapter eight, with special attention given to development, globalization and international financial institutions. We conclude, in chapter nine, with reflections on the history of human rights, their current status, and their likely future. One of the few certainties is that understanding human rights will be essential to understanding the world we live in for a long time to come.

2
Origins

The Rise and Fall of Natural Rights

Why history?

The history of human rights can be studied for its own sake and for the sake of the light that it throws on the contemporary concept of human rights. Before we can study the history of human rights, however, we must know what it is the history of. According to one view, the concept of human rights had little history before the establishment of the United Nations in 1945. On this view, the history of human rights would be the history of the UN concept. A more common view is that the contemporary concept of human rights has a much longer history. This view is better, because it enables us to investigate the historical and philosophical bases of the modern concept. It is, however, beset by controversy.

Some argue that the concept of human rights has a *universal* history in the various religions and philosophies of the world. The Code of Hammurabi (c.1792–50 BC), king of Babylon, is said to be the oldest surviving text establishing the rule of law. Cyrus the Great (died 529 BC), king of Persia, proclaimed a policy of religious toleration and abolished slavery. The Buddhist King Ashoka of India (c.264–38 BC) also promoted toleration, provided for the health and education of his people, and appointed officials to prevent wrongful punishments (Weeramantry 1997: 7–8). Thus principles now associated with human rights can be found in ancient times in many cultures around the world. These examples weaken somewhat the common claim that the concept of human rights is Western. They must be treated with caution, however, since they appear to be, at best, evidence of liberal and benevolent rulers rather than of human rights as such.

Others maintain that the concept of human rights originated in the West, and was universalized only recently. Some go on to argue that if the *history* of the concept is Western then its *validity* cannot be universal. Others say that the history of a concept is irrelevant to its validity: there may be good reasons for universalizing a concept that has a particular history. Yet the validity of a concept depends on its meaning, and its meaning derives partly from its historical usage.

There is disagreement about the history of the concept of human rights in the West. MacIntyre has claimed that there is no expression in any ancient or medieval language correctly translated by our expression 'a right' before about 1400. He doubts whether human beings could have had rights if they could not have expressed them in their language (MacIntyre 1981: 66–7). He suggests, therefore, that the fact that there was no concept of 'rights' before 1400 means that the concept of *universal* human rights is invalid.

Some scholars have argued that classical Greek thinkers could not conceive of individuals as having rights against the state because they believed that citizens were subordinate parts of the social whole. This idea, some say, was weakened by increasing social complexity that undermined stable roles and identities, thus producing the concept of the rights-bearing 'individual'. This historical sociology of individual rights is supposed to undermine the concept of universal human rights. But is it true?

On rights and tyrants

The contemporary concept of human rights is intended primarily to protect individuals from the abuse of power by governments. Whether or not the ancient Greeks had a concept of 'rights', they certainly had the concepts of power and its abuse. This was expressed in the concept of tyranny, defined as a form of government in which the ruler governed in his own interest and treated his people unjustly. It was possible, however, for the Greeks to think about tyranny without talking about rights. In Sophocles' play, *Antigone*, for example, the king forbids Antigone to bury her dead brother because he had been a rebel. Antigone defies the king's order, but on the ground that she has a religious *duty* to bury her brother, not on the ground that she has a *right* to do so. We might see this as a human-rights drama about freedom of religious practice, but Sophocles did not express it this way.

There are reasons, however, for rejecting MacIntyre's view that the ancient Greeks had no language of rights. Aristotle had a conception of rights and a language in which to express it. He believed that constitutions could assign rights to citizens. Citizens' rights included rights to property and to participation in public affairs. When these rights were violated, the laws determined compensation or punishment. Citizens' rights would be distributed differently in different political systems. Aristotle used a range of expressions that we can properly translate as 'a right'. In particular, he used the expression *to dikaion* to mean a just claim, which we could translate as a right. Aristotle had no conception of *human* rights, however, as he believed that rights derived from constitutions, and that some men were slaves by nature (Miller, F. 1995).

Justice and rights

Roman law provides the main link between classical Greek thought about rights and modern conceptions through its influence on medieval ideas. The French historian, Michel Villey, initiated a debate on the distinction between *objective right* (that which is right) and *subjective rights* (personal entitlements). Villey argued that Roman law had no conception of subjective rights: the Latin word *ius* referred to objective right (Tuck 1979: 7–9; Tierney 1988: 4–6, 15). This view has been questioned on the ground that Roman law conceived of justice as rendering to each his right (*suum ius*). Whether *ius* was objective or subjective, it was *legal*, and not *natural* (Tuck 1979).

Scholars disagree as to whether the Stoic philosophers had a conception of human rights. Sorabji acknowledges that they believed in a universal moral community of all human beings, governed by a common natural law, but maintains that they lacked a concept of human rights (Sorabji 1993). Mitsis interprets the Stoic philosophy as requiring respect for the equality, rationality and moral autonomy of others, and consequently for their human rights. These rights would not, however, include the modern human rights to such things as health, work and an adequate standard of living, as the Stoics regarded these as matters of indifference (Mitsis 1999: 176–7). It is doubtful, therefore, whether the Stoics had the concept of human rights, and, if they did, it was much more limited than the modern concept.

The Stoic philosophy influenced early Christianity, which provided a new basis for the unity underlying the diversity of peoples. A clear shift from objective right to subjective rights took place, however, only in the late Middle Ages. According to Tierney, medieval people had the concept of rights, and a language in which to express it, at least as early as the twelfth century (Tierney 1989: 626, 629). These rights were rights of particular persons, statuses, collectivities or classes: kings, lords, bishops, communities, etc. They were not natural rights. However, according to one conception of natural law, natural right was what natural law permitted. Natural rights might be rights of individuals, but they derived not from the nature of the individual, but from the right order of society (Tierney 1989).

However, the twelfth-century encyclopaedia of Church law, Gratian's *Decretum*, referred to the *iura libertatis* (rights of liberty) that could never be lost, however long a man might be held in bondage (Coleman 1993: 109–10). The thirteenth-century writer, Henry of Ghent, held that each person had a natural right to self-preservation and property in his own body. The canonistic vocabulary of the thirteenth century was rich in terms that could, in appropriate circumstances, be translated as 'right': *libertas* (liberty), *potestas* (power), *facultas* (faculty), *immunitas* (immunity), *dominium* (lordship), and others (Tierney 1992: 63–7, 1997: 262).

One source of late medieval natural-rights theory was the dispute between the Dominicans and the Franciscans, who championed the life of poverty, and thereby called into question the legitimacy of private property. The Franciscans claimed to renounce both their will and their material possessions in order to devote themselves completely to the will of God. This presented a challenge to the Church, which was committed to the compatibility of Christian virtue and private property. The Dominicans argued that the Franciscans could not renounce their will, and they could not entirely renounce property, as they were necessarily the proprietors of the food and drink that was a condition of their survival. In 1328 Pope John XXII issued the bull, *Quia vir reprobus*, maintaining that God had granted to Adam *dominium* over temporal things. Property was therefore sanctified by divine law. By the fourteenth century it was possible to argue that to have a right was to be the lord of one's moral world (Tuck 1979; Brett 2003).

The Magna Carta (1215) recognizes 'subjective' rights by such terms as 'his right' (*jus suum*) (Holt 1965: 96, 100, 104). The concept of rights was, however, at that time embedded in customary law. The Magna Carta was, furthermore, a text whose purpose was to provide remedies for specific grievances. It was therefore not a charter of the rights of Englishmen, still less of human rights. Yet its reputation as a precursor of modern human-rights texts is not wholly unmerited. Article 39, for example, says that no free man shall be arrested, imprisoned, expropriated, exiled or in any way ruined, except by the lawful judgement of his peers or by the law of the land (Roshwald 1959: 361–4; Holt 1965: 1–2, 327). This article was more limited than it might appear, as the category of 'free men' was created by royal prerogative. However, Parliament in 1354 applied the principle of this article to all men 'of whatever estate or condition' (Coleman 1993: 113–14). The Magna Carta emphasized property rights, but not only such rights, and it extended substantial rights beyond the baronial class. It also established the principle that the king was subject to the law. It was later transformed from a limited political and legal agreement into a national myth, and in the seventeenth century it was invoked as part of early modern debates about rights in England. Against the claims of James I and Charles I that they ruled by divine right, lawyers such as Edward Coke, the Lord Chief Justice, insisted that the Magna Carta made the king subject to the law. Coke interpreted Magna Carta as a declaration of individual liberty, which was certainly not the intention of its authors (Holt 1965; Breay 2002: 33, 46).

Natural rights

There is no direct line from medieval conceptions of *ius* to early modern conceptions of rights. The humanist lawyers of the Renaissance, for example, were concerned not with natural rights but with *civil* rights (Tuck 1979). However, medieval conceptions of natural law had the most influence on the modern concept of natural rights.

In the fourteenth century William of Ockham argued that all men knew intuitively that they had a natural power to make choices. Men possessed, therefore, certain liberties that could never be alienated to church or state, and they had a natural right to the necessities of life, and to consent voluntarily to create a system of laws. Positive law was required to coerce fallen men when they did not act according to their natural knowledge of what was morally right. However, the social individual possessed certain inalienable rights and duties prior to any incorporation into a political system. The custom and law of any time and place should be judged by right reason (McGrade 1974; Coleman 1993: 116–17).

In the fifteenth century, Conrad Summenhart maintained that Man had right over himself and his body. 'Here', Brett comments, 'Summenhart introduces a notion of negative liberty which is very close to elements of the modern language of rights' (Brett 2003: 42). The association of right and freedom was developed further by Spanish thinkers of the sixteenth century. Domingo de Soto, for example, held that the proper dignity of man was to live according to reason, for through that he was free and existed for the sake of himself, *sui juris* (autonomous). The political community had the right to exercise power over its members, so that each could live well, but that public right extended to the individual only as a member of the community rather than as a separate individual. Beyond that, man must not only have his rights as an individual; he must also have their exercise within his own control: that is, he must be *sui juris* (Brett 2003).

The Spanish conquest of America raised important questions for Catholic theology and international politics. The debate on its legitimacy is a largely neglected moment in the history of human rights. Those who justified the conquest employed Aristotle's doctrine of natural slavery to deny any rights to the native Americans. They were opposed by Bartolomé de Las Casas, a Dominican priest, who argued that the Indians were in all essential respects human and therefore entitled to their land and to self-government. He sought to demonstrate that the Indians had complex cultures and that the Spanish treatment of them showed that the Spanish, not the native Americans, were the barbarians. He defended the collective cultural rights of the Indians rather than the idea of individual human rights, and, in that, anticipated the modern idea of indigenous rights. Vitoria deployed the idea of natural rights in defence of the indigenous Americans. He argued that that the cities of the Mexica and the Inca proved that they were not natural slaves, but rational, and consequently had a right to their lands.

The Spanish Dominicans developed the philosophy of Aquinas with a doctrine of subjective rights. Neither Vitoria nor Las Casas doubted the right of Spain to exercise sovereignty over the New World or the rightness of attempting to convert the Indians to Christianity. Only late in his life did Las Casas come to believe that it might be better for the native Americans to remain heathens, with their distinctive cultures, than to be brought to Christianity by force. The practical advocacy of Las Casas and the more academic philosophy of Vitoria provided an important link between Thomist philosophy and later theories of rights and a basis for using the idea of rights to criticize European imperialism (Pagden 1982; Carozza 2003; Talbott 2005: 84–5).

By the beginning of the seventeenth century there were two principal traditions of thinking about rights. The first emphasized natural, subjective, individual rights. The second emphasized objective right and/or civil rights (Tuck 1979: 54–7; Tierney 1989: 621). The Dutch jurist, Hugo Grotius, was a crucial figure in transforming medieval ideas into the modern concept of rights. He began with the proposition that the will of God was law, and was known through man's sociability, which was the basis of all other laws of nature. Men had natural rights, but these were transformed by society. He conceived of *ius* as what is just and as the ability of a person to have or do something justly. The law of nature concerned the maintenance of rights, the subject matter of justice. 'Rights', Tuck says in his discussion of Grotius' ideas, 'have come to usurp the whole of natural law theory, for the law of nature is simply, respect one another's rights' (Tuck 1979: 67). Everyone should enjoy his rights with the help of the community, which was required to defend our lives, limbs, liberties and property. Grotius held that moral obligations were owed not only to members of one's own society, but also to mankind as such. He also maintained that his theory of natural law did not logically require belief in the existence of God, providing thereby the basis for a secular theory of natural rights (Tuck 1979; Tierney 1989: 621–2).

In seventeenth-century England Thomas Hobbes drew a sharp distinction between right (*jus*) and law (*lex*). Since right was liberty, and law was restraint, right and law not only differed from each other, but also were opposites. In the natural condition of mankind, everyone had the natural right to do anything that was conducive to their preservation. There was both an obligation under the law of nature and a natural right to preserve oneself. The natural condition of mankind was one of war of each against everyone else, and therefore one of great insecurity. Reason required men to authorize a sovereign to act on their behalf. All men were obliged to obey this sovereign, provided that he did not threaten their preservation (Tuck 1979: 126–31).

We are so familiar with the use of the concept of human rights to limit the powers of government that we may be surprised to learn that most early modern natural-rights theorists argued that rational individuals would give up their natural rights to absolute rulers for the sake of social order. However, in the English Civil War the Levellers adopted the concept of individual, inalienable rights and maintained that Parliament was violating them. Richard Overton argued that all governments were trusts, because by nature every one had a 'self propriety' which could not be invaded or usurped without his consent. The concept of 'self propriety' entailed freedom of conscience, equal rights in law, and the right of at least the majority of men to vote. John Wildman thought that the concept of natural rights entailed the principle of universal suffrage. The Levellers held that persons were prior to estates, which justified the right to subsistence and the legitimation of some redistribution of wealth (Roshwald 1959: 369; Tuck 1979: 148–50; Ashcraft 1986: 155, 160–1, 163; McNally 1989: 35–7).

By grounding rights in the law of nature, the Levellers emancipated such claims from historical precedents. Overton maintained that reason had no precedent, for reason was the fountain of all just precedents. Arguments from reason were, however, mixed with arguments from history, including references to the Magna Carta. This mixture of natural law and historical argument created some ambiguity as to whether the rights claimed were those of Englishmen or universal human rights. Roshwald suggests that their practical emphasis was on the rights of Englishmen, but their logic was universalistic. The Bill of Rights (1688) was concerned with vindicating the ancient rights of Englishmen, not human rights (Roshwald 1959: 366–70; Griffin 2008: 13).

The deep ground for opposition to political absolutism in seventeenth-century England was the Protestant belief that God had made human beings rational so that each could determine their own way to salvation. The Protestant conception of reason entailed freedom of the will, the legitimacy of independent action and dissent from authority. Religion, on this view, required conscientious action that could oppose the individual to authority. This argument claimed to be based on what was common to all men and represented rational individuals as having been created in a state of equality and freedom. No one was, therefore, subject to the absolute will of any other person. Rational individuals constituted a natural moral community, since they lived under a framework of moral obligations that were owed to each other and to God. By the use of their reason, they were able to discover these obligations contained in the law of nature. This law not only imposed duties but also accorded rights to individuals, including, especially, the right to follow the dictates of one's conscience (Ashcraft 1986: 49, 66–7).

In his *Essay on Toleration* Locke argued that man was a rational and active creature. Religious faith, therefore, must be active, and required liberty of action. The political authorities ought not to interfere with religious beliefs, since they concerned only the relation between the individual and God. The individual had a natural right to freedom of religion, both because salvation was infinitely more important than any political relation, and because political authorities were fallible in matters of religion (Ashcraft 1986: 88, 93–6).

Locke held that each individual had a responsibility to God to observe the law of nature. Every man was rational in that he could know the law of nature. God willed the preservation of mankind, and this imposed on everyone the obligation not to harm the lives, health, liberty and possessions of others. In 'the state of nature', in the absence of government, everyone had the right to self-defence and to enforce the laws of nature. Since everyone was judge in their own cause, they would be partial to themselves, and this would lead to conflict. Rational individuals would therefore agree to live under a government that was entrusted to enforce the law of nature, protect the natural rights of all through the rule of law, and to promote the public good. Governments that breached this trust, and that systematically and persistently violated the rights of the people, were tyrannies, lost their authority to rule, and might be resisted by the people by force if necessary (Locke [1689] 1970).

Locke is usually interpreted as a theorist of a strictly *individualist* conception of natural rights. This interpretation is supported by Locke's belief that each individual had fundamental obligations to God, was endowed with reason, and had a natural right to freedom, which was limited only by the obligation to respect the natural rights of others. Nevertheless, he also held that God's will for mankind could be achieved, and the natural rights of men could be protected, only in a political community, and that this community should be governed for the public good. There is, therefore, an unresolved tension in Locke's political theory between the natural rights of individuals and the collective good of society. The foundation of Locke's theory in the will of God and the reason of Man supported his belief that individual rights and the public good were mutually compatible.

Locke argued that each individual had a property in himself, in his labour and in the products of his labour. Labour was the basis of the right to private property. Locke's theory of property has been the subject of prolonged controversy. C. B. Macpherson interpreted Locke as a defender of 'possessive individualism' and of the interests of the bourgeois class (Macpherson 1962). Critics have pointed out that Locke's theory of rights was set in a Christian natural-law framework, and that property rights were subject to a set of moral obligations designed to provide for the common good and the benefit of mankind. Locke's theory of property clearly allows considerable inequality of wealth, but accords to everyone the natural right to subsistence, and imposes on those who have excessive wealth the obligation to aid those who cannot meet their subsistence needs by their own efforts (Tully 1980, 1993; Ashcraft 1986; Waldron 1988).

Several scholars have linked Locke's defence of property with his support for British colonialism. Tully interprets Locke as believing that America was a state of nature. Europeans had productive agricultural practices, modern states and property laws, while native Americans had none of these. Europeans had the right, therefore, to appropriate American land without the consent of the natives (Tully 1993: 129, 141–5, 151–64). On this view Locke used the concept of natural rights to justify European imperialism. Vitoria and Las Casas show that the concept could be used to oppose it.

The age of revolutions

After the Glorious Revolution of 1689 the Lockean principles of constitutional monarchy and the rights to life, liberty and property became part of Whig (liberal) ideology, although the radical, egalitarian thrust of natural-rights theory was muted. In the later eighteenth century, however, radical Whigs appealed to the right of the people to reform or remove a government that did not protect their rights. The natural right to freedom of conscience was held to entail the principle that the state should not discriminate against anyone on the ground of religion, and that consequently everyone should be an equal citizen in a secular state. A few radicals, led by Mary Wollstonecraft, argued for the natural rights of women (Dickinson 1977).

The concept of natural rights was pervasive in eighteenth-century America. Americans linked the defence of religious liberty with the struggle for political freedom. American perceptions of the tendency of the British government towards tyranny and the fact that they were not represented in that government made it easier to justify resistance (Dickinson 1977: 225; Bailyn 1992). Although Locke was only one among many influences on the American revolutionaries, the American Declaration of Independence (1776) certainly expressed Lockean ideas:

> We hold these truths to be self-evident, that all men are created equal, that they are endowed by their creator with certain unalienable rights, that among these are life, liberty and the pursuit of happiness – that to secure these rights, governments are instituted among men, deriving their just powers from the consent of the governed. That whenever any form of government becomes destructive of these ends, it is the right of the people to alter or abolish it.

The Virginia Declaration of Rights included specific liberties that were to be protected from state interference, including freedom of the press, the free exercise of religion and the right not to be deprived of freedom except by due process of law. In 1791 the Bill of Rights was enacted as a set of amendments to the US Constitution, and included rights to freedom of religion, the press, expression and assembly, protection against unreasonable search and seizure, the right not to incriminate oneself, and the right to due process of law. These rights were based on historical precedents, the rights of Englishmen, but were justified by appeal to natural rights grounded in the laws of God. Notwithstanding the reference to God, however, the Declaration of Independence almost secularized the concept of natural rights. The Americans were also strongly constitutionalist, believing that the constitution, with its separation of powers, was the foundation of liberty. The American conception of natural rights at the time of the Revolution did not include the rights of women, and was generally considered compatible with the institution of slavery. It also offered little protection for the native peoples of the country (Becker 1966; Dickinson 1977; Bailyn 1992; Griffin 2008: 13).

The secularization of the concept of natural rights that gradually took place during the eighteenth century created an important philosophical problem. The principles of morality and politics had to be derived from nature by reason. Late eighteenth-century secular natural-rights thinkers assumed that this could be done, but their arguments were often weak.

The greatest philosopher of rights in this period was Immanuel Kant. He maintained that natural law, known to reason, not consent or consensus, was the basis of all rights and obligations, and of the authority of those who made positive law. The supreme principle of natural law was the categorical imperative. This required everyone to act only according to that maxim (principle) according to which they could at the same time will that it should become a universal law. Everyone had an innate right to freedom by virtue of their humanity. Once a civil condition was established, all natural laws should become public law. The innate right to freedom provided the basis for such human rights as those to freedom of expression and association. The categorical imperative also required that no one use another person merely as a means to his ends but must always treat him as an end. This meant that everyone was obliged to acknowledge the dignity of every other person. The moral law required everyone to make the human rights of all into an end. For Kant, the point of rights was freedom rather than the protection of interests or happiness. The totality of rights was the rightful distribution of freedom (Ellis 2005: 39, 184; Brown 2006: 663–4).

In a state of nature the validity of claims to rights was uncertain. Since no one claiming a right had the right to determine the validity of the claim, only an impartial person could have this right. A person who had the right to resolve disputes must do so on the basis of natural law. A necessary condition for acquiring a right was a guarantee by everyone to respect the rights of others. This guarantee could be provided only by external coercion. Only a civil society in which there are persons with the supreme right to make, apply and execute laws determining rights could constitute a sufficient guarantee of rights (Brown 2006: 665).

The innate right to freedom entailed the right to acquire rights to external objects. The person who first took physical possession of a thing acquired a right to it. Such a right was provisional. In the civil condition all acquired property rights depended on the determination and application of laws by the civil authorities. There was a right to private property, but not necessarily to any particular form of property relations, such as capitalism. The state had the right to tax property owners to help those unable to provide for their own basic needs.

Kant's theory of rights derived from a metaphysical concept of the person as a moral agent. It was strictly universal, and rejected any moral idea that might contingently be found in any culture that was inconsistent with it. Although Kant maintained that rights were political, not ethical, he held that positive law was bound by natural law to regard everyone as a moral person with rights. Positive law had moral ends, even though it depended on legal (coercive) means to seek those ends.

Kant was a liberal rather than a democrat, because his principle of freedom limited the rightful authority of any government, including a democratic government. The duty of government was to protect the freedom of all, not to promote happiness or religion as such. Kant believed that women were not suited to be citizens, but his reasons for this belief were weak. He was generally opposed to revolution, but supported the principles of the French Revolution because he believed them to be those of a republican constitution of freedom under law (Ellis 2005: 168). Kant also argued that international justice and peace could be achieved only through a federation of free republics. Colonialism brought about by force or deception was unjust. A cosmopolitan (global) constitution would include a set of rights for all, regardless of nationality (Ellis 2005: 95; Brown 2006).

In so far as it is convincing, Kant's universalism provides strong support for human rights. Kant's critics, however, have found his conception of universal reason potentially authoritarian and imperialistic because it rejects moral pluralism, and inhuman for its prioritization of freedom over happiness. His principle of freedom under law has been interpreted as an endorsement of capitalism and the state, and thus less protective of human rights than it appears. The categorical imperative has been criticized as having no content, until supplemented by the very cultural commitments that Kant sought to exclude. Kant's account has been interpreted as extending more widely than the concept of human rights, because it offers a comprehensive moral theory, yet also as narrower because it prioritizes freedom over other human interests. There is consequently disagreement about the merits of the theory and about its relation to human rights (Hunter 2001: 308, 311; Ellis 2005: 17; Saurette 2005; Brown 2006: 665–6; Griffin 2008).

While Kant's philosophy rested on controversial foundations and arguments, advocates of natural rights in the late eighteenth century tended to assert these rights without much attention to foundations or arguments. Critics of natural rights began to mock the fondness of their advocates for unsubstantiated declarations and their lack of arguments. Attempts to derive natural rights from a cross-cultural consensus were undermined by evidence that no such consensus existed. In the late eighteenth century, therefore, while the concept of natural rights enjoyed a practical triumph in the American Revolution, it nevertheless rested on insecure theoretical foundations.

When the French Revolution broke out in 1789, the newly formed National Assembly proclaimed The Declaration of the Rights of Man and the Citizen in order to lay down the principles upon which the new constitution of France was to be founded. The Declaration stated that the preservation of the natural Rights of Man was the aim of every political association. These rights were those of liberty, property, security and resistance to oppression. It affirmed equality before the law, freedom from arbitrary arrest, the presumption of innocence, freedom of expression and religion, the general freedom to do anything that did not harm others, and the right to property. The rights that it declared were qualified repeatedly by restrictions and conditions, and made subject to the rule of law. This ambivalence between individual natural rights and the requirements of social order reflected deep ideological differences among the revolutionaries (Baker 1994: 192–3).

The French Declaration of Rights was an act of revolutionary power carried out in the name of the popular will. The revolutionary governments faced, of course, many practical problems that threatened the stability of the new order. However, the degeneration of the Revolution from the declaration of the Rights of Man to the reign of terror had theoretical as well as practical sources. In the face of serious practical challenges, the ideological mixture of individual natural rights, popular sovereignty and commitment to the public good was insufficient to protect any of these values.

The ideology of the French Revolution was expressed in egalitarian terms. The theoretical concept of equal rights had, however, to be implemented in a society in which various forms of inequality existed. Yet in three respects the French Revolution was more egalitarian than the American. During the Revolution economic and social rights – such as those to work, education and social security – were proclaimed. The question of the rights of women was also raised, especially by Olympe de Gouges, who in 1791 published a Declaration of the Rights of Woman and the Citizen. The demand for human and civil rights for women was, however, defeated in the National Assembly, and Olympe de Gouges was guillotined in 1793. The idea of women's rights was thus suppressed. The revolutionaries also abolished slavery, which Napoleon soon restored.

Inspired by the French Revolution, English radicals adopted the concept of the Rights of Man rather than appealing to historic rights, as they were seeking reforms for which there were no historical precedents. No one sought to universalize the significance of the French Revolution more than Thomas Paine. The Rights of Man, he maintained, promised 'a new era to the human race' (Dagger 1989: 301). They were the rights that men had by virtue of their status as human beings. They owed nothing to society or the state. The state had value, and therefore claims on the obligations of citizens, only as an instrument for the protection of the natural rights of individuals. Paine's conception of natural rights was uncompromisingly individualist and universalist: the Rights of Man were the rights of everyone, everywhere, at all times (Paine 1988: 171; Roshwald 1959: 347, 375–8). Paine also believed that a free, commercial society, with its associated inequalities of wealth, could be combined with political democracy in a way that would secure both individual rights and the common good. His emphasis on individual reason as the basis of politics made him a more robust champion of popular sovereignty than Locke had been, although he never considered votes for women (Philp 1989; Dickinson 1977).

Paine argued that historic rights were indefensible because no moment in history had priority over others as the basis of rights. The origin of human rights could only be the divine creation of human beings. Equal rights were necessary to motivate everyone to fulfil his duties to others. A system of rights was necessarily also a system of duties, for, if we all have rights, we all have duties to respect the rights of others. Notwithstanding his reference to the divine origin of rights, Paine's theory of the Rights of Man was grounded in reason, and hence could support a purely secular conception of human rights (Paine 1988: 65–70, 114; Philp 1989).

Paine saw civil society as naturally co-operative and progressive, and the need for governmental regulation as limited. By contrast, the essence of the state was coercion. As civil society grew more complex and stronger, so it both needed protection from the depredations of the state and had the ability to secure it. Paine thought that the pursuit of self-interest was legitimate in civil society, but that it ought to be subordinated to the common good in the political realm. Paine, like Locke, accepted inequalities of wealth as legitimate if they were products of differential rationality and industry, but he was more concerned with the misery of poverty than Locke was. In *The Rights of Man* and *Agrarian Justice* Paine made proposals for a system of public welfare financed by progressive taxation. He anticipated the social-democratic argument that public guarantees of minimal welfare, far from violating the natural rights of anyone, sustain the rights of all (Philp 1989).

The decline of natural rights

At the end of the eighteenth century the concept of natural rights was opposed by conservatives because it was too egalitarian and subversive, and by some radicals because it endorsed too much inequality of wealth. It suffered philosophically from uncertain foundations once its theological basis had faded. The violence of the French Revolution seemed to confirm the fears of the conservatives. The Revolution discredited the concept of natural rights in England, but did not hold back the movement for reform. Conservatives and reformers, therefore, sought alternatives to natural rights from different motives.

Edmund Burke did not reject the concept of natural rights completely. He recognized the natural rights to life, liberty, freedom of conscience, the fruits of one's labour, property, and to equal justice under the law. Nevertheless, he considered the concept generally to be, at best, a useless metaphysical abstraction, and, at worst, subversive of social order. Thus, the 'real rights of men' were social not natural rights. Burke distrusted all abstract theoretical ideas in the making of public policy, as he believed politics to be essentially a practical activity that involved the making of judgements in complex circumstances. The French revolutionary doctrine of the Rights of Man was dangerous because it was simplistic and dogmatic.

Although Burke subscribed to natural-law theory, he opposed the universalism of the natural-rights concept for its failure to take account of national and cultural diversity. This cultural relativism offered little to those who had to endure tyranny. Significantly, Burke appealed to the concept of natural rights when analysing what he regarded as intolerable tyrannies, such as Protestant rule in Ireland (Freeman 1980).

Jeremy Bentham rejected the concept of natural rights more thoroughly than did Burke. Bentham sought to establish law on a rational basis. This required the elimination of all concepts that were vague or fictitious. The concept of natural rights was both. Natural rights were supposed to derive from natural law, but this was fictitious. Once natural rights had been detached from the concept of divine law, Bentham argued, they were based on nothing at all. For Bentham the only rights were legal rights. The facts of pleasure and pain were the basis upon which rational laws could be built, and the object of ethics and politics was the greatest happiness of the greatest number, or the common good. This was the principle of utility, which was an objective standard by which the goodness or badness of laws could be evaluated. Legal rights were valid in so far as they contributed to the common good. Natural rights were not only nonsense; they were also dangerous because they might make society unstable. Because claims concerning natural rights were vague, disputes over them were likely to be settled by violence. Bentham believed that this explained the co-existence of the Rights of Man and violence in the French Revolution. Moreover, no rights could be absolute, because one rights-claim might conflict with another; but, if the scope of rights was limited, there must be clear criteria for limiting rights and resolving conflicts among rights-claims. The theory of natural rights could not give a clear account of the limits of rights, whereas the principle of utility could – by evaluating rights-claims in terms of their relative contribution to the general good. Both the appeal and the danger of natural-rights discourse lay in its simple dogmatism, and its refusal to engage in the hard intellectual work of thinking through the consequences of implementing general principles in the complex circumstances of society. For Bentham, the principle of utility should therefore be adopted, and that of natural rights rejected (Waldron 1987: 35–43).

In the nineteenth century Utilitarianism superseded the concept of natural rights as the theoretical basis of reform in both England and France. In France, as in England, the concepts of natural rights and utility had been thought to be mutually compatible. As the Revolution progressed, there was support in France for the view that the concept of natural rights was anarchic. A group of philosophers known as the Idéologues sought to set aside the concept of the Rights of Man, and to show how society could be reconstructed on the basis of a science of the mind with the aim of promoting happiness. They were, however, never able to convert their psychological theories into a convincing political programme (Welch 1984).

In contrast with this psychological approach, French social science moved away from the concern with political power and natural rights to an interest in economics. Economic science would deliver what natural rights had failed to (Welch 1984). Saint-Simon developed a proposal for the organization of industrial society on a scientific basis that assigned priority to the social and economic over the political, the collective over the individual, and the scientific over the philosophical. The intellectual world of liberal political philosophy was left behind. The Lockean theory of property *rights* was transformed into the search for the *laws* of material production. The Saint-Simonians concluded that Utilitarianism under the conditions of industrialism required socialism. The cause of the poor, neglected by the natural-rights ideologists of the French Revolution, was now transformed by the organized working-class movement.

Karl Marx argued that the Rights of Man were the rights of egoistic man, separated from the community. The concept treated society as external to individuals and as a limit on their natural freedom. It purported to be universal, but in fact expressed the interests of the bourgeois class, and, by emphasizing the rights of individuals, concealed the structured inequalities of class-based societies. It assumed, further, that individuals were actual or potential enemies, which might be true under the conditions of capitalism, but was neither natural nor universal. It treated the pre-social, autonomous individual as natural, and political life as merely the means to protect the supposedly natural rights. This bourgeois conception of rights ignored the fundamental importance of labour, production and wealth to human well-being. Human emancipation, therefore, would be socio-economic (Waldron 1987: 126–32; Dagger 1989: 302–3). Marx was unclear as to whether the Communist society would need no concept of rights at all or would need only to eliminate the *bourgeois* concept of rights. This was to prove a serious defect in Marx's theory when the twentieth century witnessed the development of strong Communist states with official Marxist ideologies and no commitment to individual rights. A neo-Lockean concern with the protection of individual rights from abuse of power by the state was to play an important role in the politics of actual Communist societies.

In the nineteenth and early twentieth centuries the Founding Fathers of sociology – Marx, Weber and Durkheim – were impressed by the massive social changes introduced by modern industrial capitalism, and sought to understand the larger historical forces that had brought them about. Individuals and their supposed natural rights dropped out of the picture. The first sociologists saw society as a natural entity to be understood scientifically, and not as an artificial creation to be shaped by ethical principles. If the concept of rights appeared in such analyses at all, it did so not as a fundamental philosophical category to guide ethical and political action, but rather as an ideological construct to be explained by social science. Rights survived in the US Constitution, and thinkers such as de Tocqueville, J. S. Mill and Weber worried about individual freedom in the age of large-scale, impersonal organization. However, as noted above, Utilitarianism generally replaced natural rights as the basis of movements for social reform (Waldron 1987: 17–18, 151–3). The working-class and socialist movements nevertheless played a vital role in the struggle for economic and social rights.

While the concept of individual rights survived in the late nineteenth century, rights were defended, not as natural rights, but as conducive to the common good, either on Utilitarian or neo-Aristotelian grounds transmitted through the philosophy of Hegel (Dagger 1989: 303). Certain practical political questions – such as those concerning slavery, minorities and colonial rule – were sometimes discussed in the language of the Rights of Man, and some predecessors of modern human-rights non-governmental organizations, such as the French Ligue des Droits de l'Homme, were set up (Waldron 1987: 154). Other social movements and developments – including campaigns for the social and political rights of women; workers' and socialist movements; and the development of humanitarian laws of war – laid important foundations for the future of human rights. These developments were important in two particular respects. Firstly, they brought to the foreground what are now called economic and social rights, although it is a common mistake to believe that these had been ignored in previous eras (the right to subsistence is probably the oldest human-rights issue). Secondly, the international solidarity of non-governmental organizations was pioneered as technological advances made international travel and communication faster and easier.

The First World War was a humanitarian disaster, but it also advanced the causes of economic and social rights, the rights of women and minorities, and the right of national self-determination against imperialism. At the end of the war the League of Nations was established, and addressed questions of justice in the colonies, minorities, workers' rights, slavery, the rights of women and children, and the plight of refugees. The Covenant of the League made no mention of the Rights of Man. Japan proposed a clause upholding the principle of racial equality, but this was defeated on the initiative of the USA and the United Kingdom.

The League of Nations turned out to be a practical failure. It took the horrors of Nazism to revive the concept of the Rights of Man as human rights.

3
After 1945
The New Age of Rights

The UN and the human-rights revival

Since the General Assembly of the United Nations proclaimed its Universal Declaration of Human Rights on 10 December 1948, the concept of human rights has become one of the most pervasive in contemporary politics. Seen in historical perspective, this is astonishing. A concept, not long ago discredited, has made a remarkable revival; furthermore, although widely perceived as Western, it has become global. The period from the French Revolution to the Second World War was the dark age of the concept of human rights. We are now in its second age.

We saw in chapter two that, although the concept of the Rights of Man was largely discredited in the nineteenth century, concern with what we now call human-rights issues continued to develop in the campaigns against the slave trade, slavery, racial discrimination and colonialism, and for workers' rights, humanitarian laws of war, the protection of minorities, and the emancipation of women. An international treaty to abolish the slave trade was concluded in 1890, and a treaty to abolish slavery itself was drafted in 1926. The International Labour Organization (ILO) addressed workers' rights, and the League of Nations attempted to solve problems of refugees and minorities, although its minority treaties applied only to a few countries and were largely unsuccessful (Donnelly 1989: 210; Thornberry 1991: 38–54).

The concept of human rights moved to the forefront of Allied discourse during the Second World War. On 6 January 1941, President Roosevelt, in his annual State of the Union address to Congress, presented his vision of a world based on 'four essential human freedoms': freedom of speech and expression, freedom of worship, freedom from want, and freedom from fear. 'Freedom', he declared, 'means the supremacy of human rights everywhere' (Franklin D. Roosevelt Presidential Library and Museum). In August 1941, Roosevelt met the British Prime Minister, Winston Churchill, to discuss their common purposes. This meeting produced an eight-point declaration that became known as The Atlantic Charter. It set out as a common aim, among other things, the establishment of a peace which would afford assurance 'that all the men in all lands may live out their lives in freedom from want and fear' (Avalon Project). In the Declaration by the United Nations on 1 January 1942, the Allied governments asserted that victory was essential 'to preserve human rights and justice' (Nickel 1987: 1; Morsink 1999: 1). President Roosevelt, in his State of the Union message of 11 January 1944, announced 'a second Bill of Rights' that included the rights to health, education, work, food, clothing, housing, and recreation (Newman and Weissbrodt 1996: 49–50).

The immediate cause of the human-rights revival, however, was the growing knowledge of Nazi atrocities in the Second World War. Neither Utilitarianism nor scientific positivism – the two philosophies that had undermined the concept of natural rights in the nineteenth century – was well suited to explain the evil nature of Nazism. The language of human rights seemed more appropriate. The Nuremberg trials of Nazi leaders created a favourable context for human-rights thinking, even though they were restricted to war crimes.

The United Nations Organization was set up to establish a new world order in accordance with the principles upon which the war had been fought. Support for a strong human-rights commitment came mainly from smaller countries, in Latin America, the West and the third world, and from non-governmental organizations (NGOs). Opposition came mainly from the great powers, especially the USA and the USSR. Partly as the result of determined lobbying by NGOs, the UN's San Francisco conference of 1945 included a number of human-rights provisions in the UN Charter (Cassese 1992: 25–7).

The preamble to the Charter declares that one of the chief aims of the organization is 'to reaffirm faith in fundamental human rights, in the dignity and worth of the human person, in the equal rights of men and women and of nations large and small'. Article 1 states that one of the principal purposes of the UN is 'to achieve international co-operation ... in promoting and encouraging respect for human rights and fundamental freedoms for all'. Article 55 provides that the UN shall promote 'universal respect for, and observance of, human rights and fundamental freedoms for all without distinction as to race, sex, language or religion'. Article 56 tells us that all members of the UN pledge themselves to take joint and separate action in co-operation with the UN for the achievement of the purposes set forth in Article 55. Article 68 required the Economic and Social Council to set up commissions in economic and social fields and for the promotion of human rights, and, on this basis, the Council set up the Commission on Human Rights that was to draft the Universal Declaration. Article 62 said that the Council 'may make recommendations for the purpose of promoting respect for, and observance of, human rights', and this was the basis on which it recommended to the General Assembly that it adopt and proclaim the Declaration (Robertson and Merrills 1996: 25–6; Morsink 1999: 2–4).

These provisions were qualified by Article 2, paragraph 7, which says that nothing in the Charter shall authorize the UN to intervene 'in matters which are essentially within the domestic jurisdiction of any state'. The question as to whether violations of human rights are such matters has been one of the most controversial in the law and politics of human rights. The UN's persistent concern with apartheid in South Africa shows how Article 2 (7) has, from the earliest days of the UN, been no barrier to international action if there is sufficient will and unity in the international community. The General Assembly has not been much inhibited by Article 2 (7) in discussing human-rights issues, and 2 (7) has not prevented the establishment of UN procedures to investigate human-rights violations, although it may have been a barrier to their effectiveness (Cassese 1992; Robertson and Merrills 1996: 31).

The Universal Declaration of Human Rights

Since the Universal Declaration of Human Rights is sometimes treated as a quasi-sacred text by its supporters, and as a clumsy piece of bad philosophy by its critics, it is worth noting how it was made. A Canadian lawyer, John Humphrey, produced a first draft, based on a comparative survey of national constitutions. The Commission on Human Rights then held 81 meetings over almost two years. The Commission approved the final draft almost unanimously. Then the General Assembly Third Committee on Social, Humanitarian, and Cultural Affairs held more than 100 meetings between September and December 1948. In this process, 1,233 individual votes were cast. The Third Committee adopted the Declaration by a vote of 29 to 0 with seven abstentions. The General Assembly adopted the Declaration on 10 December 1948, with 48 states voting for, none against, and eight abstaining (six Communist states, Saudi Arabia and South Africa). Thus, most UN members endorsed most of the Declaration, but those states were mainly from Europe, North and Latin America, with a few states from Africa and Asia.

Some states that played leading roles in drafting and approving the Declaration had colonial empires, and much of the world's population lived under colonial rule. Since the adoption of the Declaration, UN membership has more than trebled, with new members coming overwhelmingly from Africa and Asia. This has raised the question as to the applicability of the Declaration to these countries. In this connection, it is worth noting that even in 1948 the UN included capitalist and socialist states, rich and poor countries such as the USA and Ethiopia, and societies that were predominantly Christian, Muslim, Hindu and Buddhist. The Western states may have been dominant, but 'third-world' states strongly supported the human-rights project as a means to fight colonialism and racism, and to promote social justice. Some of the most innovative features of the Declaration – for example, racial and gender equality, economic and social rights – were promoted by states other than the dominant Western powers, which, in various ways, viewed them with misgivings. The common view that 'the West' imposed human rights on the rest is not only historically inaccurate but also exaggerates the West's commitment to human rights (Morsink 1999; Cassese 1992; Waltz 2001: 65, 70–2).

It is important not to confuse the nature or motives of those responsible for the Declaration with their reasons. The Universal Declaration was intended to prevent a repetition of atrocities of the kind that the Nazis had committed. This is expressed particularly in the second paragraph of the preamble, which states that 'disregard and contempt for human rights have resulted in barbarous acts which have outraged the conscience of mankind'. The Commission on Human Rights, aware of the religious, philosophical and ideological diversity of UN members, displayed little interest in the philosophical foundations of human rights. Nevertheless, given that Nazism violated human rights in theory and practice, the adoption of the concept of human rights by the UN in opposition to Nazi ideology clearly implied the commitment to some kind of neo-Lockean political theory. The substitution of the term 'natural rights' by that of 'human rights' may have been intended to eliminate the controversial philosophical implications of grounding rights in nature (Morsink 1999: 283, 294–6, 300–2). The Declaration set aside the traditional, but controversial, foundation of natural rights, without putting any new foundation in its place. Its strategy was to seek agreement on *norms* (rules) without seeking agreement on fundamental values and beliefs (Nickel 1987: 9). The concept of human rights is, however, sufficiently similar to the Lockean concept of natural rights to be located in the Western liberal tradition. This makes it doubly controversial: because it is Western, and because it is liberal. However influential the concept of human rights may be, and however appealing to many people, it is philosophically ungrounded (Waldron 1987: 151, 166–209). The problem of 'grounding' *any* concept philosophically is, however, notoriously difficult, and concepts may still be morally and politically useful, even though they are philosophically controversial. The actions of those who heroically resisted the Nazis may have been philosophically ungrounded, but no worse for that.

The Declaration allegedly reveals a Western bias in its emphasis upon rights rather than duties, individual rather than collective rights, civil and political rather than economic, social and cultural rights, and in its lack of explicit concern with the problem of imperialism (Cassese 1992: 31). The Declaration did, however, include the economic and social rights – such as the rights to work, health and education – that had been won in several industrial countries in the nineteenth and early twentieth centuries. Donnelly has challenged the view that the Declaration prioritized civil and political rights (Donnelly 2007b: 38).

The Declaration was not intended to impose legal obligations on states, but rather to set out goals for which states were expected to strive (Robertson and Merrills 1996: 28–9). It was, nonetheless, the first declaration of moral and political principles that could make a *prima facie* plausible claim to universality (Morsink 1999: 33). Locke's theory and the French revolutionary Declaration may have been universal in principle, but the UN Declaration was endorsed by political powers with global reach. Whatever its philosophical limitations, the Declaration has had great legal and political influence. Before the Second World War there was almost no international law of human rights. There are now approximately 200 international legal human-rights instruments, of which 65 acknowledge the Universal Declaration as a source of authority. The Declaration is also the source of an international movement, and of numerous national movements, of political activists who struggle against oppression, injustice and exploitation by reference to this document (Morsink 1999: xi–xii, 20).

Article 1 announces that all human beings are born free and equal in dignity and rights. They are endowed with reason and conscience, and should act towards one another in a spirit of brotherhood. Notwithstanding the echoes of Locke and the French Revolution, this is not unreconstructed natural-rights theory, but a liberal riposte to Fascism (Morsink 1999: 38). Article 2 says that everyone is entitled to all the rights and freedoms set forth in the Declaration 'without distinction of any kind, such as race, colour, sex, language, religion, political or other opinion, national or social origin, property, birth or other status'. This is both an explicit statement of the egalitarian implications of the concept of human rights, about which classical natural-rights thinkers had been so evasive, and a direct rejection of Nazi racist ideology (Morsink 1999: 39). Article 2 is elaborated by Article 7, which states that all are equal before the law, and are entitled to equal protection of the law without any discrimination.

Articles 3–5 deal with what are sometimes called 'personal integrity rights'. Article 3 restates the classic rights to life, liberty and security of person. Article 4 forbids slavery, servitude and the slave trade. Article 5 forbids torture and 'cruel, inhuman or degrading treatment or punishment'. Torture is widely condemned in the contemporary world, and widely practised, but the interpretation of the phrase 'cruel, inhuman or degrading treatment or punishment' has proved to be controversial.

Articles 6–12 deal with legal rights. These provisions are not controversial in general, although their particular applications may be, but the balance between legal rights, on the one hand, and social and economic rights, on the other, has been criticized for being excessively influenced by the Western history of rights as legal protections for private individuals against the state rather than as positive contributions to the life of dignity.

Article 14 says that everyone has the right to seek and to enjoy in other countries asylum from persecution. This article was influenced by Nazi treatment of the Jews, but the right of asylum has become one of the most important and controversial of human rights in recent times, as gross violations of other human rights have generated massive refugee flows, and many countries that claim to be champions of human rights are reluctant to defend the Article 14 human rights of foreigners.

Article 16 states that men and women of full age have the right to marry and to found a family without any limitation due to race, nationality or religion. They are entitled to equal rights as to marriage, during marriage and at its dissolution. Marriage shall be entered into only with the free and full consent of the intending spouses. This is the liberal view of marriage, and was a reaction against Nazi racial marriage laws. However, since the family is often at the centre of religious ethics, considerable tension has developed between this liberal conception of marriage rights and others, especially those that endorse 'arranged' marriages. Article 16 (3) asserts that the family 'is the natural and fundamental group unit of society and is entitled to protection by society and the state'. This unusual example of a collective right in the Declaration was understandable in the light of Nazi family policy. However, families, like all collective bodies, can be violators of human rights, for example through domestic violence against women and the abuse of children, so that 16 (3) is more problematic than it first seemed to be.

Historically, the concept of rights had been closely associated with that of property. The socialist movement that arose in the nineteenth century had made that association problematic. Article 17 of the Declaration states that everyone has the right to own property alone and in association with others, and that no one shall be arbitrarily deprived of his property. This is a relatively weak right to property, and is compatible with a wide variety of property systems.

Article 18 says that everyone has the right to 'freedom of thought, conscience and religion' and 'to manifest his religion or belief in teaching, practice, worship and observance'. This has been, historically, one of the most fundamental liberal rights, but it carries the potential problem that some religions may not respect some other human rights, and thus there can be a conflict between Article 18 and some other Declaration rights. Similarly, Article 7, which proclaims equality before the law, includes the right to equal protection against incitement to discrimination. This might conflict with Article 19, which says that everyone has the right to freedom of expression. This gives rise to the question as to whether so-called 'hate speech' – speech expressing hatred or contempt for specific groups – can be made illegal without violating the right to freedom of expression.

It is commonly said that the Universal Declaration was innovative in including economic and social rights, which are largely missing from earlier rights declarations. We saw in the last chapter, however, that the idea of economic rights is much older than it is usually thought to be. The right to subsistence emerged in late medieval Christian thought. In the nineteenth century the working-class movement demanded, and secured, a number of economic and social rights, although debates about these were not typically conducted in natural-rights terms. Before the Second World War, the International Labour Organization, established in 1919, worked for fair and humane conditions of labour. The ILO did not, however, apply the term 'human rights' to its work until after the Second World War. Only a few ILO conventions are officially classified as human-rights treaties. These deal with freedom of association, the right to organize trades unions, freedom from forced labour and freedom from discrimination in employment. In recent years, the ILO has increasingly emphasized the importance of civil and political rights for the protection of labour rights. Some commentators have argued that all the ILO's work concerns human rights, for it seeks to implement the right to fair conditions of work that is included in the Universal Declaration (Leary 1992: 582–4).

Economic, social and cultural rights were anticipated by the UN Charter. Article 55 says that the UN shall promote higher standards of living, full employment, conditions of economic and social development, and international cultural co-operation to create the conditions of stability and well-being necessary for peaceful and friendly relations among nations. Economic, social and cultural rights were included in the Declaration because they were thought to be necessary to prevent a resurgence of Fascism and to promote the goals of the UN. The recognition of these rights represented a marriage between the tradition of liberal rights and that of socialism.

Article 22 says that everyone is entitled to realization of the economic, social and cultural rights indispensable for his dignity and the free development of his personality, 'through national effort and international co-operation' and 'in accordance with the organization and resources of each state'. Article 25 states that everyone has the right to a standard of living adequate for the health and well-being of himself and of his family, including food, clothing, housing and medical care and necessary social services, and the right to security in the event of unemployment, sickness, disability, widowhood, old age or other lack of livelihood in circumstances beyond his control. Article 22 makes the realization of economic, social and cultural rights dependent on the resources of each state, whereas Article 25 does not. Critics of economic and social rights argue that many states lack the resources to implement these rights, and therefore they cannot have a duty to do so. It follows that there cannot be human rights to these resources. The inclusion of the right to 'periodic holidays with pay' in Article 24 is often ridiculed because it universalizes a right that is relevant only to limited social conditions. This shows the difficulty in distinguishing between *human* rights and other rights.

The League of Nations had had a minority-rights regime, but the UN decided not to include minority rights in the Universal Declaration, although it did set up a Subcommission on the Protection of Minorities. The only concession in the Universal Declaration to minority concerns, apart from the prohibition of discrimination, was Article 27, which says that everyone has the right 'to participate in the cultural life of the community'. This is, however, ambiguous as to whether 'the community' is the national community or includes minority communities, and it is therefore not very helpful to minorities.

Article 29, paragraph 1, states that everyone 'has duties to the community in which alone the free and full development of his personality is possible'. Paragraph 2 allows the limitation of human rights in order to secure the rights of others and to meet 'the just requirements of morality, public order and the general welfare in a democratic society'. This article is extremely vague. The Declaration is vulnerable to the objection that the concept of human rights under-values the importance of duties. This objection can be overcome, but only with a careful argument. The Declaration gives little help in developing such an argument.

The Universal Declaration has attracted criticisms on various grounds from philosophers, social scientists and politicians. We should remember that it was intended to be a manifesto, and neither a philosophical treatise nor a social policy for the world. It was written for a popular audience in relatively simple terms, and it is therefore necessarily oversimplified as a guide to policy-making (Morsink 1999). The test of its value is to be found in its consequences, and it is to these that we now turn.

From theory to practice

The Cold War

The Universal Declaration of Human Rights is only a declaration. It makes no provision for its implementation. It allocates rights to everyone. It says little about who is obliged to do what to ensure that these rights are respected. In 1948 the UN was committed to state sovereignty and human rights. It could not decide what was to be done if sovereign states violated human rights. At that time virtually all governments said that the Declaration was not legally binding. No human-rights violations except slavery, genocide and gross abuses of the rights of aliens were illegal under international law. The UN established a Commission on Human Rights, but it was composed of the representatives of governments, and NGOs had limited access to it. The Commission's mandate was largely confined to drafting treaties and other legal texts. In 1947 the Economic and Social Council declared that the Commission had no authority to respond to human-rights violations in any way. A procedure was established to channel the thousands of complaints that the UN received each year, which the head of the organization's human-rights secretariat described as 'the world's most elaborate waste-paper basket' (Alston 1992: 128–9, 140–1; 1994: 375–6). From 1948 until the late 1960s the ability of the UN or the 'international community' to take effective action to protect human rights was extremely limited (Alston 1992: 139).

The Cold War reinforced the reluctance of states after 1948 to submit to the international regulation of human rights, and, consequently, notwithstanding the Universal Declaration, human rights returned to the margins of international politics in the 1950s. The two main Cold-War protagonists, the USA and the USSR, used the concept of human rights to score propaganda points off each other, while directly or indirectly participating in the gross violation of human rights. Plans to introduce binding human-rights treaties were delayed until the mid-1960s.

In the 1950s and 1960s the world-wide decolonization movement created many new member states of the UN with new priorities and issues for the human-rights agenda: decolonization, the right to self-determination, and anti-racism. The Convention on the Elimination of Racial Discrimination was adopted by the General Assembly in 1965. The arrival of new states at the UN thus injected a new activism, although it was very selective: South Africa, Israel and Chile received particular attention. The new anti-colonialist and anti-racist agenda helped to diminish the apparent 'Western' bias of human rights, while, at the same time, the selectivity of the new human-rights politics threatened the universality of the concept.

Even this selective activism, however, advanced the cause of universalism, because it set precedents that were broadened later. For example, in 1965 the Special Committee on Decolonization asked the Commission to respond to the petitions that the Committee had received about the situation in southern Africa. The Council then asked the Commission to consider violations 'in all countries'. In 1966 the General Assembly asked the Economic and Social Council and the Commission on Human Rights 'to give urgent consideration to ways and means of improving the capacity of the United Nations to put a stop to violations of human rights wherever they might occur' (Robertson and Merrills 1996: 79). This led to the adoption of two new procedures. In 1967, Resolution 1235 of the Economic and Social Council authorized the Commission to discuss human-rights violations in particular countries. In 1970, Resolution 1503 of the Council established a procedure by which situations that appeared to reveal 'a consistent pattern of gross and reliably attested violations of human rights' could be pursued with the governments concerned in private (Donnelly 1989: 206). The post-colonial states had wanted the Commission to deal with racism. The Communist states thought that this would embarrass the West. The West did not want to appear to condone racism, but neither did it want racism to dominate international human-rights debates. Thus Cold-War and third-world politics generated new procedures and wider powers for the UN Commission on Human Rights.

The work of the Commission under its 1235 powers was very selective in the 1970s. It was, for example, very concerned with South Africa, Israel's occupied territories, and Chile, but did not respond to gross human-rights violations in East Pakistan (now Bangladesh), Uganda, the Central African Empire, Cambodia, East Timor, Argentina, Uruguay, Brazil and many other places. In the 1980s the 1235 work of the Commission broadened considerably. The Commission was criticized for lack of political balance, but its scope became much wider than it had been, and much wider than it could have been before the adoption of 1235. Its response time was slow, and potential sanctions were remote. The 1235 procedure was an advance in the implementation of UN human-rights standards, but it worked unevenly, and remained marginal to the world's human-rights problems (Donnelly 1989: 208; 1998: 9; 1999: 76, 101; Alston 1992).

The 1503 procedure enabled individuals to petition the UN about human-rights violations, but offered them no redress. The Commission named countries that it had considered, and might, therefore, put some pressure on governments by publicity. However, the procedure could be brought fully into effect only at least two years after receipt of the complaint. Stalling tactics by governments, and the internal politics of the Commission itself, could delay action much longer. As a consequence, Resolution 1503 has had little impact on situations of gross human-rights violations (Alston 1992; Robertson and Merrills 1996: 79–89; Donnelly 1998: 9, 53–4). There is a consensus that the 1503 process has been slow, complex, secret and vulnerable to political influence. There is a difference of view among experts as to whether it has done more harm than good (Donnelly 1989: 208; Alston 1992: 150–5).

In 1966 two international treaties – the International Covenant on Civil and Political Rights and the International Covenant on Economic, Social and Cultural Rights – were adopted unanimously, and opened for signature and ratification. They entered into force in 1976 when the necessary 35 ratifications had been received. The 1966 Covenants leave out the right to property, but include the right to self-determination. The Universal Declaration and the two Covenants, together known as the International Bill of Rights, constitute the core of international human-rights law. By 3 September 2010 each Covenant had been ratified by more than 80 per cent of the 192 UN states. The fact that Western NGOs were strongly represented in the drafting process, whereas civil-society organizations from many non-Western societies were not, raises questions about the cultural legitimacy of international human-rights law.

The Human Rights Committee was established in 1976. It is supposed to consist of independent experts whose task is to monitor compliance with the Covenant on Civil and Political Rights. The states that are parties to the Covenant are obliged to submit reports on what they have done to implement the rights in the Covenant. The Committee can also receive complaints from states under the Covenant, and individual complaints under its Optional Protocol. NGOs have played an increasing role as sources of information. Co-operation with the Committee by states is variable, but the Committee has brought about legislative changes in some countries, and can contribute to human-rights improvements through discussion, debate and advice. In a few cases, individual complainants have benefited from a decision of the Committee (Donnelly 1989: 208–10, 1998: 57–9; Opsahl 1992; Robertson and Merrills 1996: 45–6, 66, 71). There are also committees that monitor the implementation of the five other 'core' UN human-rights treaties: those on economic, social and cultural rights, racial discrimination, discrimination against women, the convention against torture, and children's rights. There are differences of detail in the resourcing, working methods and effectiveness of these committees, but their achievements have been limited. The main obstacles to their greater effectiveness have been the inability or unwillingness of some governments to co-operate with them, and the unwillingness of governments generally to provide them with adequate resources (Alston and Crawford 2000).

During the 1970s, new initiatives to implement human rights were taken in the foreign policies of certain states. In 1975 US foreign aid policy was required to take account of the human-rights practices of recipient countries. When Jimmy Carter became President in 1977, he introduced human rights into his foreign policy. This was an innovation, although the policy was implemented unevenly in practice (Donnelly 1998: 10). Meanwhile, human-rights NGOs were increasingly making an impact. Amnesty International, for example, was awarded the Nobel Peace Prize in the year in which Carter became President. The UN adopted the Convention on the Elimination of Discrimination Against Women in 1979, the Convention against Torture in 1984, and the Convention on the Rights of the Child in 1989. New 'thematic' procedures evolved. A Working Group on Enforced or Involuntary Disappearances was established in 1980 in response to events in Argentina and Chile. A special rapporteur on summary or arbitrary executions was appointed in 1982. In 1985 a special rapporteur on torture was appointed. Other special rapporteurs have dealt with religious intolerance and human-rights violations by mercenaries, and a Working Group on Arbitrary Detention was set up in 1991. Almost all the early thematic procedures applied only to civil and political rights, but, more recently, special procedures have been introduced for human rights and extreme poverty (1998), structural adjustment and foreign debt (2000), and for the rights to education (1998), food (2000), housing (2000) and health (2002). Special rapporteurs were appointed to study the human-rights situations in a growing number and increasingly diverse range of countries. By 2007, 22 experts were reporting to the Commission as special representatives or rapporteurs. These represented procedural advances in the UN implementation of human rights, but they have been thinly staffed, poorly funded, and not often successful in remedying human-rights violations. They remain marginal to the protection of human rights world-wide (Alston 1992: 180–1).

Developments in the UN were overshadowed by the impact of the Cold War, which was overwhelmingly adverse for human rights. The Communist states were gross violators of human rights, while the Western powers, led by the USA, supported regimes around the world that committed grave human-rights violations. Ironically, however, the instability of the Cold-War 'balance of power' created an opening for human-rights progress. In the early 1970s the Communist bloc sought agreements with the West on security and economic matters. The West demanded human-rights guarantees in return. In 1973 the Conference on Security and Co-operation in Europe (CSCE) was convened, later to become the Organization for Security and Co-operation in Europe (OSCE). This led to the Helsinki Final Act of 1975, in which the Communist states accepted a range of human-rights commitments. In the following years, Helsinki-based human-rights NGOs were established in the USSR, but were severely persecuted. In 1977 the human-rights group, Charter 77, was set up in Czechoslovakia. The short-term, practical effects of these events appeared slight, but they increased the intensity of international debates about human rights, and such groups later played a role in the dismantling of the Communist system in Eastern Europe (Donnelly 1998: 78–82; Forsythe 2000: 124–5).

The admission to the UN of a large number of poor, non-Western states introduced a new emphasis on economic rights into international debate. In 1974 a number of texts concerning the so-called New International Economic Order were approved. These texts sought to draw attention away from human-rights violations in individual states to the structural causes of human-rights violations in global economic inequality. This third-world approach to human rights led to a controversial conceptual development: the so-called 'third generation' of human rights. According to this new thinking, civil and political rights were the first generation of 'liberty' rights; economic and social rights were the second generation of 'equality' rights; and there was now a need for a third generation of 'solidarity' rights. These were the rights to development, peace, a healthy environment and self-determination. In 1986 the General Assembly adopted a Declaration on the Right to Development.

'Third-generation' rights have been criticized on several grounds, including the following: 1) the language of 'generations' is inappropriate, because generations succeed each other, but so-called generations of human rights do not; 2) the concept of 'generation' presupposes a questionable history of human rights: the supposed first two generations were both recognized in the Universal Declaration; 3) it is not clear whether the holders of these rights are individuals, peoples, states or some combination of these; 4) it is not clear what the bearers of these rights have a right to; 5) it is not clear who the corresponding duty-bearers are, nor what their duties are; 6) these rights-claims provide cover for authoritarian governments to violate established human rights; 7) what is valid in third-generation rights is already contained in established human rights: for example, the right to development is covered by taking economic and social rights seriously (Donnelly 1993).

In the 1980s and early 1990s the theme of 'cultural relativism' became more salient in UN debates about human rights. In 1984 the Islamic Republic of Iran announced it would not recognize the validity of any international principles that were contrary to Islam. In the run-up to the UN World Conference on Human Rights that was held in Vienna in 1993 there was much talk of a conflict between 'Asian values' and human rights. The final declaration of the Vienna conference reaffirmed the universality of human rights, but conceded that human rights 'must be considered in the context of a dynamic and evolving process of international norm-setting, bearing in mind the significance of national and regional particularities and various historical, cultural and religious backgrounds'.

After the Cold War

Although the end of the Cold War brought some immediate human-rights improvements, such as the establishment of civil and political rights in former Communist societies, the new world order produced complex human-rights patterns. Both the General Assembly and the Commission on Human Rights became more active. The challenge to Western domination of the human-rights agenda by the poorer states of the so-called South weakened. The UN goals of peace-keeping and human-rights protection became increasingly combined. The Secretary-General's office negotiated a human-rights agreement between government and rebels in El Salvador, which involved intrusive monitoring by UN civil and military personnel. Similarly, in Haiti and Liberia, the UN became involved in monitoring respect for human rights as part of political settlements. In Namibia and Cambodia, the UN had a more comprehensive role in protecting human rights in the context of overall political re-organization. Initiatives by the Secretary-General or mandates from the Security Council provided bases for UN supervision of elections in Nicaragua, Haiti, El Salvador, Namibia, Angola, Cambodia and elsewhere. In 1991 Operation Desert Storm reversed the Iraqi military occupation of Kuwait, and was followed by military interventions in northern Iraq to create a 'safe haven' for the persecuted Kurds, and in southern Iraq in an attempt to defend the Shi'a population. In the following year the UN intervened in the civil war in Somalia to end the fighting and provide humanitarian assistance. It was more successful in the latter operation than in the former, but the intervention was problematic for the UN, the intervening states, especially the USA, and the intended beneficiaries.

If the intervention in Somalia had only limited success, the wars in the former Yugoslavia presented an even more complex challenge. The dissolution of the former Yugoslavia left a Serb minority in Croatia, three minority populations in Bosnia-Herzegovina (Serbs, Croats and Muslims), and an oppressed ethnic Albanian minority in Kosovo. Serbia launched a war against Croatia, ostensibly to protect the Serb minority, and intervened in Bosnia on behalf of the Bosnian Serbs. The war in Bosnia involved 'ethnic cleansing' (forcible moving of populations in order to create ethnically homogeneous territories) and other gross human-rights violations, including massacres and mass rapes. The UN, and particularly the major powers, were reluctant to intervene militarily, partly because of their experience in Somalia and partly because of the perceived military and political difficulties. Considerable success was achieved in delivering humanitarian assistance, but the UN's failure to prevent gross human-rights violations was catastrophic. In 1999 NATO intervened militarily in Serbia – when the UN could not because of Russian and Chinese opposition in the Security Council – in order to prevent violations of the human rights of ethnic Albanians in Kosovo. The immediate effects were worse violations against the Albanians, considerable war casualties among Serb civilians, and, after the NATO military victory, reprisals by Albanians against Serbs. The brutal and corrupt regime of the Serbian President, Slobodan

Milošević, was overthrown, and Milošević himself arrested and charged with crimes against humanity, war crimes and genocide by the International Criminal Tribunal for the Former Yugoslavia. He died before the tribunal could reach a verdict. The legality of the NATO intervention was dubious, and controversial, even among human-rights observers. After several years of UN administration, Kosovo declared independence in February 2008. In July 2010 the International Court of Justice ruled that Kosovo's declaration of independence did not violate international law. At that time 69 countries, including the USA and most European Union states, had recognized Kosovo's independence, but most UN states, including Russia and Serbia, had not.

The establishment of international criminal tribunals, both for the former Yugoslavia and for Rwanda following the genocide of 1994, were further innovations by the UN. In 1998, 120 states adopted the Rome Statute establishing the International Criminal Court. The Statute entered into force in 2002. The success of this combination of law and politics remains controversial and is still uncertain.

The UN has had for a long time a small and poorly funded programme of technical assistance for human rights, for example in legal institution-building. In the early 1990s this was somewhat expanded. Some observers prefer this constructive assistance for human rights to more adversarial pressure, while others believe that such programmes achieve little, and can divert attention from human-rights violations. The UN also acts to mitigate the effects of human-rights violations through the High Commissioner for Refugees (UNHCR). Although UNHCR does extremely valuable work, it acts typically after gross human-rights violations have taken place, and the problem of refugees is, despite its efforts, becoming worse, not better.

The Vienna conference of 1993 reaffirmed the universality, indivisibility and interdependence of human rights. It also emphasized the special vulnerability of certain groups such as women, children, minorities, indigenous populations, disabled persons, migrant workers and refugees. Among the consequences of these concerns were the appointment in 1994 of a Special Rapporteur on Violence Against Women, the International Convention on the Rights of Migrant

Workers, which entered into force in 2003, and the Convention on the Rights of Persons with Disabilities, which entered into force in 2008. The conference also opened the way for the appointment of a High Commissioner for Human Rights.

9/11 and after

On 11 September 2001 the militant Islamist group, Al-Qaeda, carried out an attack, using hijacked civilian airliners as missiles, on the World Trade Center in New York, and the Pentagon in Washington, DC. Another plane was brought down by its passengers in Pennsylvania. Some 3,000 people were killed.

Al-Qaeda had been formed by Osama bin Laden, son of a wealthy Saudi Arabian businessman, during the resistance to the Soviet invasion of Afghanistan. After the withdrawal of Soviet troops from Afghanistan, bin Laden turned his attention to his own government, and its superpower ally, the USA. He appears to have been particularly angered by the willingness of Saudi Arabia to allow US troops to use that country, the homeland of Islam, as the base for its invasion of Kuwait to expel the occupying Iraqi forces in the Gulf War of 1991. Al-Qaeda is a loose network rather than a disciplined organization, and its supporters have various ideologies. Bin Laden's ultimate goal, however, is the reversal of Western intrusions into 'Muslim lands' that took place after the dismantling of the Ottoman Empire after the First World War.

The USA, and some of its allies, responded to 9/11 by helping the Northern Alliance to overthrow the Taliban regime in Afghanistan, which had been sheltering Al-Qaeda. In March 2003 the USA invaded Iraq on the ground that its President, Saddam Hussein, had 'weapons of mass destruction' in violation of Security Council resolutions, that he was supporting terrorism, and that he was a dictator whose removal from power was justified. The US administration hinted that Saddam Hussein was somehow linked to 9/11. The war was extremely controversial, because no weapons of mass destruction were found, no links with Al-Qaeda were established, and the result of the invasion was extremely bloody conflict in Iraq. Although Iraq acquired a democratically elected government, both its stability and its commitment to human rights are uncertain.

The 'war on terrorism' was not only military. A number of countries passed anti-terrorism laws that were criticized by human-rights groups, and sometimes by courts. The most notorious human-rights issues arising from the 'war on terrorism' were the detention without trial of several hundred suspected terrorists at Guantánamo Bay in Cuba, and allegations of torture and/or inhumane treatment of prisoners in Afghanistan, Iraq, Guantánamo, and by 'extraordinary rendition' to countries where torture is common. The USA and its allies supported governments with poor human-rights records in exchange for their collaboration in the 'war on terrorism'. At the same time, the US Congress and NGOs continued to criticize the human-rights records of their country's anti-terrorism partners.

There is a growing concern that 'globalization' is a threat to human rights. Concern for 'globalization' has shifted the human-rights agenda somewhat in favour of economic and social rights, and has raised questions about the human-rights obligations of non-state actors, such as multinational corporations. Another human-rights problem associated with globalization is that of the increasing numbers of asylum-seekers and the reluctance of the governments into whose jurisdiction they flee to respect their rights in full. A related issue is that of climate change. The connections between climate change and human rights are not yet well understood, but it is possible that climate change has already had an impact on economic and social rights, civil conflict and refugee flows. These issues are analysed further in chapter eight.

In March 2006 the UN General Assembly decided to abolish the Commission on Human Rights and replace it with a Human Rights Council. The origin of this reform was widespread dissatisfaction with the Commission on the grounds that some of its members represented governments with very bad human-rights records, that the Commission had become too politicized, and that it had lost credibility as a human-rights institution (Lauren 2007: 308–9). In formal, bureaucratic terms, this was a 'promotion' for the main UN human-rights body, as, instead of reporting to the Economic and Social Council (ECOSOC), it would report directly to the General Assembly, and become an equal with ECOSOC in the UN hierarchy. A number of other reforms were instituted: whereas the Commission met for only six weeks each year, the Council will have at least three sessions, meet for at least ten weeks, and be able to convene additional sessions; candidates for membership are supposed to have contributed to the promotion and protection of human rights, and are invited to make pledges to continue to do so on the Council; membership has been reduced from 53 to 47; the Council is required to review periodically the human-rights record of *all* states (the Universal Periodic Review); any member that commits gross and systematic violations of human rights can be suspended by the General Assembly.

It is too early to evaluate this reform with confidence. Some argue that the Council has achieved some progress by, for example, excluding some of the worst violating states and subjecting all states to the Universal Periodic Review. Others emphasize the fact that some serious violators are elected to the Council, it remains biased and has failed to address some gross violations. A key problem is that UN member states have stronger loyalties to their regions than to human rights, and consequently violating states are voted onto the Council by fellow regionals. The Council's limits were indicated when the Democratic People's Republic of Korea accepted none of the Universal Periodic Review's 167 recommendations on human rights in that country (International Service for Human Rights 2010). The Council certainly has its critics who claim that it 'plays politics' and protects human-rights violators. The change from the Commission to the Council has not solved the problem that the UN is an association of states that have varied human-rights commitments and interests.

Conclusion

Since 1945 the UN has done a lot of 'standard-setting', institution-building and human-rights promotion. The concept of human rights is one of the most influential of our time, and many poor and oppressed people appeal to it in their quest for justice. The capacity of the UN to implement its own standards is still modest, however. The concept of state sovereignty and the realities of international power politics still make the implementation of human-rights standards uneven, and generally weak. There is widespread lip-service to human rights by governments, and also much hypocrisy. This may nevertheless have the advantage that human-rights violators can be shamed into making human-rights improvements. Lip-service may, however, be a substitute for action. There is an important role for NGOs in converting lip-service into effective action.

It is difficult to evaluate the success of the UN human-rights project precisely. Its achievements have clearly been limited, but it may be that the combined effect of UN agencies, governmental policies and NGOs has improved the human-rights situations in many countries, although gross human-rights violations are still common. The failure of the UN to respond effectively to the situation in Rwanda, despite the fact that it received early warning of the genocide, shows that its limitations can still lead to disaster. The UN carried out a human-rights revolution in world politics, but it is a long revolution in its early stages, and success is not guaranteed. The international politics of human rights is part of international politics. This means that it is characterized by a considerable amount of self-interest, pragmatism and short-term crisis management, rather than systematic implementation of principles (Forsythe 1995: 309–10).

The UN has also failed to sustain its own commitment to the indivisibility of human rights. Economic, social and cultural rights have been neglected in the main UN agencies, especially the General Assembly and the Commission, although in recent years there are signs that they are being taken more seriously. The International Labour Organization has done much to convert economic and social rights into relatively precise standards, but it is somewhat marginal in the UN human-rights system and its global impact on human rights is limited (Leary 1992: 619; Donnelly 1998: 62–4).

The international human-rights regime has been strong on declarations and weak on implementation and enforcement.

This reflects the interests of the principal international actors: *states* (Donnelly 1989: 211–12). Nevertheless, the regime has some prestige in world politics that gives it some influence. It can improve human rights if a strong alliance of states exerts pressure on an offending state with an interest in conforming to the demands of the international community (Donnelly 1998: 82–4). The regime is political, not philosophical. It responds pragmatically to circumstances, and consequently operates inconsistently. The relatively coherent ideals of the Universal Declaration are, therefore, in practice unevenly implemented. The legal institutions of the UN may be more impartial, but are procedurally restricted and diplomatically cautious. The political organs have more freedom of action, but may be more selective.

We should not forget that the very existence of an international human-rights regime is astonishing, given the controversial philosophical history of the idea of human rights and the realities of international power politics. We should remember, too, that, in addition to the international regime, there are regional regimes in Europe, America and Africa. These vary greatly in their effectiveness: the European being relatively strong, and the African very weak. In addition, there are, of course, human-rights provisions in the constitutions and laws of many states. Many of these are impressive on paper, but bear little relation to what happens in the streets and the fields.

The concept of human rights is a concept whose time has come. But what is it precisely that has come? How should we evaluate it in the light of (a) the criticisms that were made of its historical predecessors; and (b) its uneven record of success in practice? In the next chapter we shall examine theories of human rights that have attempted to clarify and justify the concept, and that have offered relatively precise answers to these questions.

4
Theories of Human Rights

Why theory?

The revival of human rights by the UN ignored the criticisms that had been made of the earlier concept of natural rights. Its practice of human-rights declarations, promotion, standard-setting and institution-building has been carried out by diplomats and lawyers, prompted and assisted by activists. They have not been much concerned with the theoretical justification of this practice. They may have considered theoretical justification unnecessary. Human-rights practice was addressed mainly to obvious human wrongs – such as racism, colonialism and political oppression – and it might be tempting to follow the American Declaration of Independence and to consider the truth of human rights to be 'self-evident'. This is quite unsatisfactory, however, because the concept of human rights is clearly controversial and in need of justification. The history of the concept shows why this is so.

Since the classical concept of natural rights had been based on Christian natural-law theory, the secularization of the concept called its foundations into question. When the validity of the concept could no longer be guaranteed by the will of God, the Rights of Man were said to be derived from reason and/or nature. However, this derivation was very controversial. The critics of the Rights of Man – such as Burke, Bentham and Marx – could appeal to reason and nature in different ways in order to reject the concept. In the nineteenth century 'reason' came to mean 'scientific reason' and science was hostile to the concept of natural rights. There was also a reaction against the individualism of natural-rights theory, and a revival of the Aristotelian idea that society was the primary concept of political philosophy. Thus, *social science* was hostile to natural rights on two grounds: the concept was unscientific and it was anti-social. From the perspective of modern philosophy and social science, the UN revival of the concept was very problematic.

Scepticism about human-rights theory can be defended theoretically. Rorty has argued that there is *no* theoretical foundation for human rights, because there is no theoretical *foundation* for any belief. This is not, however, something we should regret, both because it is a necessary philosophical truth, and because the cause of human rights does not require theory for its success, but, rather, sympathy (Rorty 1993). Rorty's argument, however, confuses *motivation* and *justification*. Sympathy is an emotion. Whether the action we take on the basis of our emotions is justified depends on the reasons for the action. Rorty wishes to eliminate unprovable metaphysical theories from philosophy, but in his critique of human-rights theory he goes too far, and eliminates reasoning. We need reasons to support our human-rights actions, both because it is often not clear which actions human-rights principles require and because opponents of human rights can support their opposition with reasons, and we must understand whether our reasons are superior, and, if so, why.

A different kind of objection to human-rights theory has been put forward by the political scientist, David Forsythe. He argues that philosophical theories are inherently controversial, and that concern with theory will undermine human-rights practice (Forsythe 1989). Forsythe is interested primarily in the politics of human-rights law. However, human-rights politics is influenced by its implicit theory, and the neglect of theory will lead to an inadequate understanding of the politics as well as an insufficient justification of the practice. Forsythe implicitly admits this when he says that for many actors in world politics, the philosophy of human rights matters (Forsythe 1989: 60).

Burke, Bentham and Marx all believed, for different reasons, that declarations of rights such as that of the French Revolution should be severely criticized. Their arguments could be applied to the Universal Declaration of Human Rights. It would be irresponsible to assume dogmatically that such arguments are mistaken. Theoretical criticisms of rights declarations require a considered theoretical response. Practical agreement among those with different theories is certainly, as Forsythe maintains, desirable in international politics. However, if we wish to understand why such agreements are desirable, how they are possible, and why they are difficult to implement, we should examine the different theories that support or undermine the concept of human rights.

Forsythe suggests that human-rights law and practice should be evaluated, not by ideal standards, but by 'real possibilities' (Forsythe 1989: x). However, political theorists now commonly distinguish between 'ideal theory' and 'non-ideal theory'. Ideal theory does not describe reality, but puts forward reasoned arguments for certain standards with which to evaluate reality. Non-ideal theory introduces reality, and thereby analyses 'real possibilities'. Ideal theory directs us to the 'real possibilities' that are *worth realizing*. Ideal theory is very practical, therefore. It endorses standards for evaluating practical reality and for guiding our actions. Reality may well limit the pursuit of the ideal quite strictly, but we cannot understand how it does so if we have no conception of the ideal. Forsythe rightly says that the concept of human rights is contested, and that its meaning is established through an interminable process of moral, political and legal debate and review (Forsythe 2006: 253); but the task of human-rights theory is to make available the best arguments for evaluating that process. Clarity and good reasons are necessary to reduce the possibilities for the political misuse of the unclear and contested concept of human rights.

Gewirth has given the following arguments for human-rights theory. All claims of human rights assume that they are justified. However, the reasons for this belief are often not clear, and, if they are not clear, we cannot know whether or not they are good reasons. Also, different persons may make conflicting human-rights claims, and, without a theory of human rights, we cannot rationally choose between them.

Human-rights theory seeks to answer questions such as the following. Are there any human rights? What is their content and scope? How are they related to each other? Are any of them absolute, or may they all be overridden in certain circumstances (Gewirth 1981)? Donnelly proposes that the theory of human rights must explain the meaning of the concept, its justificatory basis, to which obligations they give rise, and the relation between human rights and other values (Donnelly 1985a: 1). We can give *legal* answers to these questions, but such answers only give rise to the further question as to whether the law is what it ought to be (Griffin 2008: 204). Human-rights law presents the conclusions of certain arguments. Human-rights theory provides the arguments.

While the Universal Declaration was being drafted, UNESCO, the UN cultural organization, undertook an inquiry into the theoretical problems of such a declaration. In his introduction to the published results of this inquiry, Jacques Maritain described the project as a search for the philosophical bases of human rights, that is, the correct interpretation and justification of the concept. Maritain suggested that there was a need to provide a justification for the concept, but a consensus on the justification was impossible in view of the diversity of philosophies in the world. There could be agreement on what human rights there were, but not on why there were these rights. Practical agreement would be combined with theoretical disagreement. There must, therefore, be a diversity of ways to justify human rights philosophically. The different underlying philosophies might well generate disagreement about the proper limits to the exercise of human rights and the correct way to relate different human rights to each other. He warned the world not to expect too much from an international declaration of rights. It might be possible to reach an agreement on words, but agreement on the implementation of human-rights standards would require agreement on values. Given the value diversity of the world, this would be difficult. The best hope was that agreement would be reached on practical rather than theoretical values (Maritain 1949).

Several UNESCO contributors were concerned with the relation between rights and duties. Mahatma Gandhi suggested that all rights had to be deserved by the performance of corresponding duties (Gandhi 1949). E. H. Carr argued that rights implied duties, because governments could not protect the rights of citizens if citizens failed to support their governments and to provide them with the necessary resources (Carr 1949: 21–2). We shall see that most human-rights theorists now say that the performance of duties is not a *precondition* of human rights, but that human rights entail duties both to respect the human rights of others and to fulfil other moral and social obligations.

Margaret Macdonald, in an essay written at the time the Universal Declaration was being drafted, questioned the concept of natural rights from a positivist point of view. How, she asked, could propositions about natural rights be validated? They could not be verified by empirical observation. Natural-rights theorists claimed that these rights were known to 'reason'. Macdonald thought that this appeal to 'reason' was tautological, for to say that human beings had human rights because they were human beings was equivalent to saying that human beings were human beings. Natural-rights theorists might reply that human beings have natural rights because they are rational. Against this Macdonald argued that the supposed fact that human beings are rational does not logically lead to the conclusion that they have natural rights. There was a gap between 'reason' and natural rights that natural-rights theorists had failed to bridge. The appeal of the concept of natural rights, she thought, derived from the emphasis on the individual suffering from bad social conditions. Nature, however, provides no standards of evaluation. Such standards are the product of human choices. There are many ways to characterize human nature, and philosophers have derived different conclusions from different conceptions of human nature (Macdonald 1963). Macdonald's argument that natural rights are neither empirically verifiable facts nor deductions from self-evidently true premises clarifies the challenge that a justificatory theory of human rights has to meet. Her conclusion that human rights are the products of human choice, however, leaves them with no justification at all. As a response to Nazism, this is not satisfactory.

The United Nations thus introduced the concept of human rights into international law and politics at a time when its philosophical justification was very uncertain. This uncertainty was produced both by the historical critique of the concept of natural rights and by the lack of any philosophical consensus on the basis of human rights. Worse, the concept of human rights was called into question by the following arguments, among others.

1. Human rights do not exist in nature: they are human constructions. They are, therefore, neither 'natural' nor 'self-evident', but are morally compelling only if they follow from a morally compelling justificatory argument.
2. Aristotle was right to say that human beings are social animals. A theory of human rights must, therefore, *follow from* and not *precede* a theory of the good society.
3. Since the good of society is prior to the rights of individuals, the duties of individuals to society are prior to the rights of individuals.
4. There are different conceptions of the good society, and there are different conceptions of rights that can be derived from them: there is no universal conception of rights.
5. International human-rights law is the product of political power, pragmatic agreement and a limited moral consensus. It has no deeper theoretical justification. Verbal agreement on general principles may conceal disagreement on the meaning and policy implications of those principles.

The justification of human rights has to confront these arguments. This is the task of human-rights theory.

Human-rights theory

Rights

Human rights must be a special kind of rights. They are often contrasted with *legal* rights or *civil* rights that derive from the laws or customs of particular societies. It is commonly said that human rights are the rights one has simply because one is a human being. This is, however, not a satisfactory formulation. It is not clear why one has *any* rights simply because one is a human being. It is particularly unclear why one has the rights listed in the Universal Declaration. Indeed, this formulation seems ill suited to explain this list. Article 21, for example, says that everyone has the right to take part in the government of his country; but one does not have that right simply because one is a human being, since children do not have this right. Article 22 says that everyone, *'as a member of society'*, has the right to social security.

The point of rights discourse, which distinguishes it from other moral discourses, such as those that emphasize duties and/or benevolence, is that if you have a right to x, and you do not get x, then this is not only wrong, but it is also a wrong to *you*. The discourse of rights draws our attention to persons who have *rightful entitlements*. The distinctive value of a right is that it gives the right-holder a special entitlement to press the relevant claims if enjoyment of the right is threatened or denied. This distinguishes having a right from simply enjoying a benefit or being the beneficiary of someone else's obligation (Donnelly 1985a: 1–6, 12–13; 1989: 9–12). Some theorists claim that unenforceable rights are not rights at all. One can, however, have a moral right to something even if that right is unenforceable. The Jews in Nazi Germany had many moral rights that were not enforceable. The recognition of moral rights that are unenforceable now may help to get them enforced in the future.

Human rights may not be rights one has simply because one is a human being, but they are rights of exceptional importance, designed to protect morally valid and fundamental human interests, in particular against the abuse of political power. They carry special weight against other claims, and can be violated only for exceptionally strong reasons. Dworkin has made the influential suggestion that rights are 'trumps', but this is misleading if it is interpreted to mean that rights always defeat other moral and political considerations. Dworkin's view was that rights 'trump' only 'the routine goals of political administration', which is a relatively weak conception of rights (Dworkin 1978: xi, 92). Human rights may be 'trumps' in a stronger sense, in that they override more than routine political policies, but it is not plausible to claim that they override all other considerations. Article 29 of the Universal Declaration provides for the limitation of human rights to meet 'the just requirements of morality, public order and the general welfare in a democratic society'. This provision is very vague, and seems to provide a worryingly broad permission to limit human rights.

There is a consensus that human rights have three distinctive characteristics: 1) they are universal: everyone has human rights; 2) everyone has them equally; 3) they are the rights of individuals. Each of these characteristics presents challenges to the justificatory theory of human rights. To show that there are universal rights, we must offer plausible, cross-cultural reasons for such rights. To show that everyone is equal in rights, we have to clarify, and to justify, the sense in which everyone is equal, and which social inequalities, if any, are nevertheless justifiable. The view that human rights are always the rights of individuals is widely held; but the idea that there are collective rights in the field of human rights – for example, the rights of indigenous peoples – has also achieved increased acceptance in recent years.

Justifications

The simplest justification of human rights is the claim that they are 'self-evident'. Some hold that there is something morally wrong with demanding reasons for the belief that, for example, genocide violates the human rights of its victims. This is not so much a justification of human rights as the claim that no justification is necessary. This argument is unsatisfactory, however, because the concept of human rights is, in fact, controversial and therefore stands in need of justification.

Human rights are sometimes justified on the ground that there is an international consensus on most rights found in international law (Donnelly 1989: 21–4, 1999: 85, 2003: 40–1, 51–3). This is, however, a weak argument for several reasons. The apparent consensus on international human-rights law is neither complete nor sincere. There is no consensus on the rights of women. The partial consensus on the abstract formulations of international legal texts does not mean that there is consensus on even the most fundamental moral issues: for example, there may be a consensus on 'the right to life', but there is certainly no consensus on the morality of abortion. The partial consensus exists among state elites, who do not necessarily represent the people they rule. There is no consensus on human rights even among Western philosophers. The limited consensus on human rights among state elites is undermined by their neglect of human rights in their political and economic policies. Finally, and most fundamentally, consensus is a matter of fact, and justifies nothing in the absence of independent reasons showing why the consensus is good.

A common argument is that human rights derive from the fundamental value of human dignity. The concept of human dignity is vague, however, and could provide the basis for moral theories that ignore human rights in favour, for example, of a system of duties. In some cultures, to affirm the dignity of women is to challenge the dignity of men. Human rights may be grounded in the value of human dignity, but the justification of human rights must provide arguments that lead us from human dignity to human rights.

The classic justification of natural rights derived from arguments based on the will of God, the claims of reason, and/or beliefs about nature. Some still base their support for human rights on one or more of these foundations. To many contemporary philosophers, however, the original form of such arguments is now unconvincing. There has, nevertheless, been an attempt to defend human rights in terms of natural law. Such attempts usually avoid controversial metaphysical claims. Modern natural-law theorists argue that there are objective goods that cannot rationally be rejected, such as life, society and knowledge. These things are good, whether or not this is endorsed by consensus or positive law. These goods are said to be objectively necessary conditions for human flourishing, and consequently form the basis of moral obligations. The natural-law theory of human rights claims to reconcile the common good with individual rights, since it holds that the common good enhances individual freedom by providing it with stable social conditions, while individual freedom enhances the common good by promoting the flourishing of all. Human rights are, on this account, not subject to, but components of, the common good. As such, they may be limited by each other and by other aspects of the common good. They may also limit what can be done for the common good (Finnis 1980).

This theory seeks to combine an Aristotelian conception of the common good with a Lockean theory of individual rights. It is vulnerable to a number of objections. Claims about objective goods are either too vague to be useful or too controversial to be objective. Even those who agree that there are objective goods do not agree on what those goods are. The claim that the common good has been reconciled with individual rights is asserted, but not demonstrated, and begs many questions about conflicts between individuals and society.

A similar approach is taken by the theory of 'capabilities', which was introduced, not to justify human rights, but to replace the concept of 'development' as the increase of national wealth with a focus on improvements in the quality of life (Nussbaum and Sen 1993). It is also Aristotelian in that it is based on the value of human flourishing. It is liberal in that it values the flourishing of each human individual. A person's capabilities are their abilities to do and be certain things that are fundamentally important to any human life, whatever else the person wants. Capabilities are intrinsically valuable because they make life fully human. Each capability is valuable, and there are therefore limits to the extent to which they may be traded against each other. The theory can set some priorities when capabilities conflict by requiring that basic capabilities 'trump' non-basic capabilities (food is more important than play, for example), but it can do so only to a limited extent. In this, however, it is like many accounts of human rights. Like the concept of human rights, that of capabilities is said to be valid cross-culturally. The emphasis on cross-cultural validity means that the list of capabilities is always open to challenge through cross-cultural dialogue. Capabilities theorists argue, however, that liberal freedoms, democratic rights and basic welfare are all required by a plausible account of human flourishing.

The theory of capabilities, like that of natural law, claims to have identified objective, basic human goods. The concept of capabilities can be associated with that of human rights in so far as everyone has the right to have their capabilities protected. Both capabilities and human-rights theories hold that governments are the primary bearers of the relevant obligations, although capabilities theory is somewhat less tied than the concept of human rights to the doctrine of international law that such obligations are borne solely, or mainly, by states. Both capabilities and modern human-rights theories are secular, and seek to avoid controversial metaphysical or religious commitments. Capabilities theory is well suited to integrate civil, political, economic, social and cultural rights, as the concept of human rights seeks to do in theory and in practice (Nussbaum 1997).

Capabilities theory has been very influential in recent thinking about development, especially at the UN. Its relation to human rights, however, has not been fully elaborated. The theory raises several problems, the most fundamental of which is that capabilities are (actual or potential) facts about human beings, and their moral status is therefore questionable. It may be, for example, that practical reason is a capability necessary for human flourishing, but this capability can be used for good or bad purposes, and hence we seem to need a different moral theory to distinguish between good and bad capabilities. Since capabilities theory is universalistic and egalitarian (all human beings have and need capabilities, equally), good capabilities are those that do not diminish the capabilities of others, and that may indeed enhance them. Imagination, for example, is a capability that can be used for art and for torture, but art is generally friendlier than torture to the capabilities of others. However, even if we can define the good capabilities, the theory of corresponding obligations is undeveloped. Capabilities theory, like the concept of human rights, seems to be a theory of *minimal entitlements* and not of distributive justice, because it cannot tell us what is a *fair* distribution of capabilities (Pogge 2002b). There are problems of identifying, weighting and prioritizing capabilities. The best way to solve these problems may be context-dependent. This raises the further problem as to whether capabilities provide a basis for criticizing cultures or whether cultures provide the basis for identifying capabilities (Clark 2005: 7).

Both contemporary natural-law and capabilities theory reject the metaphysical commitments of classical natural rights while retaining the idea of the human individual as an autonomous, rational agent. Gewirth has placed the concept of agency at the centre of his theory of human rights. He has argued that, although there are many, diverse moralities in the world, morality itself presupposes agency (purposive action), and all agents must regard the proximate necessary conditions of their actions as necessary goods. These necessary goods are freedom and well-being. Freedom consists of choosing one's actions without external coercion on the basis of adequate information. Well-being consists in having the other general abilities required for agency. Logically, all agents must claim, at least implicitly, rights to freedom and well-being grounded in their needs as agents who want to pursue their purposes.

The necessary goods of action are equally necessary goods for all agents, and so all agents must logically admit that others have as much right to these goods as they do. The rights to freedom and well-being are therefore moral rights, since they require of all agents that they take favourable account of the most important interests of all other agents. It follows that everyone ought to refrain from interfering with the freedom and well-being of everyone else, and that everyone ought to assist others to have freedom and well-being, when they cannot have them by their own efforts, and others can assist them without comparable cost to themselves. Such assistance typically operates best through appropriate institutions.

The rights to freedom and well-being are human rights, since every human being is an actual, prospective or potential agent. The human rights of one person may, however, conflict with those of another person, as indeed one human right may conflict with another in respect of the same person. Human rights are, therefore, only *prima facie*, not absolute rights (Gewirth 1981). There may be a tension between Gewirth's claim that it is *logically* necessary to recognize human rights and his acknowledgement that they may be overridden in certain circumstances. Despite the great care with which Gewirth presents his argument, the relation between logical deduction and empirical assumption in his theory is not entirely clear. Although Gewirth's argument from agency is more Kantian than Aristotelian, its emphasis on freedom and well-being makes it somewhat similar to capabilities theory. His argument has, however, been criticized on several grounds: he derives rights invalidly from needs; he does not make clear what necessary goods are necessary for; rights are not *logically*, but *empirically* necessary for action; the assumption of moral equality is Western and liberal, and not inherent in morality. Gewirth offers a systematic defence of human rights, but it is not as logically compelling as he claims.

One problem with the agency approach to human rights is that human beings who lack full agency – such as children and mentally disabled people – would be less than equal in rights. Some philosophers accept this conclusion, but insist that others may have strong obligations towards such persons. Others hold that human rights are proportional to the capacity to exercise them. Thus, children have the right not to be tortured, but not to vote. The main rival to agency as the ground of rights is sentience (feeling rather than thinking). On this view, torture is to be condemned because it is (unjustifiably) painful rather than because it violates agency. However, sentience does not ground a distinction between human and animal rights (an advantage, some may think), and does not ground the special importance normally given to such rights as freedom of expression and association.

Agency has a complex relation to needs. Some human rights – such as the right to subsistence – seem to be based on needs, but we do not have a right to everything we need, because some of our needs are trivial or immoral. Some have suggested the idea of basic needs as the ground of human rights. There is not, however, a human right to have all basic needs – including, for example, the need to be loved – fulfilled, for this may be impossible or too burdensome. The concept of basic needs is also better suited to the duty of charity to the needy than to the dignity of rights-holders.

Philosophers of human rights disagree as to whether the ground of human rights consists of the necessary conditions for agency or 'personhood' (Griffin 2008) or for human flourishing. The former argument holds that if human rights are to be universal and realistic they must be minimal, and thus be restricted to the conditions of a recognizably human life, but not necessarily of a good life. The latter, implied by capabilities theory and perhaps the Universal Declaration, has more ambitious aspirations for human well-being. Both seek to leave a generous space for human freedom within the field of human rights. Nickel argues that human rights set minimal standards for the conduct of governments, and thus leave most policy matters to democratic decision-making, and can accommodate considerable cultural and institutional variation (Nickel 2007: 36–7).

Attempts to derive human rights from 'human nature' have been subjected to two, quite different, objections. The first is that there are many conceptions of human nature, and there is no agreed method for deciding which is the best. The second is that 'human nature' is a biological concept that cannot generate rights. Yet even the minimalist account of human rights assumes that moral agency is a feature of human nature. There is no account of human nature that is both generally accepted and justifies human rights, but any justification of human rights requires some conception of human nature. Some say that human nature is 'socially constructed', but this presupposes a particular conception of human nature: human beings socially create their nature. This is consistent with the usual theoretical presuppositions of human rights.

There is no consensus on the best justification for human rights, and there is no reason to expect that such a consensus can be achieved. However, the fact that there are several strong justifications for human rights strengthens the moral force of the idea (Nickel 2007: 53–4).

Specification

Human-rights theory should justify the concept of human rights, and provide some guidance as to which claims and rights are human rights. The Universal Declaration is often taken to be an approximately correct list of human rights. Some philosophers who support the concept of human rights do not support the whole of this list. Rawls, for example, held that only Articles 3–18 represent genuine human rights because the other rights are either liberal, and therefore not universalizable, or presuppose particular institutions. Rawls located the concept of human rights in the context of his proposal for a 'law of peoples', which, he argued, should not be based on any particular philosophy of human nature, such as that human beings are moral persons. He did not, however, show that there are cultures which deny that human beings are moral persons nor, if there were such cultures, that they could respect human rights. Rawls offered no theory that would justify his limited set of human rights (Rawls 1999).

The concept of 'basic rights' has been proposed by some theorists who believe that the concept of universal rights might be 'imperialistic', but who do not wish to abandon the idea that governments should observe minimal standards of decent behaviour (Miller, D. 1995). Shue has suggested that basic rights are those that are necessary to other rights, but it is difficult to establish, conceptually or empirically, the necessity of one right to another. For example, although eating is necessary to the enjoyment of the right to free speech, the *right* to eat is not necessary. Also, we might think that the right to eat is more basic than the right to freedom of movement, but, in some circumstances, freedom of movement may be necessary in order to eat (Shue 1996; Nickel 2007: 131–2). The *enjoyment* of the right to subsistence is not necessary to the enjoyment of the right to security, nor is the enjoyment of the right to security necessary to the enjoyment of the right to subsistence (Pogge 2009: 118–19). Another proposal is that basic rights are those necessary for agency (Griffin 2008). Donnelly worries that the identification of 'basic rights' may lead to the neglect of other human rights, which are, according to his theory, necessary to a life of dignity (Donnelly 1989: 38–41). Many theorists, therefore, hold that some rights are more basic than others, but there is consensus on neither the justification nor the specification of basic rights.

Philosophers sometimes seek to derive specific rights from more general rights. Griffin, for example, has proposed that the right to autonomy is a fundamental, general human right, because it is necessary to moral agency. The right to autonomy entails a number of specific human rights, such as the rights to subsistence and education. It is sometimes objected that autonomy is one value among many, and that privileging autonomy is incompatible with toleration and pluralism. However, it is doubtful whether any culture denies autonomy completely, and, if there were such a culture, that it would be said to respect human rights. Griffin distinguishes autonomy from freedom. A person acts autonomously when they decide which religion to practise; they act freely when they practise their religion without coercion or deception. The general right to freedom entails familiar specific rights, such as those to freedom of expression and association (Griffin 2008).

There is a common view that only civil and political rights are genuine human rights because they require only inaction by governments (refraining from torture, for example), and therefore can be fulfilled universally, whereas economic and social rights depend on specific, not universal institutions (such as a welfare state), and are too expensive for some governments to afford. There is no duty to do the impossible; therefore, if it is impossible to meet some economic and social needs, there can be no *right* to have them met (Cranston 1973). Shue and Donnelly have answered these arguments effectively. Donnelly has pointed out that the distinction between the two types of rights is confused: the right to property is considered a civil right, for example, whereas it could just as reasonably be considered an economic right (Donnelly 1989: 30). Shue argues that failure to respect certain basic economic rights, such as the right to subsistence, would render civil and political rights worthless. Both authors also argue that protecting civil and political rights can be expensive (providing fair trials, for example) and that both types may require positive action or inaction by governments. There is thus no basis for treating only civil and political rights as genuine human rights (Shue 1996; Donnelly 1989). Mobilizing resources to implement human rights is a common problem, but it affects civil and political rights as well as social and economic rights.

There is consensus neither on which general rights there are, nor on how to derive specific from general rights. Consequently, it is difficult to specify human rights in a very determinate way. This is not necessarily regrettable however, since although it opens a space for the violation of rights, it leaves the determination of human rights to democratic debate and permits flexibility under changing circumstances.

Democracy

Institutions can play an important role in making the UN's vague specification of human rights more determinate. Which institutions are best suited to this task is partly a conceptual, and partly an empirical question. Here human rights and democracy may be integrated in that the democratic interpretation of human rights is both practicable and justifiable by democratic principles. However, although democracies generally respect human rights better than do other political systems, they do so imperfectly; and, of course, many states are not democracies. The best mix of international and national institutions for human-rights protection is therefore uncertain.

It is commonly believed that human rights and democracy are mutually supportive or related to each other by definition. The Vienna Declaration of 1993, for example, asserted that democracy and human rights were 'interdependent and mutually reinforcing'. The relations between the two are, however, quite complex. Similar values, such as respect for the dignity of the individual, may form the basis of both human rights and democracy. Democracy may also be, empirically, the best form of government for protecting human rights, although some electoral democracies fail to protect economic and social rights, while some authoritarian regimes do so quite well. Nevertheless, human rights and democracy have different, and potentially competing, theoretical foundations. Democratic theory asks who ought to rule, and answers 'the people'. Human-rights theory asks how rulers ought to behave, and answers that they ought to respect the human rights of every individual. Democracy is a collective concept, and democratic governments can violate the human rights of individuals. The concept of human rights is designed to limit the power of governments, and, in so far as it subjects governments to popular control, it has a democratic character. But human rights limit the legitimate power of all governments, including democratic governments. Human rights are consequently often protected by entrenching them in constitutions. This transfers power from democratically elected political decision-makers to judges, who are usually not democratically elected.

Waldron has made a rights-based critique of the constitutional entrenchment of rights. He argues that if the value of human rights derives from the dignity of individuals, the outcome of democratic participation by such individuals should have priority over the judgements of courts (Waldron 1993). Dahl argues, similarly, that the people are the best judges of what is good for them, and are, therefore, the safest guardians of their rights. Democracy is, in this sense, prior to rights (Dahl 1989). Dworkin, however, makes a distinction between majoritarian and egalitarian democracy. Majoritarian democracy permits the 'tyranny of the majority', and is a defective form of democracy, since it denies the equality of all citizens. Egalitarian democracy recognizes the equality of all citizens, and therefore entrenches their rights in a constitution to protect them from violation by majorities. The constitutional protection of democratic rights is, according to Dworkin, not undemocratic, because it is intended to protect democratic equality (Dworkin 1978; 1996). This dispute is difficult to resolve, partly because it involves complex empirical questions about the outcomes of court decisions. Most actual democracies entrust the protection of basic rights to independent courts. Courts always have to interpret laws, and, if they defend only the most basic rights, their limitation of democracy is minimal. However, neither courts nor elected legislatures guarantee the defence of human rights or democracy. Some theorists argue that a strongly supportive political culture is a better safeguard for human rights and democracy than specific institutions.

Some human rights, such as the right to vote, are *constitutive of* democracy. Others, such as freedom of speech, are necessary to democracy. Still others, such as the right to education, are necessary to an adequate democracy. Some human rights, such as freedom of religion, seem more remotely connected to democracy, and perhaps sometimes unfriendly towards it. In so far as human rights are necessary to democracy, democratic government must be limited to preserve democracy.

Other values

Critics of rights discourse sometimes say that there are more important moral values than rights, and that appeal to rights may undermine these values. Parents, for example, should love their children, and children should respect their parents. If parents or children appealed to their rights, this mutual relation of love and respect would be damaged. However, if parents seriously harm their children, then children, or adults acting on their behalf, may appeal to their rights. Rights kick in when other values, which may be ideally superior, fail. A principal justification of rights discourse is that it legitimates challenges to social order when that order is unjust. Where justice prevails, appeals to rights are unnecessary. This answers the objection that the concept of rights undermines social harmony.

Philosophers sometimes talk of 'rights-based' moralities, and human rights may seem to be an example of such a morality. There are good reasons, however, for rejecting this view. Firstly, if rights form the *basis* of morality, it may not be possible to defend rights against their critics by appeal to more fundamental values. Secondly, rights ought to be balanced with other values, and it would be dogmatic to assume that rights are always more fundamental than other values. We must take account of other values if we are to give a plausible account of the *limits* of rights. The question of whether I have the right to insult another person's religion, for example, cannot reasonably be answered simply by assuming that rights always trump other values, for I should identify and evaluate the moral weight of the other values at issue. Rights are important, but they are not the whole of morality. We can have the right to do something that it is not right to do: to criticize our government unfairly, for example. The relations among rights and other moral values are complex, therefore, even if it is true that human rights are especially important values.

The Universal Declaration says that human rights are the foundations of justice, but it may be that justice is the foundation of human rights. Many theorists now consider respect for human rights to be a requirement of justice, but, in so far as human rights set only minimal standards for society, they cannot fully specify the requirements of justice. A society could respect human rights, yet distribute benefits and burdens unjustly. A theory of justice, therefore, says more than a theory of human rights, but the concept of human rights makes a distinctive contribution to the theory of justice by emphasizing the entitlements of rights holders rather than, say, the duties of rulers.

Some theories of justice require that rewards be allocated according to desert. Such criteria play no role in the theory of human rights. It may be justifiable to restrict the human rights of wrongdoers, as in the imprisonment of certain criminals, but although such persons may deserve to be justly punished, they do not deserve to lose their human rights. Human rights do not depend on desert, but it has always been accepted that they do not prohibit just punishment.

Two kinds of theory of justice relevant to human rights have been much discussed recently. The first is transitional justice. This raises questions as to how the 'normal' requirements of social justice should be combined with those of justice for the victims of past injustice or gross human-rights violations. These can conflict, and in practice 'forward-looking' justice is often given priority, controversially, over justice for the victims of human-rights violations (Waldron 1992; Méndez 1997; Thompson 2002). The question first arose in connection with the transitions between various forms of authoritarian regimes and democracy at the end of the twentieth century, but has been extended to such questions as the demand for reparations and/or apologies for such past evils as colonialism and slavery. The second kind of theory of justice that has aroused much controversy recently is the theory of global justice. Most theories of global justice endorse human rights to some extent, but the extent varies from those who favour a narrow conception to those who support something like the UN conception (Rawls 1999; Pogge 2002a). Theories of global justice are controversial, but they are a means to specify human rights. We shall return to them in chapter eight.

Obligations and costs

Rights generally entail obligations. These obligations include the obligation not to violate rights, the obligation to protect others from violations of their rights, and the obligation to aid the victims of violations. Human rights do not depend on the performance of one's obligations. However, respecting human rights entails the performance of obligations, so that anyone enjoying rights without performing obligations would act unfairly. Obligations involve costs, so that the justification of rights requires the justification of imposing the corresponding costs.

There is a controversy as to who has human-rights obligations. The orthodox view (especially of international law) is that only, or mainly, states and their governments have them. Classical natural-rights theory, however, held that everyone had such obligations. Article 30 of the Universal Declaration envisages human-rights violations by non-state actors. Concerns about powerful non-state actors, such as transnational corporations, as well as feminist analyses of the private sphere as one in which the rights of women are violated, have led to a new view that human-rights obligations should be extended to various non-state actors. It may be countered that the state has the primary obligation to prevent human-rights violations by private corporations and to protect women. There is also a question as to whether, if the concept of human rights is extended to private harms, it would cover a wide range of crimes and lose its distinctiveness. States are usually thought to have human-rights obligations mainly to their own citizens; but they do also have obligations to non-citizens, although the extent of these remains controversial. If the primary obligation-bearers are unable or unwilling to fulfil their obligations, others may have an obligation to assist or to take over the responsibility, but these actors will have other obligations, and it is difficult to say how these different obligations should be prioritized. Most moral philosophers require us to make only limited sacrifices for the sake of others, but they generally agree that the sacrifices we actually make are less than those that we ought to make.

O'Neill believes that human-rights discourse fails the neediest because it fails to identify who is obliged to do what for whom (O'Neill 2005: 40). Rights must specify corresponding duties, but human welfare rights fail to do this. Welfare duties are borne by *institutions*. Because these institutions are not universal, the rights they fulfil are not human rights. Ashford argues, to the contrary, that *all* rights may need institutions to be effective: the right not to be tortured requires not only that individuals refrain from torture, but also that institutions ensure that they do so. The case for welfare rights derives from their contribution to human dignity. Institutions are necessary for their realization but not for their existence. The causes of both torture and starvation may be complex, and may involve a complex set of duties. If the causes of human-rights violations are complex, those involved in the causation share responsibility if they either knew about the violations or were culpably ignorant of them, and could have avoided them (Ashford 2006). Pogge argues that the rich and powerful are primarily responsible for the international order, which is the 'decisive' cause of human-rights violations, and therefore they bear the primary responsibility for reforming that order for the sake of human rights (Pogge 2005a: 31; 2007).

The provision of international law that states may derogate from some of their human-rights obligations in national emergencies recognizes that the cost of protecting human rights can be excessive. This provision is nevertheless controversial both because the concept of 'national emergency' is vague and because the distinction between derogable and non-derogable rights conflicts with the principle that human rights are indivisible. International law allows no restrictions of human rights in dangerous situations that fall short of national emergencies.

Conflicts of rights

Because human rights derive from interests, require resources and are indeterminate, they can conflict. Steiner argues that conflicts of rights lead to intolerable arbitrariness, and that rights therefore should be 'compossible', that is, only a theory of rights that avoids conflicts is rational. His theory of rights, however, recognizes only rights to private property that exclude most of the economic and social rights recognized by the UN (Steiner 1994). His critics complain that his theory would allow an intolerable 'trumping' of basic human rights by property rights. Most theorists of human rights acknowledge that conflicts between human rights are possible, as does Article 29 of the Universal Declaration.

Such conflicts are of two main kinds. The human rights of some may conflict with those of others and/or one right may conflict with another right of the same person. My right to security may conflict with others' right to a fair trial and/or my right to freedom of movement. Apparent conflicts of rights may sometimes be resolved by carefully specifying the scope of rights. The right to freedom of speech, for example, would not conflict with the right not to be subject to racial abuse if the former were specified to exclude the right to express some forms of abuse (Jones 1994: 199–201).

Conflicts of rights may be resolved by assigning them differential importance and determining priorities. It is difficult, however, to do this systematically without transforming human rights into a calculus of interests. One objection to this is that the required calculation simply cannot be made. Another approach is 'the utilitarianism of rights', which requires conflicts of rights to be resolved in whichever way maximizes the protection of rights. This is subject to a criticism commonly made of ordinary Utilitarianism: that it sacrifices some for the good of others. A better approach may be to respect all rights, but, when some sacrifice is unavoidable, to distribute the sacrifice fairly. This may be indeterminate, but it refuses to treat the human rights of some merely as means to the good of others. Those who ground human rights in agency give priority to those rights that are most important to agency: the right not to starve would, for example, have priority over the right to holidays with pay (Gewirth 1982). This is theoretically coherent, but it offers no resolution of conflicts between equally important rights. Those who believe that they can identify 'basic rights' would hold that to secure those rights other rights may be violated, if necessary, but basic rights may not be violated to secure non-basic rights. We have seen, however, that the concept of 'basic rights' is controversial. It may be that no theory of human rights can resolve all conflicts of rights. Life presents us with tragic dilemmas, and human-rights theory cannot change this.

Although the concept of human rights is usually thought to be incompatible with the philosophy of Utilitarianism, because the latter would sacrifice human rights for the sake of maximizing utility, Jones has suggested that rule-Utilitarianism might rescue human-rights theory from the dilemmas of rights conflicts. Rule-Utilitarianism says that we ought to live by those rules that best promote the common good. It would tell us not to violate the human rights of one person to protect the human rights of others because this would violate a justified rule, and rule-Utilitarianism says that this should not be done even if, in the short run, it did more good than harm (Jones 1994: 203–4). This is a plausible solution for those who believe that the human rights of some should never be violated to protect the human rights of a larger number of others, but it is not certain that we should always take this position.

Objections to human rights

We saw in chapter two that objections to the concept of human rights are almost as old as the concept itself. The move from 'natural' to 'human' rights eliminated some of the objections to the former in so far as those objections were to arguments from 'nature'. Nevertheless some of the objections to the classical concept have been made to the contemporary concept: it is too dogmatic, or too absolutist, or too individualistic; it lacks philosophical foundations; it stimulates expectations unrealistically and thereby promotes social conflict and disorder; it ignores the importance of responsibilities and marginalizes the value of community; it cannot resolve conflicting values; it is too legalistic and formalistic, thereby failing to address real suffering and injustice. Those who do not necessarily reject the concept nevertheless complain of 'rights inflation', which trivializes rights, imposes unreasonable burdens on duty bearers and excessive constraints on freedom, restricts the scope of democratic politics, limits the role of toleration and pluralism, and undermines valuable social relations such as those of the family.

A recent challenge to human rights has come from a group of philosophers known as 'communitarians' (Caney 1992; Mulhall and Swift 1996). These philosophers criticize liberalism for overvaluing individual autonomy and undervaluing community. It is mistaken, however, to see human rights and community as mutually exclusive. Some communities violate human rights, but others protect them. Some human rights refer explicitly to the value of community, while others, such as the right to freedom of expression, are best interpreted as requiring communities of an appropriate kind (Gewirth 1996). Communitarians raise complex issues, and not all their ideas are compatible with human rights, but the supposed incompatibility between human rights and community is often overstated. For example, persecution and poverty undermine communities and family life, and better protection of human rights could strengthen the solidaristic values that 'communitarians' like to defend. We should also remember that the value of 'community' can often be invoked to hide cruelties and injustices (especially towards women and children) that should not be defended.

Conclusion

The concept of human rights is often criticized because it is 'individualistic', emphasizes rights *rather than* responsibilities, and encourages selfishness. Locke's classical theory of natural rights, however, was based on natural law that imposed an obligation on everyone to respect the rights of others. The concept of rights can be used selfishly, but all concepts can be abused: the concept of duty, for example, can be used by the powerful to control the weak. Rights advocates often fight for the rights of others, and in doing so are not acting selfishly. Article 29 of the Universal Declaration of Human Rights assumes that everyone has social duties, and Gewirth argues that the concept of human rights entails duties to communities that sustain human rights (Gewirth 1996). It is sometimes said that the concept of human rights presupposes the concept of the non-social individual. However, the concept of human rights is primarily the basis of a theory of legitimate government. Thus, the concept is so far from being non-social that it is primarily a *political* concept.

The Universal Declaration states that recognition of human rights is the foundation of justice in the world. The relation between human rights and justice has proved to be controversial, however. Liberal theorists of justice have argued that the concept of justice is more fundamental than that of human rights, and theories of justice can say more about how rights should be allocated than the concept of human rights can. The theory of justice can, nevertheless, find an important place for human rights. Some theorists believe that whether a human-rights claim is valid or not depends on whether it is endorsed by justice. In contrast, Donnelly has argued that the concept of human rights is clearer and less controversial than that of justice (Donnelly 1982). In practice, the concept of human rights may be less controversial than any *particular* theory of international justice, and therefore politically more useful. However, we have seen that many aspects of human rights are very controversial. Liberal theories of justice usually endorse human rights, and it is a matter of practical judgement rather than theory whether a rights-based or justice-based approach to international politics is more effective.

A common objection to the concept of human rights is that rights cannot be derived from nature, but only from the culture and institutions of particular societies. This objection has been made to at least some of the rights in the Universal Declaration. Jones points out that Article 22 says that 'everyone' has the right to social security and to realization, *in accordance with the organization and resources of each state*, of the economic, social and cultural rights indispensable for his dignity. He suggests that Article 22 sets out citizens' rights rather than human rights (Jones 1994: 160–3). This should be read, however, as a statement of universal rights that allows their implementation to vary according to the organization and resources of different states. In so far as human rights have limits, society sets those limits, and in this sense human rights must be socially and therefore variably specified (Jones 1994: 192–4). Article 29 of the Universal Declaration allows that human rights may be limited by law for certain purposes, though, unfortunately, the wording of this provision is exceptionally vague.

Rights derive from rules governing the relations among human beings. In this sense, rights are essentially social. This is consistent with the idea that rights empower rights-holders. Power is a social relation, and legitimate power is restrained by rules that protect rights. The empowerment of rights-holders is, however, the distinctive feature of rights as a concept. To emphasize human rights rather than human duties is to emphasize the moral worth of the rights-holder without denying that the moral status of human individuals also entails duties to others. The concept of human rights demands respect for human individuals as moral agents and concern for them as vulnerable creatures. It is neither egoistic nor anti-social. It denies neither individual responsibility nor the value of community. It is a concept that affirms human solidarity while respecting individual autonomy. Maritain and Forsythe may be right to say, that, given the religious and philosophical diversity of the world, and the 'essentially contested' nature of philosophy itself, consensus on the 'philosophical foundations' of human rights may be impossible to achieve. There is probably no single philosophical foundation of human rights; different human rights may have different justifications, and the very concept of human rights may have various justifications. This is not a serious blow to the concept, however, because the very idea of philosophical foundations is itself problematic. There are various strong reasons for supporting human rights, based on respect for human dignity (Donnelly), the bases of moral action (Gewirth), the demands of human sympathy (Rorty), or the conditions of human flourishing (Nussbaum). It has been doubted whether a consensus on human rights can be based on a consensus on liberalism in the foreseeable future, but it may be that a 'consensus' may be based on diverse grounds, while the best arguments for human rights are liberal arguments. Human rights do not constitute the whole of morality or politics: they have to be balanced with other values, such as social order. They are not absolute, for human rights can conflict with each other. The moral and humanitarian case for assigning the concept of human rights a leading role in political theory is, however, very powerful.

Human rights are thus not 'natural', although they must rest on a conception of human nature and well-being. Nevertheless, as 'social constructions' they are as 'valid' as the reasons for supporting them are strong. Talbott has questioned what he calls 'the proof paradigm', which requires that all justified beliefs be rationally beyond question. The fact that human rights are not beyond question does not make them morally invalid, or more doubtful than many other beliefs that it is reasonable to hold (Talbott 2005: 23). The distinction that is commonly made between the individualism of rights and the good of society is misleading in that the concept of human rights entails a conception of how the good of individuals is best reconciled with the good of society. The distinction between rights-based and duty-based theories is also misleading in that a theory of human rights must also be a theory of duties. The *justification* of human rights should be distinguished from *consensus* about human rights, because the consensus is worth supporting only if the justification is compelling. The concept of human rights is a basis for articulating the wrongs done to individuals by unjust and oppressive uses of power. It gives rise to a number of moral dilemmas and philosophical puzzles, but the moral force of its core meaning remains extremely powerful and deservedly influential.

5
The Role of the Social Sciences

Introduction: human rights and social science

The concept of human rights originated in theology, philosophy and law. The concept of natural rights was first developed from Roman law in the late Middle Ages to provide a theological defence of property, then both to defend and condemn European imperialism, and, in the seventeenth century, to defend property and what we now call civil and political rights against absolute, monarchical government. This concept was *normative*: it prescribed how people were permitted and obliged to behave. The contemporary concept of human rights has inherited this normative character: it is designed primarily to prescribe to governments what they ought and ought not to do. Between the French Revolution and the establishment of the United Nations, the concept of natural rights was challenged by the philosophy of scientific positivism that strongly influenced the emerging social sciences. According to this philosophy, science is not normative: it does not tell people how they ought to live. The tension between the concept of human rights and social science became apparent in 1947, when the Executive Board of the American Anthropological Association submitted a statement to the UN Commission on Human Rights expressing concern that a universal

declaration of human rights might show insufficient respect to the different cultures of the world (American
Anthropological Association Executive Board 1947). The
statement was criticized within anthropology on the ground
that the Association, as a scientific organization, should not
speak about human rights, for there was no scientific
approach to human rights (Barnett 1948).

Human-rights law bridges the gap between the normative
concept of human rights and social science. Law is normative
in that it prescribes rights and duties. Social science can,
however, study why and how human-rights law is made, and
why and how it is or is not implemented. The interpretive
social sciences can supplement the legal discourse of human
rights by explaining how human-rights problems are understood in different cultural contexts. Interpretive social science
bridges the gap between legal abstractions and the everyday
lives of the ordinary people it claims to defend.

The legalization of human rights is often the best way to
implement them, but it is neither necessary nor sufficient.
Sometimes law can achieve what morality cannot. To benefit
from human rights, however, people need secure access to
what they offer, not legal rights as such. The legalization of
human rights may even hinder their implementation if it
provides formal institutionalization without effective protection (Nickel 2007: 50–1, 92–3; Pogge 2005a: 13–14).
Social scientists have studied empirically the actions and
impact of those involved with human-rights law, such as
governments, intergovernmental organizations and non-
governmental organizations.

The dominance and critique of law

Before the 1970s almost all academic work on human rights
was done by lawyers, and most articles were published in
law journals. A survey of journals published between the
early 1970s and the mid-1980s conducted by the UN
Economic, Social and Cultural Organization (UNESCO)
found that almost all human-rights journals were predominantly legal, and that the social sciences contributed little to

other journals that carried articles on human rights. Several surveys on the teaching of human rights in universities have shown that the legal perspective is overwhelmingly dominant. The legal approach to human rights cannot, however, adequately analyse the ethical, political, sociological, economic and anthropological dimensions of human rights. Human-rights law has social and political origins, and social and political consequences, and legal analysis cannot help us to understand these. Social science has substantive interests and research methods that are quite different from those of legal studies, and that can illuminate the practice of human rights (Pritchard 1989). The social sciences have, however, until recently largely neglected human rights.

Lawyers make *judgements* as to whether human rights have been respected or violated. Social scientists seek to *explain* why human rights have been respected or violated. Judgemental disciplines sometimes make assumptions about the measures that will improve respect for human rights. Social scientists test causal hypotheses empirically, and can thereby contribute to effective policy-making.

Political philosophers have long argued that politics should be subject to the rule of law, and that law stands above the politics of interests and power. However, in so far as law places limits on government, it is political. Law cannot abolish power, but it can conceal or legitimate it. International human-rights law has been criticized because it rests on the fiction of universal equality, and, by masking structural inequalities, conceals the causes of many human-rights violations. It can, however, have a partial autonomy, and thereby provide justice to those subject to power, but this autonomy is never complete. Law appears to be impartial and objective, but this may be illusory. The illusion may be appealing, in so far as it seems to provide certainty in an uncertain world, but such certainty is illusory, because the interpretation and application of law is contested both legally and politically. The existence, nature, interpretation and implementation of human-rights law unavoidably raise contentious political questions.

The empirical evidence as to whether law protects human rights is surprisingly slight. Keith, in a study of the period 1977–96, found that constitutional provisions for freedom of speech, assembly, association, religion and the press generally produced no observable improvement in human-rights behaviour. However, provisions for fair trials did lead to an improvement in personal integrity rights. The evidence suggested that constitutional protection of human rights had less effect than lawyers and activists assumed, but more than sceptics believed (Keith 2002). Blasi and Cingranelli, however, found that constitutions did have a positive effect on human rights if they provided for appropriate institutions, such as an independent judiciary (Blasi and Cingranelli 1996).

Moravcsik found that the success of the European human-rights regime resulted from a combination of a free civil society and an independent judiciary. The regime did not liberalize illiberal regimes; it improved the human-rights records of democratic regimes that already had good records. The most effective institutions for international human-rights implementation rely on a prior ideological and institutional support. Human-rights implementation is most difficult when it is most needed. Comparison between the European and the American human-rights regimes shows that consensus on human-rights values is more important than institutions in protecting human rights (Moravcsik 1995: 158–9, 178–82).

Hathaway claims that international lawyers are reluctant to assess systematically whether human-rights law is effective. She found that the human-rights practices of countries that have ratified human-rights treaties are generally better than those of countries that have not. However, non-compliance with treaty obligations is common, and countries with the worst human-rights records often have high rates of ratification. Treaty ratification is often associated with *worse* human-rights practices. Since enforcement of human-rights treaties is extremely weak, and states can gain some prestige from ratifying them, treaty ratification may be *a substitute for* improving human rights. Some claim that human-rights treaties have diffuse, positive effects that cannot easily be measured, but the long-term effects of ratification are unknown. Hathaway concludes that declarations of rights that are not easily defined and measured, and are not accompanied by an effective means for securing remedies for violations, may be counter-productive. Efforts to secure universal ratification of human-rights treaties are therefore problematic (Hathaway 2002). Goodman and Jinks have challenged Hathaway's findings on methodological grounds (Goodman and Jinks 2003). Keith found that although states that ratified the International Covenant on Civil and Political Rights (ICCPR) had better records than non-ratifiers, economic and political factors, not ratification itself, explained this difference (Keith 1999).

Neumayer found that ratification of human-rights treaties had a beneficial effect in conditions of democracy and a strong civil society. In the absence of those conditions, treaty ratification had no effect, and might be associated with more human-rights violations (Neumayer 2005). Hafner-Burton and Tsutsui found that states which ratify more human-rights treaties are not more likely to protect human rights than states which ratify a small number of treaties. Ratifiers are, indeed, more likely to violate human rights than non-ratifiers. States that ratified the ICCPR and the Convention Against Torture were not more likely to implement the rights set out in these treaties. Neither treaty had a systematic effect on the human-rights behaviour of repressive states even 15 years after ratification. Thus the argument that ratification takes time to have an effect is not supported (Hafner-Burton and Tsutsui 2007). Landman concludes that there is strong empirical support for a limited effect of international human-rights law on state behaviour (Landman 2005a: 6, 137, 146–7). Simmons found that ratification of human-rights treaties sometimes has positive effects on the executive branch of government, legislatures, judiciaries and civil society, especially in countries that are neither autocratic nor fully democratic, but where there is space for public debate about human-rights reforms. She found also that some human rights are harder to implement than others for various reasons, not only because of scarce resources (Simmons 2009).

International human-rights law may conflict with politics. Human-rights advocates support prosecutions to end impunity for human-rights crimes and deter further violations. Rodman argues, however, that international criminal tribunals cannot deter human-rights crimes in the midst of conflict. The experience of the former Yugoslavia and the recent indictment of Sudan's President, Omar al-Bashir, by the International Criminal Court (ICC) for war crimes and crimes against humanity in Darfur show that prosecution cannot deter violations if the co-operation of the perpetrator is necessary for peace. In Bosnia, Kosovo, Rwanda and Sierra Leone it was force not law that stopped the violence. Flint and de Waal argue that the arrest and prosecution of Bashir are unlikely because domestic opposition to his regime is weak and the international community is unwilling to use force. China, Russia, Arab and many African states, have economic and political interests in supporting Bashir, and against these the ICC has little power. Flint and de Waal believe that the only solution to Sudan's political conflicts is a compromise power-sharing deal. In conflicts such as that in Darfur, politics overwhelms law. International criminal tribunals can contribute to improved respect for human rights, but only if combined with politics (Rodman 2008; Flint and de Waal 2008).

The recent development of international criminal tribunals for the former Yugoslavia and Rwanda, and the establishment of the ICC, have precedents in the trials after the Second World War in Nuremberg and Tokyo. International tribunals have both advantages and disadvantages compared with national tribunals. International tribunals may conform better with international standards for fair trials. But national courts may have both more legitimacy and more impact with the people concerned. Human-rights advocates support criminal tribunals for human-rights crimes in principle, but states may sometimes favour them as cheap concessions by realism to idealism, a middle way between high-risk interventions and doing nothing (Rudolph 2001; Barria and Roper 2005: 358). The ICC was established in 1998. The USA has opposed the court and taken measures to prevent it from trying any US citizen. The court became fully operational in June 2003 and began its first trial – of the Congolese militia leader, Thomas Lubanga – in January 2009. The ICC has been criticized because all its formal investigations have been in Africa. The court has no police force, and generally must rely on the co-operation of governments in whose countries it is operating. It is also dependent on international support for funding, intelligence and evidence, the arrest of suspects and pressure on recalcitrant governments. Often that support is not forthcoming. On its value the jury is still out.

Because international and national tribunals have different advantages and disadvantages, hybrid tribunals, with national and international components, have been tried in Sierra Leone, Kosovo, East Timor and Cambodia. Finding a satisfactory combination of the merits of international and national courts can, however, be difficult. Some national courts assert 'universal jurisdiction' over the most serious violators. The 1999 case concerning the extradition of former Chilean President, Augusto Pinochet, in London set an important precedent for this approach. However, while universal jurisdiction exists in limited form in some treaties and national laws, it has gone into relative decline.

Some worry that human-rights trials are political 'show trials'. Wilson has argued, however, that the charge of genocide enabled the tribunal for the former Yugoslavia to combine a fair trial with a broad, historical narrative (Wilson 2005). In contrast, Futamura doubts whether the Tokyo trial gave an adequate account of the Second World War in Asia, and also whether its mixture of collective political aims and individual legal responsibility has helped the Japanese people to come to terms with their past (Futamura 2008). In Cambodia, although the trials took many years to establish, and some of the worst perpetrators had died, there is evidence that surviving victims felt that justice too little and too late was much better than no justice at all.

Some argue that although law can protect the human rights of the poor, their problems may not require legal solutions, law may oppress rather than liberate them, legal reforms intended to benefit them may not be implemented and/or they may find it difficult to access the courts. The UN Development Programme estimates that more than four billion people (two-thirds of the world's population) live outside the rule of law. There is, therefore, a need for legal empowerment of the poor. The legal-empowerment approach may have limits: for example, women's rights in areas dominated by Afghan warlords. Legal procedures may obscure the structural causes of violations and the best remedies.

Nevertheless, a combination of human-rights education, popular social movements and legal action may offer the best hope for the powerless. External assistance can facilitate local initiatives.

Human-rights tribunals, international and national, have been part of 'transitional justice', discussed briefly in the previous chapter. In transitions from repressive to democratic regimes policies on the prosecution of violators have varied. In some countries nothing has been done about past violations; in others violators have been given amnesties. Where there have been trials, sentences have sometimes been light. Truth commissions have sometimes been set up as alternatives to trials, but sometimes they have been combined with trials. One problem with combining truth commissions with trials is that truth commissions may need the co-operation of violators, and violators are not likely to co-operate if they face trial.

The nature of the transition is likely to influence the adoption and nature of transitional justice: negotiated transitions are likely to lead to weak or no transitional justice, whereas the take-over of collapsed regimes is likely to encourage more severe measures. The balance of forces determining whether trials and/or truth commissions are held may change over time, so that transitional justice is sometimes delayed for years. The UN has had no consistent policy on the punishment of human-rights violators. It set up criminal tribunals for Yugoslavia and Rwanda, but required none for South Africa, even though it had often condemned apartheid. Transitional justice began with the end of the military regimes of the late twentieth century in Latin America, spread to Africa, most notably with the Truth and Reconciliation Commission in South Africa, and to Asia. It has played little role in Europe, although in some former Communist countries 'lustration', the barring from office of former Communist officials, has been introduced, often controversially.

The 'truth' of truth commissions is not the same as that of criminal trials: the looser rules of evidence at truth commissions mean that more truth can be told but more of what is told may not be true. This is particularly problematic if alleged perpetrators are named without a fair trial. Truth commissions can go beyond questions of individual guilt to the structural causes of violations and recommendations for institutional reform. Truth commissions can give a voice to the victims, and, it is claimed, treat them with more sympathy and dignity than a criminal court, where they may be subject to hostile cross-examination. They may also award reparations, although their record in this is not generous. Truth commissions vary considerably in their mandates and their resources, but most have limited resources, especially of time. Truth commissions have been favoured because they counter denials, acknowledge the wrongs done to victims, and are thought to be less divisive than criminal trials. They have been criticized for failing to deliver justice, while their supposed contribution to reconciliation and stability has been doubted (Hayner 2002).

Snyder and Vinjamuri investigated empirically whether prosecutions deter further human-rights violations. They doubt whether they do. The tribunals for the former Yugoslavia and Rwanda did not deter subsequent gross human-rights violations in the former Yugoslavia and central Africa, while formal or tacit amnesties curbed violations in El Salvador, Mozambique, Namibia, South Africa and Afghanistan. They argue that if democrats do not dominate anti-democrats, prosecution of human-rights violators increases the risk of violent conflict and further human-rights violations, and hinders the institutionalization of the rule of law. Trials are most effective in stable democracies with a well-institutionalized rule of law, that is, when they are least needed to prevent human-rights violations. Human-rights campaigns against 'impunity' may, therefore, often be bad for human rights (Snyder and Vinjamuri 2003–4).

This argument has been challenged empirically by Sikkink and Walling. They point out that Latin America has the longest experience with human-rights trials, and here they have neither undermined democracy nor led to an increase in human-rights violations. Trials have been held in countries with the worst human-rights violations, and, in most cases, human rights *improved* after the trials. The more trials that were held, the more human rights improved. Trials are positively associated with human rights, independently of the level of democracy. There is no evidence that trials exacerbated conflict. Where transitions took place without trials, human rights *worsened*. There is no evidence that amnesties *caused* human-rights improvements, even where, as in El Salvador, both are found together. We do not know whether the Latin American experience could be repeated elsewhere, but the sceptical view of trials has been excessively influenced by a small number of cases and a short time-frame (Sikkink and Walling 2007).

Another recent development in efforts to implement human rights has been the establishment of national human-rights institutions (NHRIs). These have now been set up in more than 100 countries, a four-fold increase since the early 1990s. NHRIs work under guidelines adopted by the UN General Assembly in 1993, known as the 'Paris Principles'. They advise governments, investigate complaints, make recommendations for the resolution of particular cases or for legislative reform, and engage in human-rights education. They do not usually have the power to make binding decisions, but may be useful where the judiciary is ineffective. In 1993 an International Co-ordination Committee of National Institutions, endorsed by the UN Commission on Human Rights, was established. NHRIs may play a useful role in areas of the world lacking a regional human-rights regime, such as Asia. They may, however, be weakest where they are most needed, and, at worst, may be public-relations exercises for repressive governments. They are probably most effective in democracies as one component in a complex of governmental and non-governmental institutions designed to protect human rights. Nevertheless, NHRIs may have some success in countries with weak human-rights institutions, especially in transitions to democracy. NHRIs have so far made only a modest contribution to the prevention of serious human-rights violations, but they can promote human rights in a way that is not too legalistic and yet based on the standards of international human-rights law (International Council on Human Rights Policy 2000).

International human-rights law is inherently political. Decisions to hold or not to hold human-rights trials are always politically motivated. Law plays a role in human-rights promotion, but understanding that role requires political analysis.

Political science

Political science neglected human rights between the adoption of the Universal Declaration in 1948 and the mid-1970s, except for some descriptive studies. This neglect is explained by two main influences on the discipline: Realism and positivism. Realism taught that politics was overwhelmingly the pursuit of power and that ethical considerations, such as human rights, played at most a marginal role. Positivism taught that social scientists should eliminate ethical judgements from their work because they were unscientific. This situation began to change in the 1970s as human rights became more salient in international politics. A recent study of leading political-science journals calculated that only 34 articles on human rights were published before 1980; 36 were published in the 1980s; 60 in the 1990s; and 459 between 2000 and August 2008. Nevertheless, since the end of the Cold War only about two per cent of articles in these journals have been about human rights, and most of these have been in only two journals. Thus the study of human rights in political science has increased but remains marginal (Cardenas 2009).

In 1976 Claude argued that human rights could not be understood by the analysis of legal processes alone. Social scientists should investigate the social forces underlying human-rights development. This would involve both historical and comparative approaches. Claude described the 'classical' pattern of human-rights development in France, Britain and the USA. He argued that in the process of the development of a mature human-rights regime, four problems must be solved: the securing of political freedom; the guarantee of legal rights; the establishment of equal rights to political participation; and the recognition and implementation of social and economic rights.

Claude developed several empirical hypotheses from his comparative historical analysis:

1. The more people engaged in private economic activity, the more likely were legal guarantees for freedom of expression.

2.   The stronger the demand for citizenship equality, the stronger the state became.
3.   The more elites competed for support, the more they would encourage popular participation and civic equality rights.
4.   The more poor people participated in politics, the more likely the implementation of economic and social rights.

The 'classical' model, therefore, proposed that the emergence of private, capitalist economies provided an economic basis for the institutionalization of human-rights law. The development of a mature human-rights regime involved the sequential introduction of three forms of decision-making: market exchange that required legal security; bargaining that extended rights to new social forces; and central decisions to regulate and administer an increasingly complex set of rights. Human rights developed in these countries in a context of relatively gradual social and economic change, and conclusions drawn from the study of these processes might well not apply to those countries that were undergoing, or at least attempting, rapid change. Claude suggested that this might lead to more centralized decision-making that would prevent the emergence of a human-rights regime according to the classical model (Claude 1976). In the same volume Strouse and Claude found by statistical analysis that rapid economic development had a negative effect on political rights. They concluded that developing countries often faced painful trade-off dilemmas between the protection of civil and political rights, on the one hand, and rapid economic growth, on the other (Strouse and Claude 1976).

Donnelly examined the relation between economic development and human rights with a different method. He identified three supposed trade-offs in this relation. The *needs* trade-off sacrifices basic needs to investment. The *equality* trade-off is based on the belief that great inequality is necessary for rapid economic development. The *liberty* trade-off assumes that political rights encourage populist policies that obstruct economic growth. Donnelly tested the proposition that such trade-offs are necessary to economic development by a comparative study of Brazil and South Korea.

South Korea achieved more rapid economic growth than Brazil between 1960 and 1980 with much less inequality and relatively good protection of social and economic rights. This case refutes the hypothesis that the needs and equality trade-offs are necessary for rapid economic development. South Korea's record of civil and political human-rights violations during this period was, however, very bad. This shows that political repression may accompany economic development but not that it does so necessarily. Donnelly argued that repression may lead to a crisis of legitimacy as, for example, in Indonesia: the liberalization and democratization of developed authoritarian societies may therefore help to stabilize them (Donnelly 1989: 163–202). Liberalization and democratization may, however, sometimes be destabilizing, as the cases of the USSR and Yugoslavia show.

In 1986 Gurr showed how positivism could be used to study problems related to human rights. He bypassed the problem that human rights is a normative concept by studying state violence. He did this by using a model of regimes and their challengers. He treated violence as one of many policy options for states seeking to establish and maintain their authority. He then put forward 14 hypotheses about the state, its challengers, ethnicity and class, and the global environment. Examples of these hypotheses are: the greater the threat posed by challengers, the more likely the state is to use violence; the greater the ethnic diversity and the social inequality, the more likely the state is to use violence; states facing external threats are more likely to use violence internally (Gurr 1986). Gurr left the relations among the hypotheses unclear. For example, threats to the state tend to increase state violence, but democratic institutions tend to reduce state violence. Gurr did not explain what happens if there is a great threat to a democratic state. The hypotheses also do not explain the dynamic of violence. For example, in the former Yugoslavia, ethnic diversity may have been correlated with state violence, but this explains very little about what happened in that society after the fall of the Communist regime.

Whereas Gurr sought to explain state violence by reference to the state and its challengers, Foweraker and Landman asked how social movements establish rights regimes. Social movements do not necessarily improve rights; in fact, they can provoke increased repression. States may, however, seek to buy legitimacy by granting rights. Rights are best guaranteed by the combination of active non-governmental organizations and an independent, competent and non-corrupt judiciary. Social movements seek to close the gap between law and politics, between 'rights-in-principle' and 'rights-in-practice'. However, as societies move from authoritarianism to democracy, the protection of rights may move to the legal sphere, and social movements may lose their pre-eminent role. Foweraker and Landman claimed that comparative, empirical, quantitative analysis showed that popular social forces could be the makers of democratic rights (Foweraker and Landman 1997).

Landman maintains that the idea of universality in human-rights theory and law implies the need for cross-national, empirical comparison. Comparative studies can help explain the gap between what is claimed in principle and what is observed in practice. He acknowledges that the meaning of the legal standards is uncertain and consequently measuring empirical compliance with normative standards is problematic. However, empirical studies show that democracies and rich countries are less likely to violate personal integrity rights, and that countries involved in international or civil war are more likely to violate them. Thus, wealth, democracy and peace are the best determinants of human-rights protection. Statistical relations that hold globally, however, do not always hold for all regions: for example, the positive relation between economic development and human rights does not hold for Latin America (Landman 2002, 2006).

It has been suggested that the empirical relationship between democracy and human rights is not straightforward, and that more gross human-rights violations are found in regimes that lie in the middle, between full democracy and full autocracy (Fein 1995). Davenport and Armstrong have challenged this finding, however, and argue that below a certain level, democracy has no discernible impact on human rights, but above this level it improves respect for human rights (Davenport and Armstrong 2004). Old democracies violate civil and political rights less than new democracies (Landman 2005a: 92, 117–18). Davenport points out that, although it is well established that democracy generally reduces repression, we do not know whether all aspects of democracy reduce repression, whether democracy reduces all types of repression, or whether democracy reduces repression in all circumstances, particularly in circumstances of violent conflict. He found that, generally, the mass aspects of democracy were more effective in reducing repression than its elite aspects; democracy was more effective in reducing state violence than in preventing restrictions on civil liberties; and mass democracy was less effective in civil wars (Davenport 2007).

Comparative statistical analysis provides a rigorous means to identify variables that are associated with different levels of respect for human rights, but it does little to illuminate the *causal mechanisms* by which human rights are improved. Risse, Ropp and Sikkink seek to make good this deficiency with a causal model of human-rights change (Risse, Ropp and Sikkink 1999). Risse and Sikkink propose a theory of the stages and mechanisms through which international norms can lead to human-rights improvements. Their five-phase 'spiral model' seeks to explain variations in the extent to which states have internalized these norms. The five phases are: 1) repression; 2) material and normative pressures met by resistance; 3) tactical concessions, empowerment of domestic opposition, and dialogue; 4) legal reform; 5) internalization of human-rights norms in routine behaviour. The model does not assume evolutionary progress: governments may return to repressive practices.

The diffusion of international human-rights norms depends on the establishment and maintenance of networks among domestic and transnational actors connected to the international regime. Advocacy networks serve three purposes which constitute necessary conditions for sustainable human-rights change: 1) they put repressive states on the international agenda; 2) they assist domestic opposition groups; 3) they apply pressure to repressive governments. These processes may create a 'boomerang effect', whereby domestic NGOs mobilize international actors, who in turn empower domestic NGOs and put pressure on their governments. The process of change through socialization involves the social reconstruction of identities and interests by reference to norms.

Each of the five stages makes the next stage more likely. The third stage is crucial, because instrumental adaptation (by which states make some concessions from practical motives) involves 'talking the talk' of human rights, and this may lead to 'walking the walk' by institutionalizing human-rights norms in the fourth and fifth stages (Risse and Sikkink 1999). This model provides a useful framework for comparing the processes by which international human-rights norms may or may not be institutionalized in national legal systems. However, it has little predictive, and therefore little explanatory, value.

Hawkins has sought to produce a stronger explanation of human-rights change by what he calls a 'process tracing' method in a case study of Chile. There was an international campaign against human-rights violations in that country during the rule of the military junta headed by General Pinochet. The success of this campaign depended on a split in the Chilean elite between those prepared to rule by force and those who sought legitimacy through the rule of law. A combination of domestic and international pressures led the regime to move from repression to constitutional reform. Hawkins argues that absence of domestic security or economic crisis, elite divisions, and cultural receptivity to human rights are each necessary and are jointly sufficient to explain variations in the Chilean government's strategies in the face of strong human-rights pressures (Hawkins 2002).

Sociology

Sociology has traditionally been concerned with national societies rather than international relations and consequently taken very little interest in international human rights. Turner has sought to construct a sociological framework for the analysis of human rights by viewing human rights as a global ideology and their institutionalization through the United Nations as part of the social process of globalization. The concept of citizenship has been closely linked with the modern nation-state, but globalization has created problems that are not wholly internal to nation-states, and so the concept of citizenship rights must be extended to that of human rights. Sociologically, the concept of human rights can be explained by the need to protect vulnerable human beings by social institutions, which in their turn pose threats to those human beings. The social and legal institutionalization of human rights is the predominant modern attempt to resolve this dilemma that is inherent in modern societies (Turner 1993).

Waters argues that a sociological theory of human rights must take a social-constructionist approach that treats the universality of human rights as itself a social construction. On this view, the institutionalization of human rights reflects the prevailing balance of political interests (Waters 1996). This approach fails to explain why human rights were chosen to legitimate interests.

Stammers criticizes legalistic and statist approaches to human rights on the ground that human-rights violations occur at the sub-state, social level. The power perspective on human rights that he advocates can show that economic and social rights are often violated by private economic agencies, and that the human rights of women are violated by men. Those who see states as the solutions to human-rights problems may be mistaken, because they locate human-rights obligations where the power to solve human-rights problems may be lacking. Also, in looking to states to solve human-rights problems, statists may have to advocate an increase in the power of states, which is the original source of human-rights problems. The power perspective requires us to consider the impact of institutions and social movements on the distribution of power, and not merely on the legal formalization of rights (Stammers 1999).

Howard argued that there are social-structural causes of human-rights violations and barriers to improvement. In Commonwealth Africa post-colonial rulers inherited authoritarian government from their colonial predecessors. State elites controlled the economy and were consequently intolerant of oppositional actors, who were potential economic and political challengers. This inhibited the rise of bourgeois challengers to the state. The dispersal, low educational levels and economic hardships of the peasants made it difficult for them to mobilize in social movements for human rights.

African states were also authoritarian because they lacked the legitimacy and administrative structures to regulate society, and so resorted to rule by coercion. The legitimacy of the state was weakened by its failure to build nations from diverse ethnic groups, but the ethnic conflict that was common in Africa could not be explained only by ethnicity but had to be understood by reference to state power and social inequality.

Howard's structural approach did not exclude culture. Pre-colonial Africa was generally characterized by communalistic cultures, in which human worth was recognized by reference to social roles and statuses rather than to individual rights. Modernization had, however, substantially disrupted traditional social organization, and thereby much of its traditional culture. Consequently, many Africans had to deal with the modern African state and dominant class as modern individuals without the support of traditional institutions. Modern elites appealed to traditionalism to control modern challengers, but, although traditional culture was incompatible with human rights in some respects, most Africans faced modern problems of structural political and economic inequality. The structural changes of modernization make the development of a human-rights culture possible (Howard 1986).

Woodiwiss rejects Howard's suggestion that modernization tends to create a convergence on similar conceptions of human rights. The economically successful societies of East and South-East Asia have patriarchal cultures that assume the legitimacy of social inequalities. Liberal rights would be unenforceable in such societies. Patriarchalism is, however, compatible with human rights, Woodiwiss says, because rights can be expressed in values and institutions that do not endorse autonomy. Human rights, therefore, do not require liberal-democratic states or individualistic values. Patriarchalism is as compatible with human rights as liberalism, except in regard to gender relations. This claim that human rights do not require liberal values derives from a *reconceptualization* of 'human rights' that severs it from equality and autonomy, and the exception of gender relations is a large one. Woodiwiss also assumes that patriarchalist cultures are unchangeable, whereas his own analysis shows that they are not. He maintains that such Asian values as hierarchy and benevolence should be incorporated into international human-rights discourse as additional or alternative sources of virtue so that it can be truly cosmopolitan (Woodiwiss 1998). The concept of human rights does not, however, aspire to be a comprehensive social ethic, but a limited set of norms opposing abuses of power: other social virtues lie outside its scope.

Capitalism, Woodiwiss believes, subverts human rights because it distributes freedoms unequally according to individuals' positions in the relation of capital and labour, whereas human rights requires that individuals are treated equally regardless of social position (Woodiwiss 2005). Human rights do not, however, require that all freedoms are distributed equally, only that human rights are. It is questionable whether this can be fully achieved in capitalist societies, but some capitalist societies have relatively good human-rights records, and Woodiwiss proposes no better, feasible alternative.

Social psychology

It may be thought that psychology is not a *social* science at all, since it is a science of the (individual) human mind. However, human-rights behaviour is the product of the human mind, and psychology therefore should contribute to our understanding of it.

Governments may violate human rights 'rationally', as an efficient means to achieve certain ends. Some violations, however, are not efficient in this way, and exhibit cruelty that is inefficient or even counter-productive. Cruelty cannot explain human-rights violations by itself, for it is developed, channelled, inhibited or let loose in particular social situations. Human-rights violations are socially structured but the cruelty of individuals may initiate and/or aggravate them.

Some human-rights violations may be partly explained by scapegoat theory, which derives from frustration-aggression theory, according to which a frustrated person will tend to become aggressive. The obvious target for this aggression is whoever is responsible for the frustration (the frustrator). The frustrator may, however, be unknown (e.g., world markets), inaccessible (the World Bank), too powerful (the army) and/or morally protected (the Church). If aggression cannot be directed at the frustrator, scapegoat theory says that it is likely to be displaced onto a target that is known, accessible, weak and despised. Ethnic minorities often have these characteristics, which is why they are often the target of irrational aggression.

Experimental psychology has shown that ordinary individuals are likely to conform to the standards of their group or to the orders of a person in authority, even if doing so violates their own moral values (Milgram 1974). These experiments suggest that gross human-rights violations are likely to occur when murderous leaders mobilize the co-operation of ordinary followers, who do not question their social environment or their leaders. However, studies of those who rescued Jews during the Holocaust suggest that actions to defend human rights may be motivated not by rational and independent moral thinking, but by conformity to groups or authority figures that are themselves humane (Oliner and Oliner 1988).

Anthropology

We have seen that anthropology in the USA after the Second World War was dominated by a mixture of positivism and relativism. In the 1960s relativism was picked up by radical anthropologists to challenge the authority of the discipline's elites and their supposedly 'imperialist' approach to other cultures (Washburn 1987).

In these debates human rights played little role. Some anthropologists, however, began to combine the 'committed' anthropology of the radicals with human rights. In the UK, Survival International, and in the USA, Cultural Survival, were activist organizations that brought together academic anthropology and a concern for indigenous rights. Cultural Survival published a volume entitled *Human Rights and Anthropology* in 1988. The editors acknowledged that the peoples whom anthropologists studied were often victims of serious human-rights violations. Anthropologists had expressed concern for human rights through their professional associations but the discipline of anthropology had neglected human rights. Anthropologists should investigate state policies directed towards eliminating cultural pluralism. Such investigations were both scientifically and ethically justified (Downing and Kushner 1988).

Downing suggested that anthropology could contribute to the understanding of human rights by showing how conceptions of rights functioned in different cultures and how cultures incorporated external ideas (Downing 1988). Barnett argued that anthropologists were sensitive to the value of different cultures to those whose cultures they were, but could also recognize that they might be internally oppressive. The recognition of cultural difference, therefore, did not rule out intervention in other cultures, but it did impose the obligation to respect the context into which that intervention was to be carried out (Barnett 1988). Doughty pointed out that in Latin America the concept of 'citizenship' had traditionally been defined so as to exclude indigenous peoples, with the result that these peoples had become victims of gross human-rights violations. Anthropologists had ignored state policies towards cultural difference. This was a scientific and moral error (Doughty 1988).

Messer has argued that anthropologists should no longer study 'cultures' as local, isolated entities, but as part of an interactive and interdependent global system of cultures. International human-rights law must be implemented in a world of diverse cultures, some of which are at least partly incompatible with human rights. Anthropologists can help the cause of human rights by clarifying the relations between international human-rights law and particular cultures (Messer 1993).

Wilson has complained that the legal positivism favoured by the human-rights community misrepresents the subjective experiences of the victims of human-rights violations. Human-rights universalism often ignores local contexts and thereby misunderstands the social and cultural dimensions of conflicts over rights. Human-rights law speaks in a clear and certain voice, while human-rights experience is complex and uncertain. In order to move beyond subjectivity to authoritative objectivity, human-rights discourse paradoxically dehumanizes its subjects. The task of anthropology is to put the human back into human rights (Wilson 1997a; 1997b).

Both Schirmer and Stoll argue that decontextualized universalism can lead to counter-productive international interventions for human rights, either because of undue emphasis on legal reform with neglect of social consequences, or by oversimplifying what may be complex social and political relations. Anthropology can help to make human-rights interventions more effective by providing them with a deeper understanding of their cultural, social and political contexts (Schirmer 1997; Stoll 1997).

There is a tension between the normative demands of human rights and the ethnographic practices of anthropology, since anthropology encounters cultures that lack the concept of individuals as bearers of rights. Anthropologists can study 'cultures' to examine whether they do or do not conform with human rights and also the 'cultures' of human-rights practitioners. They can study how social movements incorporate human-rights discourse into their legal and political strategies and how transnational actors may modify their practices as they encounter local cultures (Goodale 2006a, 2006b; Merry 2006).

Merry has added that anthropology can tell us where and how human-rights concepts and institutions are produced, how ideas circulate, and how they shape everyday lives. The concept of rights moves from the local to the global, and then back to the local. Yet even the concepts of 'local' and 'global' may be problematic, since global discourses such as that of human rights have their local sites, such as the committee rooms and assembly halls of Manhattan and Geneva. The interaction between 'global' and 'local' discourses is mediated by 'translators' who act as double agents, interpreting the 'global' to the 'local' and the 'local' to the 'global' in a field of unequal power. We may ask whether human rights get lost in translation. Translating one set of cultural categories and meanings into another transforms them. There are limits to the capacity of the producers of discourses to control their meanings. Whether local actors adopt a human-rights approach depends on their perceptions of its success. Human-rights discourse may be rejected by local actors; it may merely decorate local practices; it may combine with local discourses in a hybrid; or it may subvert and displace prior discourses (Merry 2006). A theory of culture, Merry argues, as contested, historically produced, and continually defined and redefined in a variety of settings would enhance our understanding of human-rights processes as promoting gradual cultural change rather than as law without sanctions confronting intractable cultural difference (Merry 2006: 100).

International relations

The academic discipline of International Relations neglected human rights for many years, except for some studies of human rights in US foreign policy. The introduction of human rights into International Relations was pioneered by Forsythe in the USA and Vincent in the UK. Forsythe sought to persuade sceptics that international human-rights law made a difference to international politics, while maintaining that politics set limits to the influence of law (Forsythe 1983). Vincent acknowledged that human rights were marginal to international relations, and that states often used the idea to promote their own interests, but noted, nevertheless, that the concept of human rights had become part of global law and morality. After the Helsinki Conference on Security and Co-operation in Europe in 1975, at which the USSR accepted human rights in principle, human rights became a salient feature of Cold War international relations. The concept had been incorporated into international relations in such a way that no state could ignore human-rights considerations in its foreign policy. Nevertheless, foreign-policy professionals were typically wary of human rights, preferring standard-setting to implementation, generalities to specificities, and viewing human rights as one of the *problems* of foreign policy rather than as the solution to problems. Against this view, Vincent argued that the cautious incorporation of human rights into foreign policy might promote the interests of states (Vincent 1986).

Human rights can be incorporated into International Relations through regime theory. The international human-rights system is a regulatory regime. Donnelly has classified such regimes as declaratory, promotional, implementation, and enforcement regimes, each of which can be classified as relatively weak or strong. The international human-rights regime is a relatively strong promotional regime, a relatively weak implementation regime, and at most a minimal enforcement regime. Declaratory regimes with weak enforcement powers are attractive to states because they can appear moral with little risk to their important practical interests. International human-rights regimes can nevertheless help states that wish to improve their human-rights performance by political support and technical assistance. The European regime is relatively strong because the moral commitment of European states is relatively strong, and the risks to states' interests are small. The Inter-American regime has been quite active. Africa has a very weak regime, and Asia and the Middle East have no regimes, because moral commitment to human rights among elites is weak, and state interest in not having such a regime is strong. Human-rights regimes are therefore strongest where they are least needed, and weak or non-existent where they are most needed. Regime analysis supports the view that moral concerns play some role in international relations, but generally a marginal one (Donnelly 1989: 206–18, 223, 227–8, 252–8).

Human rights also enter international relations through states' foreign policies. States may be reluctant to include human rights in their foreign policies because they do not see them as serving their interests and/or because they generally share an interest in not interfering with each other's internal affairs. These motives are not always decisive, however, because states may have a moral or practical interest in promoting human rights, for example to stabilize a country that may threaten its neighbours or the wider international community. States have a range of means to influence human rights in other societies, from 'quiet diplomacy' through economic sanctions to military intervention. All these methods may fail because the intervenors are self-interested and/or the target states resist intervention (Donnelly 1989: 229–37, 242–9; 1998: 85; 1999: 90–1).

The 'right of humanitarian intervention' has been debated for a long time. Military interventions with a human-rights dimension – such as NATO's bombing of Serbia to protect the ethnic Albanians of Kosovo in 1999 and the US-led invasions of Afghanistan and Iraq in 2001 and 2003 – have been very controversial. Such interventions may improve human rights in some respects, but often at great human and material costs, and the difficulty of establishing a stable, rights-respecting society may be formidable. Yet failures to intervene have also been very controversial, as in the cases of the Rwanda genocide of 1994 and the repression of Darfur by the Sudanese government.

The United Nations has accepted the doctrine of 'the responsibility to protect', which suggests that the international community may intervene, even with military force, when governments fail to protect the human rights of their citizens. The legal and political status of this doctrine remains uncertain, however. There is some consensus that if military intervention for human rights is ever justified, it is only for the most serious violations (Donnelly 2003: 258–60). Weiss points out that the UN Security Council approved military interventions in Haiti (1994) and Sierra Leone (1997) to reverse the overthrow of democratic governments. A survey conducted by the International Committee of the Red Cross in 12 war-torn societies found that two-thirds of civilians wanted more intervention, and only ten per cent wanted none (Weiss 2004: 139, 142). The problems of 'the responsibility to protect' are well illustrated by the debate between de Waal and Reeves over Darfur. De Waal argues that the application of the doctrine to Darfur is dangerous, as military intervention would cost more lives than it would save. Reeves emphasizes the ongoing humanitarian catastrophe and argues that the UN's failure to intervene more forcefully has enabled what he calls 'genocide by attrition' and damaged the UN's credibility as a human-rights organization. Both agree that Sudan's problems must be solved by a negotiated peace, but disagree on what form of short-term intervention can lead to that solution (de Waal 2008; Reeves 2008).

The United Nations promotes human rights through many agencies: for example, the Commission on Human Rights (now the Human Rights Council), the treaty-monitoring bodies, special rapporteurs and working groups, the Office of the High Commissioner for Human Rights, the High Commissioner for Refugees, the International Labour Organization, the General Assembly, the Security Council, and the specialized agencies and programmes such as the World Health Organization, the UN Development Programme, the World Food Programme, etc. Its impact has been limited, however, mainly because powerful states have been reluctant to fund it adequately and have sometimes obstructed its work. There has been an attempt in recent years to 'mainstream' human rights by incorporating them into all UN programmes, but the UN system lacks coherence: the relations between the Human Rights Council, the treaty bodies and the High Commissioner are, for example, not settled. The UN has increasingly recognized the close connection between peace and human rights, so that the Security Council has taken more interest in human rights, and UN peacekeeping operations have included a significant human-rights component (Forsythe 2006; Mertus 2005).

However, LeBor has charged the UN with complicity with gross human-rights violations in Bosnia, Rwanda and Darfur, by pretending to intervene, but intervening ineffectively. At least one permanent member of the Security Council in any given case has had an interest in not intervening and so has been able to prevent effective action. The Commission on Human Rights and the Human Rights Council have often been more influenced by political interests than concern for human rights (LeBor 2006). Donnelly has argued that because the UN has been the source of international human-rights law, its importance in implementing human rights has been exaggerated, and the contribution of comparative political science to our understanding of variations in respect for human rights in different societies has been underestimated (Donnelly 1989: 260–9).

The so-called 'war on terror' has had a considerable impact on human rights in recent years. After the Cold War the USA remained the world's only superpower. Osama bin Laden, a Saudi dissident, formed an organization known as Al-Qaeda to support the Afghan resistance to occupation by the USSR. After the withdrawal of Soviet troops from Afghanistan, Al-Qaeda redirected its hostility towards the

USA on the ground that it had 'invaded' the homeland of Islam, Saudi Arabia, in the Iraq war of 1991. Al-Qaeda launched a series of attacks on US targets that culminated in the notorious events of '9/11' (11 September 2001), when Al-Qaeda agents flew two passenger planes into the World Trade Center, New York, and a third into the Pentagon in Washington, DC, with the loss of about 3,000 lives.

On 20 September 2001 President Bush declared that the 'war on terror' would begin with Al-Qaeda, but would not end until every terrorist group of global reach had been defeated. Congress passed a joint resolution authorizing the President to use force against terrorism. The US government responded by leading an invasion of Afghanistan, bombing Al-Qaeda training camps and supporting the Northern Alliance rebellion against the extreme Islamist government of the Taliban, who were overthrown. The USA and its allies arrested hundreds of suspected supporters of Al-Qaeda and the Taliban, who were then detained in Afghanistan or the US military base at Guantánamo Bay in Cuba.

The US Congress passed the Patriot Act, which was signed into law by President Bush on 26 October 2001. The Act contained a wide definition of 'terrorism', permitting wiretapping and granting the authorities the power to detain foreigners on suspicion without the protection of the US Constitution. About 5,000 foreign nationals were placed in preventive detention (Cole and Lobel 2007: 10–13). In 2006 Congress passed the Military Commissions Act, which denied to Guantánamo detainees both US constitutional rights and rights under the Geneva Conventions. The US government has admitted that less than half of the Guantánamo detainees had conducted any hostile act towards the USA (Cole and Lobel 2007: 29). According to a US Congress report, up to 14,000 people may have been victims of 'rendition' and secret detention since 2001. Some reports estimate that there have been twice as many (Campbell and Norton-Taylor 2008). Other countries passed various laws designed to help detect and prevent terrorist plots. Human-rights groups alleged that these laws violated human rights, as did the practices of assassination, detention without trial, interrogation techniques amounting to torture, and so-called 'extraordinary rendition', which involved the deportation of suspected terrorists to countries where torture was routinely practised (Foot 2005: 299). Many countries, democratic and undemocratic, collaborated in these practices.

The 2003 US-led invasion of Iraq, which the Bush administration tried to link to the 'war on terror', generated many allegations of arbitrary arrests, detentions and the use of torture by US, allied and Iraqi forces. The use of torture at Abu Ghraib prison in Baghdad was only the most notorious of these practices. Many governments, which were previously committing serious human-rights violations, used the cover of the 'war on terror' to legitimate, and to intensify, repression of dissidents.

The 'war on terror' disturbed human-rights advocates because countries thought to be strongly committed to human rights were apparently prepared to abandon its principles so easily. The International Committee of the Red Cross concluded, in a report of 2007, that interrogation methods used by the CIA 'categorically' constituted torture. President Bush's decision to remove the protection of the Geneva Conventions from Guantánamo detainees indicated that the US would wage the 'war on terror' outside the rule of law. Only low-level participants in US human-rights violations were brought to justice, despite strong evidence that the policies had been approved at the highest level.

The policies of Western governments in 'the war on terror' met resistance from various quarters, including the judiciary. A number of court decisions in the USA and the UK placed some restrictions on their governments' anti-terrorism policies. Critics argued that the very concept of the 'war on terror' was counter-productive as it would recruit participants to the anti-Western cause, especially among Muslims.

When President Obama took office in January 2009 he shut down the CIA's secret prisons, banned torture and rendition, renewed the US commitment to the Geneva Convention on the treatment of detainees, ordered the closure of the camp at Guantánamo within a year, and called for an end to military trials there. At that time there were 245 detainees at Guantánamo; by 20 July 2010 there were 178 remaining. In 2010 hundreds were reported to be held without trial and abused at Bagram airbase, Afghanistan (Andersson 2010). In

June 2009 the Obama administration abandoned the term 'global war on terror'.

Malcolm Evans has argued that while the war on terrorism led to human-rights violations and the weakening of international human-rights norms, it has also, through democratic debate and judicial decisions, led to a reaffirmation of those norms. Both courts and parliaments have resisted some of the human-rights restrictions proposed by executives (Evans 2006: 196). There is an apparent consensus that terrorism should be addressed with respect for human rights, but less consensus on how to do this. Cole and Lobel argue that US post-9/11 policy has failed to reduce terrorism, in fact has probably increased it, and that there is no evidence that the human-rights violations committed by the US and other governments in their anti-terrorist campaigns have been effective overall, even if they have foiled specific terrorist plots (Cole and Lobel 2007).

Conclusion

Nietzsche called ethical idealists 'emigrants from reality' (Glover 1999: 29). The task of the social science of human rights is to bring human-rights supporters back to reality. This reality is one both of objective structures and processes and of subjective meanings and values. A social science of human rights demands both sympathy and scientific rigour. The concept of human rights lies in a domain in which normative philosophy, law and social science meet. The field of human rights has been dominated too much by legal texts. Law has an important place in the creation, interpretation and implementation of human rights, but it has more severe limits than human-rights activists often realize. Social science is necessary to connect law to reality.

Social science by itself is, however, not enough, for it cannot tell us how we ought to live. Philosophy may offer to do so, but it is a weak motivator to action. Understanding human rights requires us to understand both the contribution and the limits of philosophy and science. Social science is itself a social process and its connection with human rights is problematic. Science has been historically connected with the idea of emancipation from authority and ignorance, and therefore with freedom and well-being. But the scientific philosophy of positivism can lead down the path of moral indifference, while the 'interpretive' social sciences, such as anthropology, can lead to moral relativism.

Hirschman has argued that the modern social sciences have been characterized by an 'anti-moralist petulance' that can be traced back to Machiavelli's anti-moralistic political science. Social scientists have a 'trained incapacity' to take morality seriously. Somehow the analytical rigour of science and ethical seriousness have to be brought together (Hirschman 1983: 21–4, 30). Bellah maintains that the division that we make between social science and philosophy arises from an attempt to 'purify' these disciplines. There may be advantages in this differentiation, but the division between science and ethics has costs that can be met only by intellectual activity that crosses the boundaries we have set up. Positivism in social science sought to reject ethics in order to improve the quality of knowledge it produced. Ironically, it failed because it failed to understand itself as a social practice that was inescapably ethical. Like all social practices, social science takes place in a field of power. If it fails to recognize this social fact, it is more likely to serve the powers that be. A social science of human rights must have other purposes, and thus must be self-conscious about its ethical commitments (Bellah 1983). In short, human-rights law is inadequate without support from the social sciences; and the social sciences are inadequate without support from philosophy.

6

Universality, Diversity and Difference

Culture and Human Rights

The problem of cultural imperialism

The Universal Declaration of Human Rights states that all human beings are born equal in rights. The Vienna Declaration of 1993 affirmed that all human rights are universal. Human-rights theorists commonly say that all human beings have human rights simply because they are human beings (Gewirth 1982: 1; Donnelly 1985a: 1; 1999: 79).

However, claims that human rights are universal are not literally supported by the text of the Universal Declaration. Article 25, for example, says that motherhood and childhood are entitled to special care and assistance. According to the Declaration, some human rights belong only to special categories of human beings. The Vienna Declaration recognized a number of special categories, such as women, children, minorities, indigenous people, disabled persons, refugees, migrant workers, the extremely poor and the socially excluded. We need to understand how there can be special categories of human-rights holders if everyone is equal in rights 'without distinction of any kind' as the Universal Declaration proclaims.

Some human rights are simply universal: the right not to be enslaved, for example. Other human rights are universal only *potentially*. There are two kinds of these rights. The first consists of rights that are activated only in certain unusual situations: the right to a fair trial, for instance. The second consists of rights that are activated when human beings meet some criterion – becoming an adult, for example – that most human beings meet. The other special categories mentioned in international texts, such as women and minorities, do not have special human rights, but are thought to be especially vulnerable to human-rights violations.

Since the end of the Cold War the most controversial topic in human rights has been the relation between universality and cultural difference. Western domination has recently been challenged on the basis of the anti-universalist celebration of cultural difference. As a result, human-rights universalism has to compete with alternative cultural perspectives, and the view that there are different cultural interpretations of human rights (Chan 1999; Othman 1999). Some Western scholars argue that the concept of human rights belongs to 'the Enlightenment project' of philosophical rationalism and an outdated 'social modernism' (Woodiwiss 1998), which have been superseded by the politics of 'difference' based on a 'post-modern' philosophical 'deconstruction' of universalism. However, the objection to human rights on the ground that it represents Western imperialism is often very implausible: for example, opposition to the dumping of toxic waste in poor, non-Western countries by multinational corporations on the ground that it violates the human right to health does not express a distinctive Western value or interest. The World Bank's survey of 60,000 poor people around the world showed substantial support for the principles of the Universal Declaration (Darrow 2003: 90).

We saw in chapter four that human rights have also been criticized in the West by 'communitarian' philosophers who argued that the concept of human rights is too individualistic and undervalues the common good. The response to this is that human-rights advocates can value the common good; that the concept of 'the common good' can hide abuses of power that should be opposed; and that communities based on the common good can respect human rights. There is, therefore, no necessary incompatibility between common-good communitarianism and human rights, although different societies strike the balance between individual rights and the common good differently.

Some scholars are sceptical of the claim that the concept of human rights has universal origins. Donnelly argues that problems now discussed in terms of human rights were traditionally treated in non-Western cultures, as in the pre-modern West, in terms of 'the right' and of duties, but not of human rights. In these cultures, there might be rights derived from the community and its different status-positions, but not *human* rights (Donnelly 1985a: 49–51, 86). There is merit in Donnelly's argument, but it is overstated. Islamic scholars who derive human rights from our obligations to God are employing an argument similar to Locke's. Islam may be reluctant to recognize that Muslims and non-Muslims are equal in rights, but Locke was reluctant to recognize equality between Protestants on the one hand and Roman Catholics and atheists on the other. Donnelly might say that the modern concept of human rights is more egalitarian than Locke's, but if Western natural-rights theory could evolve into the modern concept of human rights, Islam might evolve in a similar way. Donnelly is correct to distinguish the concept of human rights from different concepts such as justice and obligation, but, in his treatment of non-Western cultures, he underestimates the capacity for various moral concepts to develop into human-rights conceptions. Recently he has taken this point, arguing that, although traditional Islam did not recognize the concept of human rights, Islam is not fundamentally incompatible with human rights, and may provide a foundation for human rights as Christianity did, and still does, for many Christians (Donnelly 2003: 75).

The concept of human rights is, however, Western in origin, and some would say that the West remains hegemonic in the production, interpretation and implementation of human-rights norms. Some critics say that the supposed universality of human rights is an illusion produced by this Western hegemony. The 'universality' of human rights is an ideological disguise for 'cultural imperialism'. The tension between universality and difference in the concept of human rights was expressed in the Vienna Declaration, which affirmed the universality of human rights, but qualified this by insisting that 'the significance of national and regional particularities and various historical, cultural and religious backgrounds must be borne in mind'. The idea that human rights express Western hegemony is, however, somewhat undermined by the fact that the West does rather little to implement human rights in non-Western countries. Also, the West has no monopoly on hegemony: local hegemonies – for example, of male religious elites – may be more important and more oppressive for millions of people (Simmons 2009: 369–71).

Donnelly holds that human rights are universal partly because the conditions that produced them in the West – the nation-state and capitalism – have become globalized. Globalization has, however, consisted not simply of the spread of Western culture, but also of *domination* by the West and the denigration of non-Western cultures. Many non-Western peoples wish to adopt much of Western culture, especially technology and certain forms of social organization, such as the nation-state and some form of capitalist economy, but the colonial experience has often produced ambivalent attitudes to the West. Cultural assertiveness may, in these circumstances, be an expression of dignity. This may appear as the defence of conservative against liberal values, but, in historical context, it can also be a claim for equality against domination. Resistance by some non-Westerners to the concept of human rights, or their insistence on developing their own conception of human rights, may be part of this self-emancipation from Western domination. These attitudes do not invalidate the concept of human rights, but they may be relevant to its interpretation and implementation.

In the run-up to the Vienna Conference certain Asian states and intellectuals argued that there was a distinctively Asian conception of human rights. The idea of 'Asian values' as the basis for a challenge to human rights was implausible, however, both because Asia is itself culturally diverse, and because many Asians are supporters of human rights. Although some human-rights supporters believe that these appeals to difference are ideological disguises for oppressive practices of authoritarian governments, some universalists believe that universalism has to take cultural diversity seriously (Donnelly 2003: Part II).

It is said either that non-Western societies value communities more than individuals or that each society should balance communities and individuals according to its history and culture. This does not necessarily entail the rejection of human rights, but it may entail that each society interpret human rights in its own way. It is sometimes further claimed that the West is morally decadent and that it deploys the idea of human rights in its own selfish interests. It is accused of hypocrisy on several grounds: the selective way in which it expresses its concern for human rights; its failure to recognize that it has historically restricted human rights for the sake of national security and economic development; its emphasis on civil and political rights, which cost it little, at the expense of economic and social rights, which could be expensive to implement.

There may be merit in these arguments, but there are also weaknesses. The supposedly non-Western values are often conservative values that many Westerners support. Likewise, many non-Westerners support Western, liberal values. The appeal to non-Western values typically fails to distinguish the interests of states, governments, communities and individuals.

A strong argument in the cultural-difference account of human rights is that each society has its unique history and culture, and must therefore have a distinctive conception of human rights. This is as true of the West as of the Rest: the Swedish conception of human rights is different from that of the USA. This variability is hidden by the abstractions of international human-rights agreements. The European Court of Human Rights has developed the concept of 'the margin of appreciation', which allows some autonomy to member states in interpreting rights. This is, in part, a concession by international human rights to national democracy. The Court has, however, been criticized for failing to develop this idea clearly or coherently. Cultural diversity is much less pronounced in Europe than it is world-wide. If the margin of appreciation doctrine is valid (and it is controversial), it provides support for culturally variable interpretations globally, at least for democratic societies.

Universality is sometimes confused with uniformity. The universality of human rights is not only compatible with cultural diversity; it also promotes diversity by protecting cultural freedom. Human dignity, the basis of human rights, is expressed in cultural diversity. Human rights should, as

Healy puts it, be implemented in 'culturally inflected ways'. Sensitivity to cultural difference is not only morally required by human rights but also may be necessary to their implementation (Healy 2006). International human-rights law cannot specify its own best interpretation. The interpretation and application of human rights must be informed by local cultures if it is not to be 'imperialistic'. Respect for local cultures is not only compatible with international human rights; it is also required by them. UN human-rights agencies often specify that rights be implemented in a way that is culturally appropriate for a particular group. There is evidence that culturally sensitive applications of human rights are more effective (Khan 2009: 129–30).

The universality of some human-rights principles is relatively uncontroversial: for example, the condemnation of racism. However, some principles of the Universal Declaration have more cross-cultural appeal than others. Article 16, for example, sets forth a liberal right to marry. Saudi Arabia objected to this on the ground that it was incompatible with Islam (Morsink 1999:. 24). Ironically, anti-universalists rely on universal principles (the value of cultural difference, for example) while some Western liberal philosophers are sceptical about strong universalist moral claims (Rawls 1999).

International human-rights institutions have generally accepted that universal human-rights standards ought to be interpreted differently in different cultural contexts. The International Covenant on Civil and Political Rights, for example, provides that in the election of members of the Human Rights Committee, consideration be given to the representation of different forms of civilization. The Committee itself has said that the right to family life may vary according to socio-economic conditions and cultural traditions (Robertson and Merrills 1996: 64). Universal standards are modified legally by reservations that states make in ratifying human-rights treaties. Neuman points out that although many reservations are motivated by hostility to some human rights, others are based on differences between treaty language and reasonable conceptions of rights in particular countries (Neuman 2002–3). Since the question of universalism is usually treated as a contest between the West and the Rest, it is noteworthy that the USA has been particularly unwilling to accept international human-rights standards.

Donnelly allows that collectivist cultures with no conception of human rights may be morally defensible in conditions of extreme scarcity, when social solidarity is necessary for survival. He argues, however, that nation-states and capitalist economies have almost everywhere separated individuals from small, supportive traditional communities to a significant extent. Appeals to cultural tradition in these circumstances are often made by authoritarian elites who have little or no regard for the traditional cultures of their societies. Modernized elites often invent pseudo-traditions to defend their repressive regimes from criticism. Many human-rights violations are the products of distinctively modern forms of rule, and have no basis in traditional culture. In such conditions individuals need human rights for the protection of human dignity, and thus the concept of human rights has 'near universal contemporary relevance' (Donnelly 1989: 59–60, 64–5). This argument, too, has merit, but it may underestimate both the oppressiveness of traditional cultures and their contribution to human dignity in modern societies.

Extreme relativism is incompatible with human rights, which entails some universal principles, but, because the concept of human rights respects autonomy, it not only allows but also celebrates considerable cultural diversity. The most difficult case for human-rights universalism is that in which those who are victims of human-rights violations support the culture that legitimates those violations. Women who are malnourished, for example, sometimes support the cultures that cause this condition. Nussbaum argues that the views of the victims are not morally decisive, because the injustice that denies them food and education denies them the ability to imagine alternative ways of life (Nussbaum 1993). Cultural relativism is biased against the weak: cultures may therefore be evaluated by principles of justice (O'Neill 1993). In these situations intercultural dialogue may be inadequate because the victims may be excluded. External intervention may be problematic because it may have undesirable consequences. There is no general solution to this problem, but the best strategy requires the kind of cultural critique proposed by Nussbaum and O'Neill, and a contextually sensitive understanding of the likely consequences of intervention.

Human rights may face the dilemma that some people find 'dignity' in a culture that is not fully compatible with human rights, and the human-rights response thus requires difficult and uncertain judgements. Local cultures are, however, often contested by those whose cultures they undoubtedly are. Respect for culture should not entail taking the interpretations of elites or majorities as representing cultures at the expense of subordinate groups or minorities. It may be hard to draw the line between respect for culture and subverting human rights. Getting the balance between universality and cultural difference right is helped by having clear reasons for the universal principle and for the local interpretation.

Human-rights universalism is sometimes accused of 'cultural imperialism'. The concept of human rights is, however, universal and *egalitarian*: all human beings are equal in rights. Imperialism is by its nature *inegalitarian*, and objections to imperialism normally assume some form of egalitarianism. Thus, the concept of human rights, far from being imperialistic, provides the basis for criticizing imperialism. Those who criticize human rights for being imperialistic assume that anti-imperialism is a universal principle, but typically do not make clear to which universal principles they are appealing. The principles of universal equal rights are strong candidates for being the best available anti-imperialistic principles. It is a common fallacy that cultural relativism supports anti-imperialism, but in fact it does not, for cultural relativism provides no basis for criticizing imperialistic cultures. The argument that human rights do not extend to non-Westerners has been used by Westerners to justify the worst atrocities of imperialism.

Cultural relativism

The anti-imperialist argument against human-rights universalism may be popular because it is thought to express two ideas that have widespread appeal: 1) everyone is equally entitled to respect; 2) to respect a person entails respect for that person's culture, because culture constitutes, at least in part, a person's identity. However, these principles are inconsistent with cultural relativism, because they are universal principles. The principle that we should respect *all* cultures is self-contradictory, because some cultures do not respect all cultures. The principle of respect for persons does not entail that we ought to respect all cultures, and therefore cultures that endorse human-rights violations cannot demand our respect simply because they are cultures. Cultures that are incompatible with human rights in some respects may have some value, but cultural relativism fails to provide a general objection to human-rights universalism. It is inconsistent to support human rights and respect cultures that violate human rights. Human-rights supporters should, therefore, realize that they are committed to not respecting some cultures, or at least some features of some cultures. Some non-Western critiques of human rights are based not on cultural relativism but on a different universalism. Islam, for example, is a universalist religion, but many interpretations of its principles, for example on gender relations, are incompatible with some human rights.

It is important to distinguish between disapproval of a cultural practice in principle and the best strategy for changing the practice. Simple condemnation may be futile or counter-productive: dialogue and support for internal reformers may work better. Outside reformers should realize that those engaged in cultural practices incompatible with human rights may resist pressure to change either because they are committed to those practices or because, even though they would prefer the human-rights alternative, the social cost of defying the prevailing custom is too high.

The argument against human-rights universalism on the basis of cultural relativism is often confused with arguments based on state sovereignty, because both are used to keep outsiders from interfering with the internal affairs of a society. The logics of these two arguments are, however, quite different and, to some extent, mutually incompatible. The appeal to state sovereignty is not an appeal to cultural relativism, because the principle of state sovereignty is as universal as that of human rights. The principle of state sovereignty may have some value in discouraging unwarranted interference and in keeping the peace among states, but it may also protect human-rights violators, and it may help states to crush cultures. It is important, therefore, to distinguish arguments about sovereignty from arguments about culture.

Cultural relativism may appeal to some because the 'philosophical foundations' of human rights are supposed to be problematic. The philosophical foundations of beliefs about human rights are problematic, however, because the philosophical foundations of all beliefs are problematic. It follows that the philosophical foundations of cultural relativism are also problematic. In this situation, it may be helpful to ask whose interests are served by human rights and whose by cultural relativism. Human rights are designed to protect the fundamental interests of everyone. Cultural relativism may protect vulnerable cultures from 'imperialistic' invasion, but it can also protect oppressive elites.

If we are to respect other cultures, we must know what those cultures are. It can be difficult for outsiders to acquire this knowledge. Governments and intellectual elites often act as 'gatekeepers', offering an official version of the culture to the outside world. We have, however, reasons to be sceptical of the claims of elites to speak for the people. We can hear the people only if they have a secure set of rights. If some people are, for example, not free from the fear of arbitrary arrest, or if women are excluded from public life, we cannot know whether the culture of the people is being truly represented. Respect for cultural diversity, therefore, which is often represented as a threat to the universality of human rights, may, quite to the contrary, require the robust implementation of those rights.

In relating human-rights universalism to particular cultures, human-rights scholars generally start with universal human-rights standards, and then judge the various cultures of the world by those standards. This seems reasonable, as the Universal Declaration proclaims itself to be 'a common standard of achievement' for all peoples. However, some may accept the force of human-rights principles, but see the task of relating them to established cultures as one not of *judging* those cultures, but of *incorporating* human-rights standards into them. That there is some degree of consensus among state elites on human rights does not mean that integrating human rights with actual cultures is unproblematic.

Othman argues that in Western societies the increasing influence of human rights has accompanied the secularization of public life. In Islamic societies, secularization has not been as thorough-going, so that religion and modernity remain in a state of tension. In this situation, some Muslims have sought an interpretation of human rights grounded in the Qur'an. The acceptance of the UN Convention on the Elimination of All Forms of Discrimination Against Women (CEDAW), Othman says, has been difficult in Islamic societies. Conservatives can represent attempts to implement it as violations of the society's autonomy, and mobilize opposition to it on nationalist, cultural or religious grounds. These positions have to be opposed by counter-arguments from within the culture. Human-rights violations have to be shown to be incompatible with the principles of Islam (Othman 1999). This proposal has the merit that it views human-rights progress as a matter of self-emancipation and not of external imposition. It leaves unsolved, however, the problem of what external human-rights advocates should do if internal dialogue fails to lead to human-rights improvements.

According to the Qur'an, Othman maintains, Muslims are obliged to resist oppression. Thus Islam implies a conception of the person as the bearer of human rights. However, there is a gap in this argument between the *obligations* of *Muslims* and the *rights* of *all human beings*. To reconcile Islam and human rights, Islam would have to recognize the equal human rights of Muslims and non-Muslims. Othman does not show whether this is possible within an Islamic discourse on human rights. The strategy of arguing for human rights from within a particular culture raises questions about the rights of those who do not belong to the dominant culture. Shachar also argues that reliance on internal reform of illiberal cultural practices discriminates against the most oppressed members of cultural groups, especially women and children, because they have the least power to effect such reforms (Shachar 1999: 99). It also assumes that international standards are not part of the national culture.

An-Na'im has shown that Othman's project could face difficulties. Article 5 of the Universal Declaration says that no one shall be subjected to cruel, inhuman or degrading punishment. Islamic law (Shari'a) provides that theft is punishable by the amputation of the right hand. Many people would regard this as violating Article 5. However, Shari'a is based on the Qur'an, which Muslims believe to be the word of God, and which human beings may not question. An-Na'im believes that neither internal Islamic reinterpretation nor cross-cultural dialogue is likely to lead to the total abolition of this punishment in Islamic societies. There are, however, resources in the Qur'an for restricting its application, by requiring strict standards of proof or recognizing various extenuating circumstances (An-Na'im 1992: 33–6). We cannot know whether cross-cultural dialogue and/or social changes in Islamic societies will eliminate this punishment. We should recall, however, that beliefs about the will of God and appropriate punishment have changed over time in the West. There may also be some in Islamic societies who support international standards in this matter.

An-Na'im's attempt to reconcile Islam and human rights has been criticized because his interpretation of Islam is too unorthodox to influence even liberal Muslims and yet concedes too much to Islam to defend human-rights orthodoxy. In 1990 the Organization of the Islamic Conference adopted the Cairo Declaration on Human Rights in Islam. This permits or requires discrimination against women, and offers little protection to freedom of religion. Islamic states have made few reservations to the international covenants on civil and political rights and on economic, social and cultural rights, but they have made strong reservations to CEDAW. (The USA has not ratified CEDAW.) The Islamic approach to human rights differs from the perspectives of Asian or African values in that it claims authority from a source, Allah, which must, within the discourse, be superior to that of 'the international community'. Nevertheless, there are important differences between secular Muslims (those who self-identify as Muslims but who do not practise the religion), liberal Muslims who support human rights, moderate reformers and 'fundamentalists'. Some Islamic governments reject some human rights, but hide this fact behind talk of 'Islamic human rights' and the ratification of treaties with major reservations (Mayer 2007).

Although some aspects of Islam may be incompatible with some human rights, Islam and human rights are not competing belief-systems, such that Muslims must give up their religion to support human rights. Human rights set *minimum standards* for the conduct of *governments* (and perhaps other power-holders), including the right to freedom of religion. During the drafting of the Universal Declaration, Muslim countries did not generally find the Declaration objectionable on religious grounds (Mayer 2007: 12–14). The two 1966 covenants were approved in the General Assembly by a unanimous vote of more than 100 countries, including 21 Muslim countries. The West did not impose its conception of human rights on the Muslim countries, for the West did not always support liberal positions on human rights and Muslim countries did not always agree on their positions (Waltz 2001, 2004). Some conservative Muslims transfer the Muslim's duty to God to the state in a way that is not clearly mandated by the Qur'an (Mayer 2007).

Chase emphasizes the diverse and dynamic nature of the Muslim world. He argues that political, social and economic factors explain the status of human rights: Islam is neither responsible for human-rights violations nor the basis for advancing human rights. We should distinguish Islam from 'Islamism': Islam is compatible with diverse political systems, while Islamism is a modern form of religious nationalism that is not friendly towards human rights. Islamism is unpopular with most Muslims, unless the available alternatives have failed them. Attempts to justify human rights on Islamic grounds lack authority and are unconvincing, because the concept of human rights is political, legal, economic, social and cultural, but not theological. The question is not whether Islam can be reconciled with human rights, but under what political and economic conditions a liberal, human-rights regime would be attractive to Muslims (Chase 2006, 2007).

Baderin takes a different view. Islamic law is embodied in the constitutions and laws of several states. It is therefore necessary to take Islam into account in implementing international human-rights norms (Baderin 2007). Modirzadeh believes that religious conservatism is indeed the cause of human-rights violations and deploying international human-rights law against Shari'a may undermine the work of reformist Muslims (Modirzadeh 2006).

There are many different Muslim views about the relation of Islam with human rights. Although many Muslims support human rights, the governments of countries with predominantly Muslim populations tend to subscribe to human rights with reservations that render their support for universal standards seriously wanting. The failure of secular regimes in the Muslim world, and the historical imposition of Western culture, have for many called into question the legitimacy of human rights, together with other ideas perceived to be Western. Nevertheless, repression by governments in the Muslim world is similar to repression by governments in other countries, and many Muslims object to it for reasons that are similar to those advanced by non-Muslims against human-rights violations. The Beirut Declaration on the Regional Protection of Human Rights in the Arab World (2003) affirmed the universality of human rights and rejected the use of culture or Islam to restrict them. The dominant Islamic conceptions of human rights reflect power struggles between traditionalist elites and liberal modernizers more than inherent features of Islam (Mayer 2007).

Debates about cultural relativism often fail to distinguish states from cultures and to analyse the complexity of cultures. Falk has argued that international human-rights law has been slow to recognize the values and needs of individuals and groups that are not adequately represented in the system of nation-states, such as ethnic minorities, indigenous peoples, women, children, gays and the poor (Falk 1992: 48). The respect that international law gives to nation-states potentially entails various forms of exclusion. Some, such as those of ethnic minorities and indigenous peoples, may raise questions of cultural discrimination. Others, such as those of women and children, may raise questions of cultural oppression. Thus, the concept of 'cultural relativism' is too blunt for the adequate analysis of culture and human rights.

Minority rights

It is often assumed that minority rights belong to the field of human rights, but the relations between the two kinds of rights are problematic. The United Nations, in drafting the Universal Declaration of Human Rights, decided to leave out minority rights. The League of Nations had had a minority-rights regime, but this was thought to have failed, and the concept of minority rights was believed to have been exploited by Nazi Germany as an excuse for aggression. The Universal Declaration is based on the assumption that individual human rights are sufficient to protect cultural minorities. The UN recognized that there might be a minorities problem by setting up its Sub-Commission on Prevention of Discrimination and Protection of Minorities.

The most important provision of international law relating to minorities is Article 27 of the International Covenant of Civil and Political Rights, which provides that, in those states in which ethnic, religious or linguistic minorities exist, 'persons belonging to such minorities shall not be denied the right, in community with other members of their group, to enjoy their own culture, to profess and practise their own religion, or to use their own language'. This goes beyond the Universal Declaration, but contains several problems: 1) it applies only to those states in which minorities exist, thereby encouraging states to deny that minorities exist in their jurisdictions; 2) it recognizes the rights of persons belonging to minorities, not of minorities as such; 3) it imposes on states only duties of non-interference with the rights of such persons, but no duties to assist them.

The reluctance of states to take minority rights seriously has been attributed to the following factors: 1) it would encourage outside interference; 2) minority problems are diverse and it is doubtful that there are universal solutions; 3) minority rights threaten the cohesion of states; 4) minority rights discriminate against majorities (Eide 1992: 221). Nevertheless, in 1992 the UN adopted a Declaration on the Rights of Persons Belonging to National or Ethnic, Religious and Linguistic Minorities. The title of this declaration follows Article 27 in assigning rights to *persons*, not to *minority groups*. However, Article 1 of the Declaration provides that states 'shall protect the existence and the national or ethnic, cultural, religious and linguistic identity of minorities within their respective territories, and shall encourage conditions for the promotion of that identity'. Thus, although the

Declaration does not recognize minority-group rights, it goes further than Article 27 in imposing on states the obligation to take positive measures to protect minority identities.

The political theory of liberal democracy was not designed historically to solve problems of cultural minorities. The classical conception of democracy entailed the rule of a culturally unified people. In the influential theory of the eighteenth-century French philosopher, Rousseau, any cultural differences that might exist in society should be subordinated to the 'general will' of the people (Rousseau 1968). Locke's liberal theory was designed to protect the natural rights of individuals. He assumed that, since all citizens were equal, political decisions should be taken by the majority: minorities were simply citizens who had been outvoted. He had no conception of cultural minorities. Government had a duty to respect the natural rights of every individual, but minorities as such had no rights (Locke [1689] 1970). Liberal democracy offers to members of cultural minorities individual rights, including the right to participate in cultural groups. Since all citizens have equal rights, the status of minorities is perfectly just. Actual liberal democracies are, of course, unjust in various ways, but, liberal democrats argue, this is because liberal-democratic principles are often violated in practice. The solution to this problem is the robust implementation of the principles, not their revision.

The persistence of minority claims in even the most developed liberal-democratic societies, the connection between minority problems and gross human-rights violations around the world, and the end of the Cold War ideological conflict have generated practical and theoretical challenges to this liberal-democratic solution. In response, a number of liberal-democratic theorists have reviewed the relations between politics and culture, and between majorities and minorities. The concept of 'multiculturalism' has come to occupy a central place in liberal-democratic theory. Liberal-democratic theorists are far from agreement, however, on how liberal democracies should solve the problems of multiculturalism.

Kymlicka has sought to develop a liberal theory of culture. In a multicultural society, he argues, the state necessarily promotes certain cultures and thereby disadvantages others. In a multilingual society, for example, not all languages can be official languages. This raises the question of justice for minorities. Liberals value individual choice, but individuals make their choices in particular cultural contexts. Liberals should, therefore, protect the cultures that provide the bases for individuals' choices. Under certain conditions, cultures can be protected only by recognizing group rights (Kymlicka 1995).

Cultural communities are, therefore, necessary to good individual lives, but individuals should have some autonomy from the communities of which they are members to choose the life that seems best for them. Communities are structured by inequalities of power, and are therefore always at least potentially oppressive. Liberals cannot generally approve the restriction by minority groups of the basic rights of their members. Liberals believe that individuals should have the capacity and freedom to question the culture of their community, and decide for themselves which aspects of that culture they will retain. Some restrictions of individual rights may nevertheless be justified to prevent actions that would undermine communities which are necessary for autonomous choices. What makes this justification of community restriction of individual rights liberal is that its purpose is to protect a rights-supporting community (Kymlicka 1995).

Kymlicka believes that the discourse of human rights can be an ideological disguise for the domination of minorities by majorities and that human-rights principles cannot solve some of the most important problems raised by minorities. The right to freedom of speech, for example, does not tell us what language policy a society ought to have. Even in liberal-democratic societies members of cultural minorities may suffer from unfair disadvantages, resulting from the power of majorities, without the violation of human rights (Kymlicka 1995: 4–5, 109). Human rights may even make injustice worse. For example, the rights to freedom of movement and vote may enable members of the majority to move to the traditional homelands of minorities, outvote them, and then undermine their culture. To protect themselves from this form of oppression, minorities may need collective rights to land ownership and language use, and to restrict the rights to freedom of movement and vote of the majority. Such collective rights are not fundamentally inconsistent with human rights, for liberal-democratic states claim the right to regulate immigration, land use and language policies, and such claims are not usually considered to be human-rights violations. In so far as the collective rights of minorities resemble recognized collective rights of nation-states, they should be subject to the same human-rights conditions. Kymlicka claims that minority and indigenous rights are an *extension of*, rather than a *reservation to*, the concept of human rights, but there may be in his theory an unresolved tension between individual and collective rights (Kymlicka 2001, 2007).

Kymlicka has been criticized for being a liberal imperialist, because he supports minority rights only for minorities that are liberal (Chaplin 1993). Kymlicka might reply that liberals are logically committed to disapproving of illiberal groups. His criticisms of human rights are, however, not compelling. The charge that human-rights principles cannot solve all minority problems is not apt, for the concept of human rights is intended to set *minimum standards* and not to provide a comprehensive theory of social justice. The charge that human rights might permit unjust behaviour can be answered by reaffirming that human rights are not unlimited. They may be limited for the sake of protecting human rights or for other reasons, as Article 29 of the Universal Declaration provides.

Tully has put forward an apparently anti-liberal argument about cultural diversity and justice. He argues that cultural diversity is a fundamental feature of the human condition and culture is inherent in human interaction. As citizens interact with each other, so they express their different cultures. Cultural recognition is a basic human need. A uniform political and legal system, to which all citizens are subject in the same way, denies this cultural diversity unjustly. Most liberal constitutions are unjust in this way. Constitutions should consist of a continuing intercultural dialogue. In this dialogue, each speaker should be given their due. This appears to recognize that cultural diversity goes down to the level of the individual, and therefore lays the basis for a conception of (individual) human rights: Tully's 'intercultural' constitutionalism is not as anti-liberal as it appears at first sight. Nevertheless, liberal constitutions, he argues, require cultural minorities to speak in the discourse of the dominant group. They suppress cultural differences and impose a dominant culture, while representing themselves as impartial. By contrast, intercultural dialogue aims for just cultural recognition, while repudiating unjust claims to recognition (Tully 1995). Tully does not make clear his criteria for the justice of claims to recognition, and thereby fails to answer the question to which liberal democracy provides an answer in the form of equal rights for all. Although Tully's theory of intercultural constitutionalism has a liberal core, its reliance on dialogue favours the powerful over the weak, and is therefore in this respect less just than the liberal constitutionalism that he criticizes.

Barry defends a liberal-democratic conception of justice that is 'blind' to cultural difference. Liberalism, he says, accommodates all differences that are just. Liberal democracies are just in that they treat all citizens as equals. They do not tolerate all differences, since some social practices are unacceptably harmful to others and to society. In particular, liberal democracies should not tolerate those who would undermine them. Such toleration betrays justice. Barry opposes the institutionalization of cultural differences, because he believes that this makes minorities more vulnerable to the dominant groups in society. Participation in common institutions creates solidarity, which is the best protection for minorities. Barry's defence of liberal democracy is open to the objection that liberal states cannot be culturally neutral, and that supposedly impartial justice conceals the unjust domination of particular cultures (Barry 2001).

Barry holds that liberal democracies should permit voluntary associations to engage in certain illiberal practices (for example, a religious community can refuse to have women priests) provided that their members have a genuine right to leave. However, he supports forceful intervention by liberal states to end unacceptable illiberal practices in minority communities. Few people, he argues, object to state intervention in *families* to prevent child abuse. Kymlicka is cautious about intervention for two reasons. The first is the unsuccessful historical record of liberal states in their attempts to 'improve' minority cultures. The second is that liberal state agents may be insensitive to the value of minority-group cultures to their members (Kymlicka 1989). We may also recall the argument that self-emancipation is better than emancipation by outsiders. These arguments against intervention are not decisive where the group oppression of its members is extreme.

In liberal democracies, Barry maintains, citizens have no obligation to respect each other's cultures; rather, they have obligations to respect each other as citizens, irrespective of culture. This misses Tully's point that citizens encounter each other culturally, and they cannot respect each other as citizens if they despise their fellow-citizens' cultures. Barry agrees that cultural differences are unavoidable, but maintains that liberal democracy provides the fairest way of settling disputes among cultures. What all people have in common provides the basis for universal human rights, and their cultural disagreements are best settled by liberal-democratic procedures. Minority rights tend to undermine both human rights and liberal democracy.

Barry's defence of liberal democracy underestimates the problem that actual liberal democracies have developed historically through injustices that may not be rectified by equal individual rights. Because the legitimate claims of minorities are typically the product of particular national histories, it is doubtful whether there are *universal* minority rights.

The term 'minority rights' refers to two different kinds of rights: individual rights of minority-group members and collective rights of minority groups. The first may be *required* by human-rights principles, whereas the second may be incompatible with human rights (the right to community education may, for example, discriminate against girls). Collective rights can also raise the problem of defining the group that has the rights. If indigenous peoples have rights, for example, who defines who is an indigenous people? The UN solution is to say that indigenous people should define themselves, but this assumes that (a) we already know who indigenous people are, and (b) there will be no unreasonable self-definition. A further problem of collective rights is that although it is sometimes assumed that individuals are selfish and groups are not, group rights-claims can be selfish and unjust.

Donnelly argues that although there are collective rights, there are no collective human rights. Collective rights may be necessary to protect human dignity, and therefore may be compatible with human rights, but, in the event of conflict between collective rights and human rights, the latter should generally prevail. The preservation of cultural groups may be valuable, but, if the group is violating human rights, and its members choose to leave or to abandon its culture, human-rights principles cannot defend the survival of the group. However, since human rights are not absolute, and since rights-violating groups may have some value for their members, there is no general principle governing the right of cultural groups to survival. We should remember, however, that respecting human rights is often the best way of protecting cultural minorities (Donnelly 1989: 149–57). A controversial question is whether cultural minorities have the right to state funding for their culture. It may be good policy for the state to support some minority cultural activities, but it is doubtful whether there is a human right to such support. One problem with recognizing such a right would, again, be that of identifying the right-holders. Critics of such supposed group rights to state support for minority cultures believe that it would encourage competition and division among minority groups and make them more vulnerable to hostility and exploitation by the dominant group.

Indigenous peoples

Minority rights are often confused with the rights of indigenous peoples. Some indigenous peoples' representatives, however, claim that they are not 'minorities', but *colonized peoples*. The confusion is made worse by the fact that there is no agreed definition of either minorities or indigenous peoples in international law or social science. The term 'indigenous peoples' originates from the American continent, where it refers to those who are descended from the peoples who inhabited the continent before the arrival of Europeans, and who retain significant elements of non-European culture, and are economically, socially and politically oppressed. The application of the concept to other parts of the world is problematic, since some groups who have the social characteristics of indigenous peoples are not indigenous, and some indigenous peoples do not have these characteristics. Indigenous peoples can also contain conflicting class, gender and other interests. Most, though not all, indigenous groups are relatively small, but, together, they constitute about five per cent of the world's population. Historically, they have been victims of genocide, cultural oppression and labour exploitation. Indigenous peoples do not, however, all have similar cultures nor do they all have similar social problems.

There have been two significant developments in conceptions of the rights of indigenous peoples in recent years. The first has been a move from emphasis on *integration* and *assimilation* to debates about *self-determination*. The second has been a move from the International Labour Organization (ILO) to the Human Rights Commission (now the Human Rights Council) and the General Assembly. Issues concerning indigenous peoples arose in the UN first as questions about the exploitation of indigenous labour. They were taken up by the ILO, and this led to ILO Convention 107 in 1957. This Convention was based on the premise that the problems of indigenous peoples could be solved by extending to them the citizenship rights of the dominant population. It did not recognize their specific cultures. Consequently, it was rejected by indigenous peoples. In 1989 it was amended as ILO Convention 169. Although this Convention called upon states to respect the cultures of indigenous peoples and rejected the policy of assimilation, it failed to meet those peoples' demands and was adopted without their participation (Kymlicka 2007).

Indigenous peoples rejected these statist, 'top-down' solutions, and began to mobilize with the demand for self-determination as colonized peoples. National governments and the 'international community' were for a long time reluctant to meet this demand. This reluctance was sometimes justified by the so-called 'saltwater principle', which restricts the right to self-determination to colonized peoples who had saltwater between them and their imperial rulers. Thus, Nigerians had the right to self-determination, but the Inuit of Canada did not. The UN Working Group on Indigenous Peoples, consisting of independent experts, drew up, with the participation of indigenous representatives, a Draft Declaration on the Rights of Indigenous Peoples that included the right to self-determination, but governments resisted the incorporation of this into international law. On 13 September 2007 the UN General Assembly adopted the Declaration on the Rights of Indigenous Peoples.

The indigenous demand for political self-determination is not usually a demand for an independent state, but for self-government within the state in which they live. Equally important for many groups is the demand for *economic* self-determination. Indigenous peoples are not necessarily opposed to economic development, but they wish to control the form that it takes. This often brings them into conflict with states and private corporations that have other plans for the local resources.

Indigenous peoples' representatives also claim the right to *cultural* self-determination. This raises the problem of potential conflict between indigenous cultures and human rights. The UN Human Rights Committee has sought to strike a balance between individual rights and the preservation of indigenous cultures. These decisions show that the international-law conception of human rights is far from being extremely individualistic. The individualistic conception of human rights is, however, not well suited to do justice to collective indigenous land claims (Brysk 2000: 202). Kymlicka maintains that indigenous peoples are more willing to accept adverse judgements of international bodies than of their own states' institutions (Kymlicka 1995: 169). Conflicts between collective indigenous peoples' rights and international, individual human rights may, therefore, not be as intractable in practice as they may appear in theory. The doctrine of cultural relativism may *disempower* indigenous peoples in their struggles against the state by trapping them in politically ineffectual cultures (Brysk 2000: 65).

States sometimes hold indigenous practices to be illegal on human-rights grounds as a means to control indigenous groups in ways that may violate their individual and collective rights. The international human-rights system may offer least protection to those indigenous peoples who need it most: states that have agreed to adjudication by the Human Rights Committee are those with relatively good human-rights records (Speed and Collier 2000; Thornberry 2002).

A neglected sub-field of indigenous rights consists of the rights of nomadic peoples. Since Locke, theories of property have favoured agricultural rights over those of nomads. The agricultural theory of land ownership provided a basis for the territorial theory of sovereignty and the exclusion of nomads from the protection of international law. In the *Western Sahara* case (1975), however, the International Court of Justice did hold that nomads in the Western Sahara had rights over land. Some national courts have also recognized nomadic land rights. Some have, however, been reluctant to extend indigenous rights to nomadic peoples. There is scope within the law of non-discrimination, minority and indigenous rights to protect the human rights of nomadic peoples, but this law is not yet fully developed (Gilbert 2007).

The recent movement for indigenous rights has challenged the liberal-democratic basis of human rights. This is not because indigenous groups reject human rights. Some indigenous practices violate human-rights norms, but indigenous groups also sometimes appeal to those norms to support their cause. However, in claiming various forms of autonomy, indigenous groups challenge the concept of the liberal-democratic nation-state with a homogeneous concept of citizens' rights. They do so partly because they have been conquered and exploited by the states of which they are supposed to be citizens, and partly because their experience of liberal-democratic citizens' rights has not been positive. The 'international community' of nation-states and its international law were constructed by imperial conquest. Natural law provided a basis for criticizing imperialism, but when it was replaced by positive international law in the nineteenth century, indigenous peoples were coercively included in the system of sovereign states. Liberal democracies form part of this international system and so their moral claim to the loyalty of their indigenous groups has been questioned (Keal 2003). Nevertheless, the rich liberal democracies have been able to afford limited concessions to indigenous peoples, while the 'development imperative' of less-developed countries make such concessions more difficult.

Some have questioned the very idea of 'indigenous rights' without denying that indigenous peoples have been victims of gross injustice. The argument is that it is not 'indigeneity' as such that grounds rights, but historical injustice. Some indigenous groups may be the perpetrators, not the victims, of injustice: the indigenous Fijians may be an example. The right of indigenous peoples to self-determination is, some say, in principle no different from the right of any people to self-determination. Its ground is not indigeneity, but the contingent, though pervasive, historical fact that indigenous peoples have been the victims of gross human-rights violations, and that some form of autonomy is the most appropriate remedy (Buchanan 2004).

The right to self-determination

Both the international human-rights covenants of 1966 state that all peoples have the right to self-determination, but deciding who has this right in practice has proved controversial. The orthodox view in international law is that self-determination is a right to be free from European imperial rule, and not to be subject to racist domination or alien occupation (Cassese 1995). This view is strongly influenced by particular political phenomena such as the world-wide anti-colonial movement, the campaign against apartheid in South Africa, and opposition to Israeli occupation of Palestinian lands. The right has not been extended to other peoples subject to alien rule, such as the Tibetans. The right to self-determination has been interpreted in international politics for the sake of the stability of the states system. This policy of the 'international community' has not been very successful, since conflicts over self-determination have constituted perhaps the most disorderly feature of the states system in recent years. The international community has given priority to the principle of *territorial integrity* over that of self-determination. This has left minority peoples vulnerable to majority oppression, encouraged secessionist conflicts, provoked state violence and gross human-rights violations, and threatened destabilization of the inter-state order.

Political theorists have proposed various theories of self-determination on the basis of liberal-democratic principles. The most influential is the *remedial theory*. This says that states which respect the human rights of their citizens have a right to their loyalty, and there is therefore no right of secession from such states. There is a right of secession only if there are serious and persistent human-rights violations and no solution other than secession is available (Birch 1984). This theory is *liberal* rather than *nationalist*, for the violation of individual human rights rather than national interests justifies secession, although the theory might support national self-determination if the victims of human-rights violations constitute a nation.

Beran has developed an alternative liberal theory that may be called the *voluntarist theory*. This is based on the liberal value of *individual* self-determination. This entails the right to freedom of association. Any individual who wishes to leave a political community has the right to do so. If the majority in part of a state's territory wishes to secede, they have the right to do so. Human-rights violations are not necessary to this right of secession. Nor is it necessary that the secessionists are a nation (Beran 1984, 1988). The right to secession is subject to two important conditions: 1) secessionists must respect the human rights of everyone living in the new state; 2) they must also recognize the right to secession of the majority of any territory within its borders. This generates what is sometimes called the 'Russian doll' problem. If all territorial majorities have the right to secede, the states system might split up into ever smaller states, with consequent anarchy. Beran advances four answers to this objection: 1) the risk of war may override the right to secession; 2) war apart, the right to secession overrides concerns about the number of states; 3) excessive secession would be checked by the self-interest of potential secessionists; 4) excessive secession can be checked by enlightened concessions by states to potential secessionists. Whether Beran's theory would work in practice is hard to say, since it is rejected by the international community. Theoretically, Beran has difficulty in deriving a *collective* right to self-determination from his *individualist* premises. He says that those with property rights have the right to alter the sovereignty over their property, but, since he has no theory of property rights, this argument is weak. Pavković and Radan argue that no actual secession has been based on Beran's voluntarist theory (Pavković and Radan 2007).

The collective right to self-determination may be derived from *democratic* premises. According to democratic theory, the legitimacy of government derives from the will of the people. The self-determination of nations is, therefore, equivalent to democracy. Since democratic self-government is a *collective* value, democratic theory may be better suited than liberal individualism to justify a collective right to self-determination.

A collective right to national self-determination can also be derived from *communitarian* premises. Communitarians reject Beran's assumption that national membership is voluntary. Most people are born into their nation; it forms part of their identity. Communitarians argue that if there is a right to national self-determination, it must be a collective right (Raz 1986: 207–9). Margalit and Raz argue that individuals flourish through culture; culture is maintained by groups; the prosperity of cultural groups is therefore necessary to the well-being of their members; and self-determination is necessary for the protection of groups. Human-rights violations are not necessary to justify the right to national self-determination. The right of groups to self-determination is the weaker, however, the more likely it is that recognizing it would lead to the violation of the rights either of group members or of outsiders (Margalit and Raz 1990). The communitarian right to self-determination is therefore subject to liberal conditions.

Miller argues that nations are ethical communities and states are the most effective co-ordinating mechanisms for nations. Nation-states are therefore the best available institutions for social justice, and this provides the justification for national self-determination (Miller, D. 1995). This raises several problems. There are problems, for example, in defining nations and in showing that they are 'ethical communities'. The argument also claims only that nation-states are the best institutions to provide justice *for their citizens*. This allows at best only weak obligations on the part of nation-states towards the human rights of foreigners.

Practical discussions of self-determination are more concerned with international order than with human rights. Shehadi argues that in order to achieve its goal of international order, the international community must balance the principle of the territorial integrity of states with the aspirations of aggrieved nations, and that there should be international institutions with the authority to settle self-determination disputes in accordance with the rule of law rather than the rule of force (Shehadi 1993). This proposal tries to combine principle with pragmatism, but may be too principled to be acceptable to powerful states, and too pragmatic to satisfy the requirements of justice. This shows how difficult it is to implement the right of *peoples* to self-determination in a world of *states*.

There is a consensus among more practical scholars that the right to *secession* should rarely be recognized, but that states should recognize forms of self-determination that fall short of secession (Hannum 1990). Many governments, however, fear that self-determination may be the first step to secession. Such fears are often exaggerated, but we cannot say that they always are. Self-determination problems can be extremely difficult, but their solutions are likely to require not the abolition of the nation-state, but new thinking about the forms that it might take. Some have maintained that the right to self-determination is *the most important* human right or the *precondition* of all other human rights. Some persecuted nations undoubtedly have strong claims to self-determination. However, the idea of a universal human right to the self-determination of peoples raises complex analytical problems and carries great dangers to human rights. It may even be incoherent, as the right to self-determination of one people (say, the Québécois) may conflict with the right to self-determination of another people (say, the Canadians).

The rights of women

The Vienna Declaration emphasized the human rights of particular groups, such as disabled persons, refugees and migrant workers. These are very important, but require specialized treatment, which is beyond the scope of this book. It is necessary, however, to say something about the rights of women and children, not only because of the importance of these subjects, but also because they raise particular challenges to traditional political thought.

According to the World Health Organization 70 per cent of those in extreme poverty are female; two-thirds of those who are illiterate are women; and on average women are paid between 30 and 40 per cent less than men for comparable work (Simmons 2009: 204). Certain forms of the mistreatment of women were objects of international standard-setting by intergovernmental conferences and the International Labour Organization before the Second World War. In 1945 feminists succeeded in having the equal rights of men and women written into the United Nations Charter and in establishing the Commission on the Status of Women (CSW). The prohibition of discrimination against women was included in the Universal Declaration of Human Rights. The CSW, though hampered by underfunding and the opposition of culturally conservative states, was responsible for the Convention on the Elimination of All Forms of Discrimination Against Women (CEDAW), adopted in 1979. Many states have ratified CEDAW, but it is weakened by numerous reservations. The Committee charged with implementing CEDAW is also under-resourced and relatively inaccessible to NGOs (Jacobson 1992; Reanda 1992).

Growing dissatisfaction among women's groups and Commission members about the slow pace of progress led to the Decade for Women 1975–85, which included three world conferences, held in Mexico City, Copenhagen and Nairobi. The declarations and programmes of action adopted by these conferences were endorsed by the UN General Assembly. The issues thus officially recognized included political participation, education, employment, health, nutrition, agricultural production and marketing, access to credit, housing, industrial development, and the special vulnerability of refugees, the disabled, the elderly and many others. The Women's Decade led to a shift of emphasis from activities specifically related to women to 'mainstreaming', that is, incorporating women's issues in all UN planning. UN human-rights bodies began to include gender issues in their work, an innovation that was strengthened when Mary Robinson became the High Commissioner for Human Rights (Gaer 2001). It was also recognized that the situation of women would not be improved unless women were empowered through participation in decision-making. Whether this change of strategy has led to much improvement in the everyday lives of women is uncertain (Reanda 1992; Simmons 2009).

Feminists have challenged dominant interpretations of human rights, arguing that they are biased against women, because they address violations by states, and ignore the violations that women suffer at the hands of men in the private sphere. In classical natural-rights theory, natural rights are held by all human beings and entail obligations by all human beings. This theory has been translated into international human-rights law, in which the rights are held by individual human beings, but the obligations not to violate those rights are borne mainly by *states*. This element of the dominant conception of human rights is sometimes justified as necessary to distinguish human-rights violations from ordinary crimes (Donnelly 1998: 1, 1999: 85–6).

The Universal Declaration, however, is not so statist, and imposes obligations on states, groups and persons. Article 2(e) of CEDAW imposes on states the obligation to eliminate discrimination against women 'by any person, organization or enterprise'. The Vienna Declaration acknowledged that 'gender-based violence and all forms of sexual harassment and exploitation' were human-rights violations. In 1993 the UN General Assembly unanimously adopted the Declaration on the Elimination of All Forms of Violence Against Women. Article 4 (c) requires states to exercise due diligence to prevent and punish acts of violence against women, 'whether those acts are perpetrated by the State or by private persons'. In 1994 the Commission on Human Rights appointed a special rapporteur on violence against women (Joachim 2003: 247–8). Feminists sometimes cite Article 16 (3) of the Universal Declaration, which says that the family is 'the natural and fundamental group unity of society' and is 'entitled to protection by society and the state' in order to show that the Declaration endorses the male-dominated family. Article 16 (3) does not have to be interpreted in this way, however, and there are other provisions of human-rights law that can provide the basis for feminist campaigns. Liberals can reply to the feminist criticism that by insisting on a protected private sphere, they protect the violation of women's rights by men, with the argument that liberalism imposes on the state the duty to protect everyone from violation of their rights in the private as well as the public sphere.

Feminists argue that the subjection of women in the household often leads to their disempowerment in the public sphere. The distinction between the public domain of the state and the private domain of the family is fallacious, they say, because the family is, in all societies, regulated by the state and its law. Reproduction and child-rearing, usually considered to be private activities *par excellence*, are typically regulated by men to form male and female identities so as to ensure the subordination of women. Some recognized human-rights violations, such as torture, are experienced by women in a distinctive way, for example by sexual violence and/or humiliation. Women suffer much more than men from justifications of the violations of almost all their human rights by appeals to culture. In addition, their access to legal redress is often barred by discriminatory, male-dominated legal systems (Binion 1995; Desai 1999). Some feminists criticize the concept of equality in human-rights discourse on the ground that it fails to recognize the difference of women's experience. It is valid to emphasize the difference of women's experiences, but the critique of equality for the sake of difference may be counter-productive because cultural groups often justify treating women unequally on the ground of cultural difference.

Feminism has energized the cause of women's human rights, and drawn the attention of the UN, governments and human-rights NGOs to the many serious human-rights violations that are suffered exclusively or predominantly by women. This cause was advanced at the fourth World Conference on Women, held in Beijing in 1995, despite opposition from various conservative groups, religious institutions and states. This has certainly been one of the most significant shifts in the interpretation of human rights in international politics since the end of the Cold War. Against the feminist critique of international human-rights law, Fellmeth has pointed out that there are about two dozen significant international legal texts aimed at protecting women's rights. The bias against women is much less in international law than in the difficulty of implementing it (Fellmeth 2000: 727–8).

Some feminists, however, complain that the individualism of human rights conceals the structural oppression of women. However, defending the rights of individual women does not entail denying the structural causes of their violation.

The rights of children

Although concern for the welfare of children predates the modern concept of human rights, the human-rights movement was slow to incorporate children into its concerns. The declarations of the American and French Revolutions were silent on children. In the nineteenth century the child-protection movement established orphanages, schools and juvenile courts. The Geneva Declaration of the Rights of the Child, adopted by the League of Nations in 1924, stated that 'mankind owed to the Child the best that it has to give', and proclaimed a duty to provide the necessary means for normal development, food and medicine, relief in times of distress, protection against exploitation, and socialization to serve others. The UN Declaration of the Rights of the Child, adopted in 1959, also emphasized child protection (Freeman 1997).

Michael D. A. Freeman (no relation of the present author) has distinguished three approaches to child welfare: child protection; children's liberation; and children's rights. The first treats children as objects of concern; the second emphasizes the adolescent's right to self-determination. Freeman proposes a middle way, according to which children both need protection and are capable of making autonomous choices. On this view, children move from requiring protection and nurturance to respect for their autonomy as they grow older. Some adolescents have more capacity for autonomy than many adults. The value of autonomy is compatible with the practice of compulsion, so that, for example, compulsory education can be justified on the ground that it can develop the child's capacity for autonomy (Freeman 1997).

The middle approach has been taken by the United Nations, which in 1989 adopted its Convention on the Rights of the Child (CRC) without a vote. The Convention received the 20 ratifications it needed to come into force in less than a year; for comparison, the International Covenant on Civil and Political Rights took ten years to achieve the same result. CRC has now been ratified by all UN states except the USA and Somalia. In September 2010 it had 193 state parties, considerably more than any other international human-rights treaty.

Five issues were controversial in the drafting process: freedom of religion; inter-country adoption; the rights of the unborn child; traditional practices harmful to children's health; and the duties of children. Article 14 combines the right of children to freedom of religion with the right of parents to guide their children in the exercise of this right, and the right of the state to regulate religion in the public interest. Adoption is not recognized in Islam, and there was Latin American opposition to inter-country adoption on the ground that it might amount to 'exporting children'. Article 21 permits, but does not require, inter-country adoption where it is 'in the best interests of the child' and subject to various legal safeguards. The rights of the unborn are left ambiguous by a combination of the preamble, which states that children need special protection 'before as well as after birth', and Article 1, which defines children as human beings below the age of 18. The Convention is also somewhat ambiguous about traditional practices harmful to children's health, as Article 24 (3) calls on state parties to take 'appropriate' measures to abolish such practices, while the preamble recognizes the importance of traditions and cultural values. Article 29 (1) (c) states that education should include respect for parents. Perhaps the most distinctive element in the Convention is Article 12, which recognizes the right of children to freedom of expression, especially in legal proceedings concerning their welfare. CRC also unifies civil and political rights with economic, social and cultural rights more thoroughly than any other UN human-rights treaty, but this raises the question as to which rights are to be implemented immediately, as ICCPR requires, or 'progressively', as allowed by the International Covenant on Economic, Social and Cultural Rights (ICESCR).

Although the Convention represents a substantial cross-cultural consensus on the human rights of children, it suffers from many reservations, a weak implementation system, and the lack of the right of individual petition. Its monitoring committee is very under-resourced. Ten years after the Convention came into force, the committee was almost four years behind in considering state reports, and was only saved from a worse situation because 57 states were overdue in the submission of their reports. The committee has no investigative capacity, and is therefore very reliant on NGOs for information. Notwithstanding these weaknesses, the Convention and its committee have influenced the European Court of Human Rights and some national courts (Johnson 1992; Fottrell 2000).

The Convention has also been criticized because Article 38 permits the recruitment of child soldiers once they have reached the age of 15. However, as a result of an initiative by the Convention's monitoring committee the issues of child soldiers and the impact of armed conflicts on child civilians have been 'mainstreamed' in the UN Security Council. In 1997 the Secretary-General established the post of Special Representative on Children in Armed Conflict (Fottrell 2000). However, international human-rights law has not been able to protect children in armed conflict. The United Nations Children's Fund (UNICEF) estimates that between 1985 and 1995 two million children were killed in armed conflict; more than four million were disabled; twelve million were made homeless; more than one million orphaned or separated from their parents; and ten million psychologically traumatized (Kuper 2000: 109).

Children suffer from the ideological idealization of the family that assumes that parents love and nurture their children. The case for children's rights is based on the fact that many children do not live in such conditions. In various parts of the world they are targeted by death squads, die of starvation and preventable diseases, are exploited as cheap labour, and are subjected to sexual abuse. Children without rights are objects for adults, who may be benevolent, but are often not. The idea that the autonomy of at least older children should be recognized is not universally accepted. The justification of children's rights rests both on the need to protect children from abuse, and the developing maturity of the child (Freeman 1997).

King has expressed scepticism about the Convention on the ground that it does not address the causes of children's suffering, and gives the illusion of providing a solution, whereas its vague and legalistic language permits governments to evade their responsibilities (King 2004). This criticism applies to some extent to all international human-rights law, and it has some merit. Article 3 says that the best interests of the child shall be a primary consideration in all actions concerning children. This may seem to be an attractive principle, but it makes the Convention susceptible to very different interpretations in different cultural contexts. Also, because the best interests of the child are *a* rather than *the* primary consideration, they can be overruled. This is common in immigration cases, where the deportation of adults may be carried out, even when this is not in the best interests of their children (Todres 2004). Nevertheless, it may be that the Convention, for all its weaknesses, provides a helpful framework and a form of legitimation for those who campaign for children.

Sexual minorities

The purported rights of 'sexual minorities' are very controversial, as cultures differ greatly in their views of sexual behaviour (Miller 2009). Yet those whose sexual orientation and/or behaviour does not conform with the views of those in power and/or the majority are often persecuted, and their human rights demand analysis. The term 'sexual minorities' has generally come to include lesbian, gay, bisexual and transgender persons. Paul Hunt, UN Special Rapporteur on the Right to Health, stated in 2004 that human rights included the right of all persons to express their sexual orientation (Hunt 2004).

Discrimination against sexual minorities is common. Government and other leaders often dehumanize members of these minorities in language that would be considered unacceptable if applied to racial, ethnic or religious minorities. Accordingly, punishments for sexually 'deviant' behaviour is extremely harsh in many countries, including the death penalty. Members of sexual minorities are commonly denied many of their human rights, including their rights to personal security, fair access to education, health services and employment, and freedom of speech and association. In most countries same-sex couples lack the legal, economic rights of those who are conventionally married. International human-rights law and institutions discriminate against sexual minorities by failing to take their suffering seriously. Concern for the rights of sexual minorities is often said to be a Western cultural peculiarity, but this claim, like all similar East/West claims, is at best an oversimplification. There is prejudice against sexual minorities in the West, and there are 'gay rights' movements outside the West. Appeal is sometimes made to the provision of international human-rights law (for example, in Article 29 of the Universal Declaration) that states have the right and the duty to restrict human rights for the sake of 'public morals'. However, if this (extremely vague) provision is used to persecute sexual minorities, it is part of the problem, not part of the solution. As Donnelly correctly points out, human rights are designed to protect the dignity and freedoms of unpopular minorities. Nevertheless, there is no international consensus on the rights of sexual minorities (Amnesty International 2001; Donnelly 2003).

When international human-rights law was being developed after the Second World War, same-sex sexual activity was illegal in most countries. There were no 'gay rights' even though homosexuals had been explicit targets of Nazi persecution. In more recent times, the rights of sexual minorities have crept into human-rights law. In the 1980s, for example, the European Court of Human Rights held that the criminalization of consensual adult sex between men in private violated the right to privacy. However, gays have been unsuccessful in claiming the right to family life or to non-discrimination in employment benefits in European courts. Since 1991 Amnesty International has taken up gay issues, as have some other human-rights NGOs. A group of NGOs, the Sexual Rights Initiative, operates at the UN Human Rights Council (Miller 2009: 8). In 1994 the UN Human Rights Committee held that a law in Tasmania, Australia, criminalizing private consensual sex between men violated the right to privacy. Some countries accept persecuted gays, lesbians and transsexuals as refugees. The status of refugee is sometimes granted on the basis of sexual identity, but almost never on the basis of sexual conduct.

A meeting of human-rights experts, held in Yogyakarta, Indonesia, in 2006, adopted the Yogyakarta Principles on the Application of International Human Rights Law in relation to Sexual Orientation and Gender Identity. The experts agreed that these principles reflect the existing state of international human-rights law in relation to sexual orientation and gender identity. The principles affirm binding international legal standards with which all states must comply. Generally, these principles interpret the principle of non-discrimination to mean that respect for human rights requires that sexual orientation and gender identity should in no way be a reason for reducing any person's enjoyment of human rights (Yogyakarta Principles 2006). The unsubstantiated claim by these experts that the principles 'reflect' the existing state of international human-rights law is puzzling (Miller 2009: 11, 22). The principles are morally compelling for those who accept that sexual orientation is integral to human dignity. In July 2010 the UN Economic and Social Council granted the International Gay and Lesbian Human Rights Commission consultative status, the tenth organization working primarily for lesbian, gay, bisexual and transgender human rights to gain such status.

7

The Politics
of Human Rights

The real politics of human rights

The concept of human rights belongs to the *Idealist* tradition in the study of international relations in so far as it sets high ethical standards for governments. The dominant tradition, however, has been that of *Realism*, which assumes that the principal actors in international relations are *states*, that states are motivated primarily by self-interest, and that self-interest excludes, or at best marginalizes, concern for human rights. Realism can explain the neglect of human rights by states, but it can explain neither the introduction nor the increasing influence of human rights in international relations.

We saw, in chapter five, that the concept of human rights can be understood in terms of *regime theory*. International regimes consist of rules and institutions to which states commit themselves. International human rights constitute such a regime, though implementation of the regime is relatively weak. The existence and limited achievements of the regime support the Idealist approach to international relations, whereas its limitations and failures can be explained by Realism. The international human-rights regime not only implements human rights to some extent itself, but also provides the basis for human-rights actions by both governments and non-governmental organizations (NGOs).

The international policies of states are dominated by Realist concerns, whereas NGOs are more Idealistic, but carry less 'clout' in international relations.

The principle and practice of state sovereignty are, therefore, strong barriers to the implementation of international human-rights standards. Another strong barrier is the cultural diversity of the world, and the fact that many cultures legitimate practices that violate human-rights norms. The international human-rights regime is commonly presented as the 'imperialist' imposition of Western values on non-Western societies, but the USA has been reluctant to recognize economic, social and cultural rights, and to ratify UN human-rights treaties. State sovereignty and cultural difference provide two strong defences against outside pressures for human-rights improvement, and yet the legitimacy of human rights is sufficiently strong that pressures from governments and NGOs can lead to improvements in the human-rights performance of offending governments, and even to changes of government that lead to dramatic improvements. The desire of governments to benefit economically and politically from 'good standing' in the international community may play a role in this process, but Realists would be wrong to insist that the moral appeal of human rights has no effect in international relations.

The remarkable growth of international human-rights law since 1945 and the dominance of lawyers in human-rights institutions and academic human-rights study conceal the priority of politics over law in the struggle for human rights. International human-rights law is made by a political process. Political campaigns play an important role in human-rights implementation. Powerful non-governmental economic organizations, such as multinational corporations, are now recognized as important players in the violation and, potentially, in the promotion of human rights, and *political* pressure on these organizations, especially by NGOs, has recently increased. Lawyers and human-rights activists typically assign a central role to legal processes in the protection of human rights, whereas political scientists are more likely to consider them to be marginal. Forsythe points out that the dramatic improvements at the end of the twentieth century in Latin America, the former Communist societies of central and eastern Europe, and in South Africa, owed little to legal processes, and much to politics. The dominant human-rights problem in the contemporary world is the gap between human-rights ideals and law, on the one hand, and the reality of gross human-rights violations, on the other. The causes of this gap are not primarily legal or cultural, but political and economic (Forsythe 2000).

The human-rights component of foreign policy is, Forsythe maintains, a central feature of international human-rights politics. States set up international human-rights institutions, support and/or resist their efforts to implement human rights, and are the principal targets of those efforts. NGOs have become increasingly important in international human-rights politics, but their importance derives largely from the influence they have on the human-rights policies of states. These policies may be influenced by public opinion, and not only in democratic societies. States are often criticized, especially by human-rights activists, for being 'inconsistent' about human rights, but this inconsistency may be the result not only of changing perceptions of the national interest in a changing world, but also of the selective attention of public opinion to international human-rights issues (Forsythe 2000).

International human-rights politics may seem relatively ineffective if its achievements are contrasted with human-rights ideals, but they may seem more impressive if we remember that there was almost no such politics before the Second World War. After the end of the Cold War, the centre of international action for human rights shifted somewhat from the more legalistic UN institutions to the highly politicized Security Council. The so-called 'second generation' of UN peace-keeping operations has combined politics, human rights and military force. Human-rights enforcement by the Security Council may be relatively legitimate and effective, but, because this body is highly political, agreement on action is likely to be rare and selective. This is due not, as is often said, to the 'weakness' of the UN, but to the real political divisions in the world. Military enforcement of human rights is costly in lives and cash, and may be limited by the unwillingness of public opinion to make such sacrifices. It is also not necessarily well-suited to solving the political problems underlying the human-rights violations.

Even if governments include the promotion of human rights in their foreign policies, this will be only one among several elements, and will usually be given a much lower priority than defence and trade. These governments are likely to be accused of 'inconsistency' in their human-rights policies, at home and abroad, but a foreign policy dominated by military and economic priorities will almost certainly be 'inconsistent' in its concern for human rights. Governments are also not unified actors: they consist of different ministries, subject to different pressure groups, and these will lead to inconsistency in human-rights foreign policy. In addition, although UN rhetoric says that human rights, peace and economic development are interdependent, in the real world of foreign policy, pursuing these goals consistently may not always be possible. The demand that the promotion of human rights should be a dominant goal of foreign policy is probably unrealistic. Nevertheless, states could probably do more than they do now to promote human rights without damaging the pursuit of other legitimate goals, and contempt for human rights can lead to foreign-policy disasters, as the USA learned in such countries as Iran and the Philippines, and arguably, more recently in Iraq. Thus, the strict Realist theory of human rights and foreign policy is false. More accurate is 'the principle of limited sacrifice', which says that some states will sometimes include human rights among their foreign-policy concerns, but will usually be willing to pay only a limited price for implementing them.

Armed conflict is a major cause of human-rights violations. Between 1989 and 2001 there were 57 major armed conflicts in the world. Of these, 54 were internal to states. Most of these were identity-based, and led to massive human-rights violations in such places as Bosnia, Rwanda, Sudan, Liberia, Angola, Tajikistan, Congo, Kosovo, Sierra Leone and East Timor.

The boomerang theory

We saw in chapter five that Risse et al. have attempted to show how governments which violate human rights may be subject to internal and external pressures to conform with human-rights standards, and that they may respond to these pressures from instrumental or principled motives. They may consider concessions, for example, to secure trade advantages, or because they have been 'shamed' for not conforming to the principles of the international community. It is often said that many states pay only 'lip-service' to human rights. Risse and Sikkink take lip-service seriously. Governments who 'talk the talk' of human rights may find it harder not to 'walk the walk', harder, that is, not to back words with actions, for fear of being accused of hypocrisy. If human-rights norms become institutionalized, they may become standard operating procedures (Risse and Sikkink 1999). The dynamic in this model is provided by the 'boomerang effect'. National human-rights NGOs seek transnational support that is converted into international pressure, which, under favourable conditions, strengthens the hands of the national groups. The effectiveness of the boomerang depends on world opinion, but over time 'norms cascades' have occurred: the influence of human-rights norms has spread and strengthened, so that now there are few hiding-places from human-rights activism (Risse and Sikkink 1999: 18, 21).

The model proposes five phases of change. The first phase consists of repression. Repressive states often seek to prevent news of human-rights violations from leaking out. The spread of such information is necessary for the activation of a human-rights response, and the move to phase two, which consists of 'denial'. This involves not merely the denial that violations took place, but also that external pressure is legitimate. Governments may be able to mobilize nationalist sentiment in their resistance to 'outside interference'. In response, external actors can mobilize a combination of material and normative pressures: economic sanctions, 'shaming' publicity, etc. Repressive governments may 'tough out' this pressure in the hope that it will not be sustained. However, if it is sustained, and even escalated, the 'target' state may enter phase three, which is that of tactical concessions. These can lead in two directions: they may create space for internal pressure groups to bring about further change or they may 'buy off' external pressure. Risse and Sikkink believe that governments often overestimate the extent to which they can control this process, and tactical concessions may lead to 'self-entrapment', in which governments find themselves engaged in moral dialogue with external and/or internal critics (Risse and Sikkink 1999: 22–5, 28).

In the fourth phase, human-rights norms attain 'prescriptive status': governments accept them as legitimate, even though they implement them very imperfectly. They ratify human-rights covenants, institutionalize their norms in national constitutions and/or laws, and provide their citizens with remedies for violations. Although violations occur, dialogue about them takes place in terms of human rights. In phase five, compliance with international human-rights standards becomes habitual and enforced, when necessary, by the rule of law.

There is no necessary progress towards the implementation of human rights. Governments may ignore international pressures, and seek to stamp out internal resistance. If they make some concessions to such pressures, they may return to repression when the pressures relax. The main factors that affect the chances of human-rights reform are: 1) the vulnerability of repressive states to external material and moral pressures; 2) the willingness of external actors to sustain these pressures; 3) the presence or absence of class-based, ethno-national or religious forces threatening the territorial integrity or the internal cohesion of the state; 4) the space available for internal NGOs; 5) the strength of the international human-rights regime and transnational NGOs; 6) 'norm resonance', that is, the degree of fit between international norms and national cultures (Risse and Ropp 1999).

The authors claim that their model is superior to that of Realism, which cannot explain changes in human-rights policies. Some changes have not been direct consequences of state pressures; in some cases, such as that of the Philippines, internal NGO pressure changed great-power foreign policy (Risse and Sikkink 1999: 35; Risse and Ropp 1999: 268). The 'boomerang' model may not, however, explain such changes in foreign policy as that between the policies of Presidents Bush and Obama. The model is also said to be superior to 'modernization' theory, which has been used to explain both repression and liberalization, and therefore explains neither (Risse and Sikkink 1999: 37; Risse and Ropp 1999: 269–70). The 'boomerang' model provides a framework for analysing human-rights change, but it does not fulfil its promise of explaining variations among different societies. Realism and modernization may be insufficient for this, and the 'boomerang' may add a necessary dimension by relating external to internal pressures on repressive states, but we are left with something less than a full explanation of different human-rights performance in different societies.

Risse and Ropp conclude with ten lessons for human-rights practitioners:

1. Transnational human-rights NGOs have been very influential in recent years.
2. The impact of transnational NGOs is limited by the internal politics of target states, and national NGOs have to play an important role in this arena.
3. Transnational NGOs should direct their efforts both to weakening the resistance of governments to international norms and to supporting national NGOs.
4. Different strategies may be appropriate in different phases: blaming and shaming may be more effective in the repression and denial phases, and dialogue may be more effective in the later phases.
5. Moral and legal ideas are more effective in international politics than Realists recognize.
6. Transnational human-rights NGOs have been correct to rely on international law, for appeals to international law play an important role in effecting human-rights change.
7. In so far as human-rights activists have been anti-statist, they have been mistaken, for the pressure applied by liberal states on repressive states forms an important part of the international implementation of human rights.
8. The global implementation of human rights requires the consistent and persistent implementation of human-rights foreign policy by those states that claim to take human rights seriously.
9. Economic and other material sanctions are more likely to be effective in the repression and denial phases, and

less likely to be effective in the later phases, especially if the target government can mobilize a nationalist backlash against them.

10. Dialogue or 'constructive engagement' is unlikely to work in the repression and denial phases, but may be appropriate in the later phases (Risse and Ropp 1999: 275–8).

The national politics of human rights

The failure of Risse and his colleagues to explain variations in respect for human rights in different societies results from their international-relations approach, which does not pay sufficient attention to the *internal* causes of such variations. This requires the approaches of comparative history and comparative political science. In chapter five we examined Claude's argument that national human-rights regimes developed gradually in Britain, France and the USA, on the basis of capitalist economies, popular social movements and strong states. He doubted whether this could be done when, as is widespread around the contemporary world, rapid economic development is a dominant national priority. Claude's relative pessimism is explained partly by the fact that he was writing during the Cold War, when the international human-rights regime was less effective than it is now. Donnelly showed that rapid economic development could be combined with a commitment to economic and social rights. The argument that human rights must be sacrificed for the sake of development, which would improve human rights in the future, was called into question by the fact that the rich could use their political power to prevent development benefiting the poor (Donnelly 1989: 163–202).

Gurr explained state violence not by the supposed conditions of successful development, but by state strategies for dealing with political challenges. The probability and magnitude of state violence was explained by the nature and contexts of the challenges (Gurr 1986). Foweraker and Landman also explained the violation and protection of rights by challenges to the state by social movements

(Foweraker and Landman 1997). Whereas Gurr emphasized *state strategies* in dealing with challenges, Foweraker and Landman emphasized the social bases of struggles for rights. They neglected the international dimension of such struggles, but they did point out that the concept of 'rights' was well adapted to create solidarity among social groups with different and even partly incompatible interests, such as ethnic minorities and women.

Explaining human rights violations: the quantitative approach

Foweraker and Landman used quantitative analysis of four countries to show that social movements have generally been successful in gaining rights. Others have followed the lead of Strouse and Claude in seeking to explain human-rights violations by quantitative methods. The first of these studies found that even though the US Congress had mandated that US aid be tied to human rights, US foreign policy still ignored human rights. Later, methodologically more developed research showed that human rights played a role in US foreign policy, but were trumped by strategic concerns. Generally, the role of human rights was small. Making aid conditional on human-rights performance might influence recipient governments, but the withdrawal of aid from rights-violating governments could undermine their strength and thereby *increase* violations (Carey and Poe 2004; Poe 2004). Barratt found, similarly, that in the period 1980–96 human rights had some influence on British aid policy, but only when it had little or no adverse effect on trade (Barratt 2004).

Mitchell and McCormick found that political prisoners and torture were more likely in poor countries, and in countries that were involved in capitalist international trade (Mitchell and McCormick 1988). Henderson found that the less democracy, the more poverty, the greater the inequality, the worse the repression. Contrary to the findings of Strouse and Claude, he found that rapid economic growth was associated with *less* repression (Henderson 1991). Poe and Tate found that poor states and military governments were more likely to violate civil and political rights in the 1980s. They also found that where the level of democracy declines, human-rights violations increase. They found only a weak relation between wealth or economic growth rates and human-rights violations. By contrast, the threat of both external and internal war was positively linked with human-rights violations (Poe and Tate 1994).

Cingranelli and Richards sought to investigate whether or not the end of the Cold War had brought improvements in human rights. One view would be that since Communist regimes were serious human-rights violators, and during the Cold War both superpowers, the USA and the USSR, supported rights-violating regimes, the end of the Cold War would bring considerable improvements in respect for human rights. An alternative view was that since many violent conflicts had broken out after the end of the Cold War, human-rights violations might have increased. Research had generally shown that democracy was strongly associated with human rights, so that the post-Cold War increase in democracy should have led to human-rights improvements.

However, as we saw in chapter five, Fein found that what she called 'life-integrity violations' were most likely to occur in societies that lay in the middle between democracy and authoritarianism. The democratization of authoritarian political systems might, therefore, be dangerous for the protection of human rights (Fein 1995). By contrast, Davenport and Armstrong found that below a certain level democracy had no discernible impact on human rights, but above this level it improved respect for human rights (Davenport and Armstrong 2004). Landman found that old democracies violated civil and political rights less than new democracies (Landman 2005a: 92, 117–18).

Bueno De Mesquita and his colleagues found that elections without multi-party competition and constrained executives can make human rights worse, not better. Political competition leads to governmental accountability, which in turn leads to human-rights protection (Bueno De Mesquita et al. 2005). Davenport found that political competition and participation are more effective than constraints on the executive in decreasing repression. Constraints on the executive are in turn more effective than voting. Democracy is also more effective in reducing state violence than in preventing restrictions on civil liberties (Davenport 2007). The evidence therefore suggests that although democracy is broadly good for human rights, the relations between the two are not straightforward.

Cingranelli and Richards examined a random sample of 79 countries in the period 1981–96. The level of respect for the rights to be protected from disappearance, extra-judicial killing and torture did not improve by a statistically significant amount. Indeed, the amount of torture in 1996 was more than it had been throughout most of the Cold War. However, the level of respect for the right not to be imprisoned for political reasons nearly doubled after the end of the Cold War. Almost all this improvement occurred immediately after the Cold War ended (1990–93). There was no evidence of improvement in the years 1993–96. They concluded that the strongest explanation for the reduction in political prisoners after the end of the Cold War was the extent of democratization and, to a lesser extent, the increase in participation in the global economy. Neither the substantial increase in internal conflict that occurred after the end of the Cold War nor inter-state conflicts in this period had a significant independent effect on respect for the right not to be imprisoned for political reasons (Cingranelli and Richards 1999). The statistical method tells us nothing about human-rights improvements and failures in particular countries, but it does paint for us a rather bleak picture of human rights after the Cold War, except for the finding that more democracy means fewer political prisoners. Zanger, in a study of 147 countries from 1977–93, found that violations of life-integrity rights decreased in the year of change from authoritarian to democratic government, but increased in the following year. This suggests that democratization itself produces short-term benefits for these rights, but that the consolidation of democracy may be associated with violations. She also suggested that the use of economic sanctions to improve human rights may be counter-productive, since lowering a country's economic performance is more likely to worsen than improve its respect for human rights (Zanger 2000).

Milner, Poe and Leblang found that democracies score better than authoritarian states on economic and social rights, as well as on personal security. In contrast with Cingranelli and Richards, they found that human-rights performance worsened from 1989–92, and improved in 1993. This difference may be the product of different statistical methods, rights studied, time-frames, and/or sample of countries. Technical differences in statistical methods can, therefore, lead to different substantive conclusions. The study also lends some support to the thesis that security, subsistence and liberty rights are indivisible and interdependent, and that the need for trade-offs is limited. This finding is preliminary, and further research is needed to test whether trade-offs can be avoided (Milner, Poe and Leblang 1999).

Quantitative studies show that democracies and rich countries are less likely to violate personal integrity rights, and that countries involved in international or civil war, with a large population, an authoritarian regime and/or previous high levels of repression are more likely to violate such rights. The positive relation between economic development and human rights that exists globally does not, however, hold for Latin America (Landman 2002, 2006).

NGOs in world politics

These quantitative studies demonstrate *relationships* between various social, economic and political factors and certain types of human-rights behaviour, but, with the exception of the study of Foweraker and Landman, which is confined to only four similar countries, they tell us little or nothing about the effects of *human-rights activism*. In recent years NGOs have played an increasing role in human-rights politics at local, national and international levels, and, very recently, the serious study of these organizations has begun.

NGOs working for human rights are not new. Following medieval religious and academic networks, the flourishing of liberal ideas in the eighteenth-century Enlightenment encouraged the founding of various humanitarian associations. A society for the abolition of slavery was formed in 1787, the

British and Foreign Anti-Slavery Society was established in 1839, and this, the oldest human-rights NGO in the world, exists today as Anti-Slavery International. In the nineteenth century, international societies were active in the struggle against slavery, for the improvement of working conditions, and for the emancipation of women. In 1864 the Swiss humanitarian, Henri Dunant, set up the Red Cross. From the end of the eighteenth century to the end of the nineteenth, numerous international conferences were held with both governmental and non-governmental participants, and these led to a number of international conventions. After the end of the First World War, the International Labour Organization encouraged the participation of NGOs in international standard-setting (Charnovitz 1996–7).

NGOs played an important role in ensuring that the promotion of human rights was included in the UN Charter and in the drafting of the Universal Declaration. Article 71 of the UN Charter, the product of NGO lobbying, states that the Economic and Social Council 'may make suitable arrangements for consultations with non-governmental organizations which are concerned with matters within its competence'. In 1948, 41 NGOs had consultative status with the Council. In 1992 there were more than 1,000 (Korey 1998). It has been estimated that in 1953 there were 33 human-rights international NGOs (INGOs) and in 2000 there were 250 (Keck and Sikkink 1998: 10–11; Claude 2002a: 149).

The organizations that took part in the early years of the UN were religious, business, trades-union and women's associations. During the Cold War, NGOs were not viewed favourably by the Communist or 'third-world' states. Most international NGOs were based in the West, and the very idea of independent citizens' organizations seemed to belong to the Western, liberal-democratic tradition, and was inimical to the authoritarian statism of the Communist and third-world societies (Korey 1998: 77).

Although NGOs played a significant role in the drafting of both the UN Charter and the Universal Declaration, UN human-rights institutions were suspicious of NGOs in the early years, but gradually came to recognize their value as sources of information. Over time, human-rights NGOs developed the scope of their activities, publicizing violations, campaigning to persuade governments to refrain from them, and playing an important role in UN standard-setting and implementation procedures (Wiseberg 1992: 376; Brett 1995: 103–4). NGOs were influential in drafting the two covenants of 1966; Amnesty International played a leading role in the adoption of the Convention Against Torture; and NGOs were very active in the drafting of the Convention on the Rights of the Child. This last Convention was the first human-rights treaty that explicitly allowed NGOs to play a role in monitoring its implementation (Charnovitz 1996–7: 259, 264; Breen 2005: 109). An international campaign of about 1,000 NGOs in 60 countries led to a Convention to ban landmines in 1997 (Wiseberg 2003: 347). Over 200 NGOs participated in drafting the statute of the International Criminal Court. NGOs have also played an increasingly important role in UN conferences. Baehr estimates that 1,500 NGOs attended the Vienna human-rights conference of 1993 (Baehr 1999: 114, 123). Almost 3,000 NGOs were accredited to the 1995 World Conference on Women (Otto 1996: 120). For a long time, the Security Council refused to have anything to do with NGOs, but in 1996 it agreed that members could meet NGOs in their national capacity, and since 1997 most Council members have met NGO representatives frequently (Paul 2001).

NGOs range from one-person organizations to large international bodies, and from the well-intentioned amateur to the highly professional. There are international NGOs, such as Amnesty International and Human Rights Watch, national NGOs, and local NGOs. Some international and national organizations, such as religious bodies and trades-unions, which are not primarily concerned with human rights, may play an important role in certain human-rights campaigns. Some of these organizations are genuinely concerned with human rights, but others may use the human-rights cause to further other aims. NGOs are neither opposition groups as such nor political parties, even though these may have genuine concerns for human rights. Some organizations that are apparently non-governmental are actually government-controlled. The greatly increased number of NGOs has given rise to problems of co-operation. There are, in particular, some tensions between Western-based NGOs, some of which are relatively long-established, professionalized and well-financed, and NGOs from poorer countries, which are less well-resourced, and may have different perspectives on human rights. At the end of the twentieth century, 1,550 NGOs were associated with the UN, of which only 251 were from developing countries (McDonnell 1999: 206). These tensions are not necessarily regrettable, for they can enrich the struggle for human rights. Nevertheless, NGOs can be competitors for scarce resources, and local activists can become over-dependent on the funds and priorities of richer and more experienced INGOs (Baehr 1999: 114–15, 121–4).

Forsythe identifies several difficulties in measuring the influence of NGOs. They have undoubtedly made an important contribution to the development of international law and institutions, but the effectiveness of this law and these institutions is uncertain. NGOs may well have raised world consciousness about human rights, but this is difficult to measure. He suggests the following kinds of success: 1) getting human-rights issues on the political agenda; 2) getting serious discussion of the issues; 3) getting procedural or institutional changes; 4) getting policy changes that improve respect for human rights. We cannot measure the effectiveness of NGOs precisely, but nearly everyone familiar with human-rights politics acknowledges their influence, including many governments whom they have criticized, and this suggests that the influence is significant. NGOs can sometimes be shown to have had a direct, positive effect on human rights, but often their impact, if it exists, combines with other factors, such as the media and governmental action, in such a way that the independent causal weight of the NGO is not known (Forsythe 2006: 200–6). There is evidence that although neither treaty ratifications nor NGOs are sufficient for improved human-rights protection, the two together have a positive effect (Neumayer 2005: 950).

It is often said that NGOs work by 'the moblization of shame' (Baehr 1999: 114). This may be misleading, however, for human-rights violators may feel little shame, but the publicity that NGOs give to the violation of international norms, which the offending governments may have supported publicly through declarations and ratification of covenants, may damage their standing in the international community. From a social-scientific point of view, states may be seen as concerned with their reputation in the community on which they depend for material and non-material benefits, and their responses to NGO pressures may be motivated by the calculation that this is in their national interest (Baehr 1999: 126–7). The 'boomerang' model suggests that 'shaming' governments may be counter-productive in some circumstances. Burgerman has argued that the following conditions are necessary, but not sufficient, for international NGOs to change state human-rights policies: 1) no major state opposes this aim; 2) part of the state's elite is concerned with its international human-rights reputation; 3) there is some internal pressure for such changes (Burgerman 1998).

Perhaps the most important function of international NGOs is the provision of reliable information to governments, intergovernmental organizations, politicians, news media, academics and the general public. UN human-rights institutions are poorly resourced, and very dependent on NGOs for information (Baehr 1999; Brett 1995). Governments lie. NGOs can publicize part of the truth (Brett 1995: 101–3). NGOs have also provided important information to truth commissions and human-rights tribunals, often in methodologically rigorous, statistical form (Wiseberg 2003: 357). They may also play an important role at national level in the drafting of constitutions and human-rights law (Wiseberg 1992: 376). NGO representatives are sometimes members of official delegations, and some become governmental officials with human-rights responsibilities. NGOs seek to influence governments, but they need to maintain their independence even from relatively co-operative governments. Similarly, NGOs may welcome publicity for human-rights violations by the media, but the media can distort the global human-rights agenda.

NGOs are sometimes referred to as 'grass-roots organizations', but the extent to which they are so is highly variable, and the term is somewhat misleading. Some NGOs consist of small elites of human-rights professionals; others combine professionals with concerned citizens; yet others have roots among the people whose rights they seek to defend. There are thousands of national and local NGOs around the world that combine human-rights, humanitarian and development

programmes, providing services that their states do not
provide.

This raises the question of the accountability of NGOs.
To whom should they be accountable? Their members?
Those they seek to help? Their own governments, law and/
or public opinion? The governments, law and/or public
opinion of countries they seek to influence? The international
community? This raises also the question of the relation
between the accountability and the effectiveness of NGOs:
it is unclear whether democratic organizations are more
effective than those that are elitist, and which forms of
accountability improve effectiveness (Baehr 1999: 115–24).

Bob argues that the NGO world is not simply one of
benevolent and beneficent altruists, but also one in which
diverse groups compete for scarce attention, sympathy, and
money. Rights-claimants have to market themselves to potential benefactors through charismatic leaders, the medium of
the English language, and the adoption of dominant political
styles. Thus, the global human-rights project 'works' in so
far as the victims subordinate themselves to the culture of
their INGO 'saviours' (Bob 2002). This is neither entirely
mistaken nor entirely fair. The leading INGOs attempt, so
far as they are able, to develop and implement impartial,
global human-rights policies. They derive their authority
from international moral and legal standards, their reputation for truth-telling, and the extent to which they represent
and empower the oppressed (Slim 2002). Ron et al. found
that Amnesty International's reporting was largely determined by the severity of human-rights violations in a country,
although it was shaped also by an emphasis on powerful
countries and media interest. Thus, human-rights violations
in 'unfashionable' countries might be neglected, but Amnesty
had to balance the severity of violations with the availability
of resources and the prospects for effectiveness (Ron et al.
2005). Gordon argued that the strategies of NGOs may be
less important than their social location for their effectiveness. NGOs close to, and respected by, governments may
have more influence, but at the cost of collaborating with
some human-rights violations. The distinction between the
state and civil society can become blurred as they share both
personnel and values. More 'radical' or principled groups

may have less impact in the short term, but they can 'shame' more moderate groups into more forceful action (Gordon 2008).

NGOs also provide direct help to the victims of human-rights violations through legal aid, medical assistance and financial support. They raise consciousness through human-rights education, which may be formal or informal, independent of or supported by governments, narrowly legal or broadly interdisciplinary in a way that connects the concept of human rights with the practical concerns of the people (Andreopoulos and Claude 1997; Claude 2002b). NGOs provide an important bridge between the remote world of law, politics and bureaucracy, on the one hand, and the actual experience of human-rights violations, on the other. Western-based NGOs can be very professional, and fairly effective, but there is a need for 'the democratization of human rights' through the empowerment of local organizations. Ironically, governments that complain of the Western bias of NGOs often prevent the formation of NGOs in their own countries (Brett 1995: 105–6). There is a considerable gap between UN institutions and genuinely grass-roots NGOs, many of which have few resources to gain access to, or assistance from, these institutions (Smith, Pagnucco and Lopez 1998: 412).

Human-rights NGOs have been criticized on the ground that their legalistic approach, while it may provide some short-term gains in human-rights protection, is both irrelevant to the most serious human-rights violations, such as the genocidal events that have taken place in Burundi, Cambodia, Bosnia and Rwanda, and may obscure the deeper conditions that reproduce those violations, thereby inhibiting efforts to identify and address their root causes (Korey 1998: 308–9, 312–3). There is some truth in this criticism, but it is nonetheless unfair, unless certain facts are taken into account. Firstly, NGOs have sometimes provided early warnings of human-rights disasters, and it has not been their fault that governments have failed to respond. Secondly, NGOs have been willing to adapt to changing human-rights problems: Amnesty International, for example, modified its emphasis on prisoners of conscience to campaign against 'disappearances' in the 1970s. Thirdly, NGOs have very limited resources. NGOs seek to influence governments by appearing 'non-political' and appealing to international law. This is a *politically* rational strategy for improving human rights world-wide, but it has its limits. There is room also for a more robust and confrontational politics of human rights, which will also have its achievements and its limitations. NGOs may also, and to some extent do, take advantage of academic research into the structural causes of human-rights violations, but the practical value of this research should not be exaggerated. The quantitative, empirical literature on human-rights violations tells us that democracy, economic development and peace reduce violations. These are not variables that can be easily manipulated by governments or NGOs.

Human-rights NGOs have also been criticized for being biased towards Western priorities, and emphasizing civil and political rights at the expense of economic, social and cultural rights (Mutua 2001). There is also truth in this criticism, but both Human Rights Watch and Amnesty International have recently extended their mandates beyond their previous exclusive concern with civil and political rights to include economic, social and cultural rights. This move runs the risk of over-extending the limited resources and blurring the focus of these organizations, but has the advantages of embracing the human-rights concerns of non-Western peoples and emphasizing the 'interdependence' of all human rights.

Conclusion

The international human-rights regime is a political as well as a legal institution. As such, it reflects the balance of power in the world. Since the end of the Cold War, the balance of political and economic power has been held by the West, and consequently the Western human-rights agenda has dominated the international human-rights regime. NGOs with different priorities constitute a social movement that counteracts those of the major state powers, though selectively and with limited resources. International human-rights law has been developed to modify, but not to reject the statist conception of international society. Some human-rights NGOs operate within that state-centred, human-rights regime; others challenge the 'club of states' as social movements with grass roots; yet others seek to form a bridge between these two, very different worlds. The point of NGOs is to hold states to account; it is not surprising that some states seek to limit their influence in international politics.

8

Globalization, Development and Poverty

Economics and Human Rights

Globalization

Human rights have economic implications, since implementing them requires resources, and economic policies can have massive impacts on human rights. Those concerned with human rights should understand the positive and negative effects of economic forces on human rights, and the economics of the best attainable human-rights outcomes. Economic policies can be evaluated by human-rights standards. Yet human-rights activists and scholars have neglected economics, and most economists are not interested in human rights. This is now changing, slowly.

In the nineteenth and early twentieth centuries capitalism created great wealth and great misery. This led to the creation of welfare states in rich countries and influenced the principles of the United Nations. The UN Charter proclaims that a principal aim of the organization is to promote better living standards. Article 25 of the Universal Declaration of Human Rights affirms that everyone has the right to an adequate standard of living.

During the Cold War, human rights evolved in a world divided between capitalism and socialism. They also had to address the demand of the poor, newly decolonized states for 'development'. In 1974 the UN General Assembly called for a New International Economic Order (NIEO) to rectify the perceived injustices of global inequality. The rich countries rejected the NIEO, and the idea came to nothing. Stagnation of the rich economies generated policies of deregulation and privatization. The free-market ideology of 'neoliberalism' became the dominant solution to the problems of development. After the Cold War poor states abandoned their suspicion of Western capitalism and sought loans and investment from Western banks and transnational corporations (TNCs). To achieve this they had to reduce state expenditures on social services. Many saw economic 'globalization' as hostile to human rights and participated in 'anti-globalization' protests.

Neo-liberal globalization transfers power from states to private economic actors and thus threatens the international human-rights regime which imposes obligations on states. This tension between 'globalization' and human rights is complicated by the fact that the human-rights movement is part of globalization. Globalization may raise living standards for many while acting as accomplice to human-rights violations. UN human-rights bodies have expressed concern over the impact of globalization on human rights. States may incur economic obligations incompatible with their human-rights obligations. Global economic processes tend to marginalize human rights. Economic globalization and human rights are thus poorly integrated.

Global poverty and inequality

About one-sixth of the world's population lives in extreme poverty, defined as having less than $1.25 a day, according to the World Bank. About 40 per cent live in severe poverty (less than $2.50 a day). Every day about 34,000 children die from hunger and preventable disease. Estimates of the number who die every year from poverty vary from eight to 18 million (Sachs 2005: 1; Riddell 2007: 121; Pogge 2007: 12–13, 2008: 2–3, 2010: 11–12). Global poverty violates the human rights to life, an adequate standard of living, health, food, water, sanitation and housing.

The World Bank claims that global poverty is declining. In 1981, 51.8 per cent of the world lived in extreme poverty; in 2005, 25.2 per cent. Those in severe poverty declined from 74.6 to 56.6 per cent (Howard-Hassmann 2010). Much of this poverty reduction has occurred in China. Global inequality did not change much between 1950 and 2002. World Bank poverty measures are controversial. There is nevertheless a consensus that global poverty has declined in recent years. There are, however, considerable regional and country variations: about 50 countries had lower per capita GDP in 2000 than in 1990 (Fukuda-Parr 2007: 296).

Many economists argue that, far from globalization causing poverty, isolation from the global economy explains development failure. Dissenting economists counter that protectionism can aid development and that political factors such as bad governance and conflict are significant causes of poverty (Wade 2004; Collier 2007).

Economic and social rights

Civil and political rights are sometimes distinguished from economic and social rights by Kant's distinction between perfect and imperfect duties. Negative rights not to be harmed are said to entail perfect duties not to harm others. Positive rights to benefits entail imperfect duties as no one has a perfect duty to benefit others. Some argue that economic and social rights are *not* human rights because the corresponding duties are imperfect and can be implemented only through institutions which create *special* not *human* rights. UK citizens have a right to health care because they are UK citizens, not because they are human beings.

Some counter that there is no moral distinction between the right not to be tortured and the right not to starve. Both can be negative rights not to suffer or positive rights to assistance. Civil and political rights entail both perfect and imperfect obligations. For example, the right not to be tortured entails the perfect obligation of everyone not to torture anyone but also imperfect obligations to do what one reasonably can to prevent torture. All rights require institutions to implement them. The fact that economic and social rights entail negative duties shows that they are not necessarily expensive: governments can respect the right to housing by not destroying houses. It is now common to distinguish between obligations to *respect* rights (not violate them), to *protect* rights (ensure that others not violate them), and to *fulfil* rights (ensure everyone enjoys them). The obligation to respect is negative for all types of rights; the obligation to fulfil is positive for all types, although all three types of obligation may be negative and positive. Several philosophers hold that duties to the poor include the negative duty not to harm and the positive duty to assist.

Some maintain that human rights may entail imperfect duties. The rich may have imperfect duties to the poor, but perfect duties to support institutions that have perfect duties to help the poor. Human rights of all kinds may entail duties that, as a matter of fact, are unlikely to be fulfilled. This does not defeat the case for economic and social rights; rather, it makes the case for criticizing existing institutions. If the enjoyment of economic and social rights is necessary to a life of dignity, the case for these rights is independent of the corresponding duties. On this view, rights ground the institutional duties rather than vice versa. Economic and social rights may be necessary to the enjoyment of civil and political rights: a starving person cannot participate effectively in politics. Civil rights may be *components* of social rights: there is a right to a fair hearing in a social dispute.

Economic and social rights are commonly called 'second-generation' rights, but this is unhistorical. Medieval philosophers discussed the right of the needy to assistance from the rich. In modern times economic and social rights were roughly contemporary with political rights. Social rights, especially workers' rights, preceded civil and political rights in international relations, leading to the establishment of the International Labour Organization in 1919. In 1944 President Roosevelt called for an economic bill of rights. The Universal Declaration contains economic and social, as well as civil and political rights. Economic and social rights were marginalized for a long time. This has changed somewhat. The UN Commission on Human Rights established several special rapporteurs on these rights. Amnesty International and Human Rights Watch have taken them on, and numerous NGOs now specialize in them.

The International Covenant on Economic, Social and Cultural Rights (ICESCR) requires states parties to take steps, using the maximum of available resources, to realize the Covenant rights *progressively*. States must assure the enjoyment of at least the minimum essential levels of these rights by everyone. States have *immediate* obligations to 'take steps' to implement the rights without discrimination. Retrogressive steps must be justified by Covenant rights and available resources. States have a 'minimum core obligation' to fulfil the essential levels. Rich states have an obligation to assist states lacking the resources to implement their Covenant obligations.

The 'minimum core obligation' raises a problem for human-rights universalism. Is it the same for Chad as for Canada? How is the minimum determined? The obligation of 'progressive realization' is also relative in so far as it depends on available resources. Young has argued that different philosophical bases for economic and social rights – basic needs, autonomy, or dignity – will generate different conceptions of the minimum. Thus, the minimum core fails to form an agreed bedrock of economic and social rights, but is 'essentially contested' (Young 2008).

There is a rebuttable presumption that every state has sufficient resources to meet its minimum obligations. The Covenant does not clarify how poor states should balance Covenant obligations with legitimate, non-Covenant expenditures, such as those on investment, debt reduction and defence. Budget analysis may, however, show that state expenditure on Covenant rights has fallen as a proportion of GDP or of government spending, that the allocated budget was not all spent, or that it was spent in a discriminatory way. The conceptual, methodological and data-collection problems of measuring 'progressive realization' of economic and social rights are formidable and as yet unsolved, although progress has been made in tackling them. These problems are aggravated by the fact that the evidence on the relationship between public expenditures and development outcomes is very uncertain.

Lawyers regard treaty obligations as 'binding', whereas political scientists and economists consider public policy as deciding priorities and making trade-offs. Legally, the obligation of 'progressive realization' applies to economic and social, but not to civil and political rights. Donnelly maintains, however, that all human rights are subject to progressive realization (Donnelly 2007a). It is therefore not always clear when a failure of progress constitutes a human-rights violation. The obligation of rich and poor states to realize rights progressively is hard to reconcile with the principle of universal equal rights. Economic and social rights also have a relativist element because states are expected to implement these rights in a culturally appropriate way.

The obligations to realize economic and social rights are generally limited to states' own jurisdictions. The obligation to help those outside those jurisdictions is weak. Overseas development aid is still treated as charity rather than as a human-rights obligation.

Economic and social rights are said to be not 'justiciable', that is, they cannot be decided in courts of law. A recent study, however, found almost 2,000 judicial and quasi-judicial decisions on social rights from 29 jurisdictions (Langford 2008). Some argue that judges lack the expertise and legitimacy to decide disputes with large budgetary implications. But civil and political rights also raise controversial questions, such as the detention of terrorist suspects, and judges often decide cases with huge financial implications. Legislatures often specify economic and social rights in general terms and leave judges to elaborate the law. Thus, the claim that the legalization of economic and social rights illegitimately transfers powers from democratic legislatures to unaccountable judges is not wholly justified. A World Bank study concluded that the legalization of social rights may have prevented thousands of deaths and improved the lives of millions. Legal action for economic and social rights has limits and is most effective when combined with political action.

Some worry that economic and social rights discourage individual initiative, but they are intended to support not displace self-help. The legal concept of economic and social rights must nevertheless confront economic realities and theories.

Development

Human rights and development evolved separately for many years. It was commonly said that development was a precondition of human rights. It has, however, not been shown that violating human rights is necessary to economic development. Protecting human rights may facilitate development and they have an intrinsic value in respecting human dignity. Human rights are necessary to determine what people really need. The meaning of 'development' is contested, and human rights are necessary to determine what types of development are really beneficial.

In the 1980s many saw 'structural adjustment programmes' as violating human rights for the sake of economic development. Popular protests invoked human rights. In the 1990s the UN Development Programme adopted the concept of 'human development' which partially incorporated human rights into development policy. The World Bank included some human rights in its lending policies.

The 'rights-based approach' to development treats poverty as a human-rights violation and emphasizes the *obligations* of governments rather than charity. Denial of such human rights as those to food and health are *constitutive* of poverty. Other human rights, such as the right to work, are *instrumental* to eliminating poverty. The right to political participation empowers the poor, which is the first step out of poverty. The rights-based approach emphasizes non-discrimination and accountability, and provides a relatively coherent normative basis for development policy. It has, however, been criticized for conceptual vagueness, lack of systematic practice and failure to evaluate projects rigorously. The rights approach does not always help to determine priorities when resources are scarce. Popular participation is vulnerable to capture by local elites and its effectiveness is uncertain. The human-rights culture is legalistic and individualistic, and is accused of being ill-equipped to address the structural causes of poverty. The rights-based and economic approaches to development have not yet been integrated by human-rights or development specialists.

In 2000 the UN General Assembly adopted the Millennium Declaration, which became the basis for eight millennium development goals (MDGs). The MDGs, however, constitute a set of *goals* and *priorities* rather than *rights*. They overlap with human rights, but fall short of established human rights. Development institutions refer to the MDGs with few references to human rights, while human-rights organizations refer to rights rather than the MDGs. The MDGs have therefore had limited success in integrating development and human rights.

The first MDG (MDG1) is commonly presented as being that of halving world poverty by 2015. The goal may be achieved globally, mainly because of rapid progress in China. MDG1, however, ignores regional variations. The World Bank has estimated that African countries must grow on average at least seven per cent each year to achieve MDG1. The average for the previous 15 years was 2.4 per cent. Only two of the 47 Sub-Saharan African countries have achieved seven per cent (Clemens, Kenny and Moss 2004).

Pogge argues that, morally, MDG1 is culpably unambitious. In 1996 the World Food Summit promised to halve the number of undernourished people in the world by 2015. MDG1 has reinterpreted the goal of 'halving world poverty' in three ways: 1) it aims to halve the *proportion* not the *number* in extreme poverty; 2) it aims to halve poverty in the developing countries not the world; 3) it has backdated the baseline to 1990. Pogge calculates that MDG1 increases the number of extremely poor people deemed 'acceptable' in 2015 by 496 million compared with the 1996 commitment. MDG1 will be achieved, but only because of the way the goal has been interpreted. Pogge considers extreme poverty to be a grave human-rights violation and MDG1 to be a plan for massive human-rights violations (Pogge 2010: 58–62).

The right to development

In 1986 the UN General Assembly adopted the Declaration on the Right to Development. This proclaims that the right is a human right by virtue of which every person and all peoples are entitled to participate in, contribute to, and enjoy economic, social, cultural and political development in which all human rights can be fully realized. The right has been reaffirmed by numerous international meetings.

The primary legal obligation to implement this right is that of states to their citizens. The discourse of the right to development suggests, however, that the primary obligation is that of rich to poor countries, although this obligation is unclear and controversial. It is also unclear whether the right to development is a distinct human right or a combination of pre-existing human rights, and to what it is a right (Donnelly 1985b: 474–5). Sengupta, the UN's independent expert on the right, says that it is more than the pre-existing rights: it is a *vector* of all human rights, including elements of well-being that go beyond human rights (Sengupta 2002).

Donnelly argues that there is no right to development. Individual development is the goal of all human rights. The supposed right to development adds nothing to established human rights and provides an excuse for violating them (Donnelly 1985b). Salomon concludes that the right to development is conceptually unclear and practically useless. It was an attempt to transform the NIEO into the discourse of human rights. It has failed because the rich states deny that it creates any binding obligations (Salomon 2007). Sorell and Landman suggest that the supposed right to development is not a human right because the best-off do not have the right to be better off and may have the obligation to be worse off in order to help the worst off: there is therefore no *universal* right to development (Sorell and Landman 2006: 393). Developing countries' representatives advocate the right to development but reject rights-based development. Development policy ignores the right.

The causes of development

Three types of factor may explain variations in development and poverty among countries. Geography affects natural resources, health, productivity and trade opportunities.

Culture and institutions affect attitudes to economic activity, governance and the rule of law. International politics, trade and law affect development directly or indirectly through the quality of institutions.

Evidence suggests that capital accumulation and technological progress are the proximate causes of economic growth. Research shows, however, that *institutions*, especially the rule of law and protection of property rights, are the primary independent causes. Geography may have some effect on institutions. Trade is an effect of good institutions rather than an independent cause of development. It is not clear how institutions promote development: there are considerable institutional differences among the successful economies. International factors may undermine institutions and inhibit development in poor countries by protecting domestic industries and supporting corrupt dictators (Rodrik, Subrahamian and Trebbi 2004; Sachs 2005: 189–90; Pogge 2005a, 2005c, 2007).

Knowledge of the causes of economic growth and poverty remains partial and it is difficult to infer the best policy for a particular country from cross-country comparisons. Generally, however, the more unequal countries are, the higher the level of poverty. Rapid development may accompany slow poverty reduction because inequality increases. Improving growth does not necessarily improve human rights (Besley and Burgess 2003; Sachs 2005: 165–6).

Is colonialism a cause of global poverty? Many poor countries are former colonies, but some former colonies are not poor: for example, South Korea, Taiwan, Singapore and Hong Kong. Statistical analysis shows that although colonialism probably obstructed economic growth in the short term, there is no evidence of long-term adverse effects (Sachs 2005: 191).

Democracy is not necessary for economic growth: dictatorships with smart economic policies have produced successful development. Dictatorships in poor countries have, however, had very variable growth rates. Culture does not explain development well: 'Asian values', for example, have been associated with development success and failure. Governments may, however, fail to develop human capital for economic, political and/or cultural reasons (Sachs 2005: 72, 315–17).

The World Bank claims that trade liberalization has led to a reduction in extreme poverty since 1980. Some rapid developers, such as China and India, are quite protectionist, however, and free trade has done little to benefit the poorest (Wade 2004; Sachs 2005: 326).

The contribution of aid to development is controversial and uncertain. Development is possible without aid, as China shows. Aid may fund corrupt and incompetent government, and discourage local initiative and reform. It may fail because poor countries lack the capacity to use it effectively: thus more aid will not necessarily help development (Wade 2004; Easterly 2007: 44). Well-targeted aid may, however, improve the capacity of a country to use aid well (Sachs 2005: 274).

Easterly argues that aid has failed to eradicate poverty because it has been based on top-down planning whereas bottom-up, market-based initiatives are the source of development. International planners cannot understand the social complexities that underlie economies and are not accountable to the poor. He concedes that aid can contribute to development in democracies with good economic policies, and that aid for health and education has often been successful. Aid is, however, rarely evaluated rigorously so we do not know how effective it is in reducing poverty (Easterly 2007). Much aid fails because it serves the political and commercial interests of donors. Effective aid may conflict with aid to the neediest, and aid for development may compete with aid for human rights (Collier 2007). Aid is often inefficient because there are multiple donors who are poorly co-ordinated. Aid is often effective in meeting short-term needs while its impact on long-term development is uncertain. Riddell suggests that aid sometimes works and sometimes doesn't; where it doesn't, this is often the result of non-aid factors (Riddell 2007). Clemens and Moss argue that the commonly cited aid target of 0.7 per cent of rich-country gross national income is fundamentally flawed methodologically and empirically, and that it is extremely difficult to translate the human needs of the global poor into financial assistance from the rich (Clemens and Moss 2005: 18).

Development science is underdeveloped. 'Development' and 'poverty' are contested concepts, data and methodologies are problematic, and theory is weak. Simple generalizations about human rights and development cannot be justified as we do not know enough.

Trade and investment

The UN founders believed that free trade would raise living standards and thereby promote human rights. Some, however, have come to view trade as inimical to human rights. Traded goods can violate human rights in various ways: they can be harmful to health; they can be produced by means that violate human rights (e.g., child labour); or they can be used for human-rights violations (e.g., police or military equipment sold to dictators).

The World Trade Organization (WTO) was founded in 1994 by the signatories to the General Agreement on Tariffs and Trade (GATT). Most WTO members have ratified the ICCPR and the ICESCR. The WTO is not a UN agency and has no mandate to implement human rights. Trade negotiations and the WTO dispute-settlement procedures are neither transparent nor democratically accountable. The world's poor have almost no capacity to participate in trade negotiations or the WTO. NGOs have less access to the WTO than to many UN agencies. The WTO's impact on human rights and its lack of accountability have provoked popular protests (Benedek 2007).

The WTO can impose sanctions for violations of trade agreements and thereby has more power than any UN human-rights body. However, the developing countries have resisted rich countries' attempts to incorporate human rights in WTO negotiations on the ground that they amount to trade discrimination. The 1996 Singapore Declaration of WTO ministers reaffirmed their commitment to international core labour standards but said that the ILO (a much weaker organization) not the WTO was the body to deal with these (Aaronson 2007).

The WTO Agreement on the Trade-Related Aspects of Intellectual Property Rights (TRIPS) has been especially problematic for human rights. It established pharmaceutical patents limiting the ability of developing countries to address

diseases such as HIV/AIDS. The 2001 WTO Doha conference declared that TRIPS does not prevent members
from taking measures to protect public health. The Doha
Declaration has, however, been bypassed by bilateral and
regional deals.

Bilateral investment treaties (BITs) are now common and
can have serious implications for human rights. Most BITs
prohibit regulations that reduce the value of investments.
Investment tribunals have made states pay compensation for
regulations implementing their obligations to fulfil economic
and social rights. Poor states lack the capacity to contest such
compensation claims effectively, and may consequently be
reluctant to fulfil these human-rights obligations.

The WTO has never addressed conflicts between trade and
human-rights law. GATT allows exceptions to free-trade
rules for national security, protection of public morals, human
life and health, and prison labour, but it is uncertain whether
this permits trade restrictions for human rights. The WTO
respects sanctions authorized by the UN Security Council,
and legal scholars believe it must respect *jus cogens*, the
prohibition of the gravest human-rights crimes. The WTO
has allowed trade restrictions on members that do not participate in the Kimberley Certification Scheme to combat
trade in diamonds used to finance conflict. It also accepts
trade agreements giving developing countries preferential
access to rich countries' markets on condition that they meet
certain human-rights conditions if these agreements meet the
development needs of poor countries (Cottier, Pauwelyn and
Bürgi 2005; Pauwelyn 2005).

WTO agreements make commitments to the needs of
developing countries but these countries often lack the
resources and bargaining power to make these provisions
effective. Poor countries exporting to rich countries face
tariffs on average four times higher than the barriers applied
in trade among rich countries (United Nations Development
Programme 2005: 127).

Empirical studies have found both positive and negative
relations between foreign direct investment (FDI) and trade
on the one hand, and human rights in developing countries
on the other, although most studies find a positive relation,
especially with civil and political rights (Mitchell and

McCormick 1988; Cingranelli and Richards 1999; Richards, Gelleny and Sacko 2001; Milner 2002). Hafner-Burton found that trade and FDI generally had a positive influence on human rights, but results varied with different economies and different methods (Hafner-Burton 2005). Evidence also indicates that preferential trade agreements with tough sanctions are more effective than human-rights treaties in implementing human rights, although they are not always effective (Hafner-Burton 2009).

Business corporations

The Nuremberg trials of Nazi war criminals after the Second World War convicted several industrialists of grave human-rights crimes. The Universal Declaration of Human Rights implies that corporations have human-rights obligations. Corporations may violate human rights; they may be complicit in state violations; and the privatization of traditional state functions – such as provision of security, prisons, water supply and health care – means that corporations may become quasi-state organizations. The empirical evidence on the impact of transnational corporations (TNCs) on human rights is mixed, depending on the methods used (Meyer 1996; Smith, Bolyard and Ippolito 1999).

The anti-apartheid movement pioneered attempts to get corporations to respect human rights. The Sullivan Principles (1977) proposed a voluntary code for US companies in South Africa. They were supported by more than 125 companies, but were considered ineffectual (Compa and Hinchliffe-Darricarrère 1995).

In 1974 the UN Economic and Social Council (ECOSOC) established the UN Commission on TNCs. The Commission submitted a draft code of conduct to ECOSOC in 1990, providing, among other things, that TNCs should respect human rights. Negotiations on the code collapsed in 1992, having fallen victim to the shift by developing countries from hostility to acceptance of TNCs.

In 1976 the Organization of Economic Co-operation and Development (OECD) issued non-binding Guidelines for

Multinational Enterprises to protect union rights and prohibit discrimination. They were revised in 2000 to include a general requirement to respect human rights. In 1977 the ILO published a Tripartite Declaration of Principles Concerning Multinational Enterprises and Social Policy, which was amended in 2000. It affirms an obligation to respect the International Bill of Rights. It is voluntary and is considered to be rather ineffective (Compa and Hinchliffe-Darricarrère 1995: 670–1; Murphy 2004–5).

In 1986 the US Anti-Apartheid Act prohibited US companies from doing business in South Africa. The Clinton administration proposed a voluntary code of conduct for US TNCs, which was adopted by several corporations. In 1996 the administration established the Apparel Industry Partnership workplace code of conduct for companies and overseas contractors. Social Accountability 8000 was launched in 1997 by the Council on Economic Priorities and some influential companies as an attempt to compel firms to comply with a set of labour and human-rights standards (Spar 1998: 8–10; Ratner 2001–2: 457–63). Other corporate codes have been proposed for Northern Ireland, the USSR and China, for labour standards and against child labour. Some corporations have adopted codes incorporating human rights and refused to do business with countries where serious violations occurred (Compa and Hinchliffe-Darricarrère 1995: 671–84; Frey 1997: 175–6, 187). Such codes generally include a limited range of rights, and are difficult to implement (Ratner 2001–2: 531).

In 1999 the then UN Secretary-General, Kofi Annan, proposed a 'global compact' for TNCs. This is a voluntary agreement by which TNCs undertake to abide by ten human-rights and environmental principles within their 'sphere of influence'. Nearly 5,000 companies have signed up to the compact. However, its principles are vague and its implementation mechanisms weak.

In 2003 the UN Sub-Commission on the Promotion and Protection of Human Rights approved norms on the responsibilities of TNCs and other business enterprises (OBEs) for human rights within their sphere of influence, and submitted the norms to the Commission on Human Rights. The Commission requested the Office of the High Commissioner for Human Rights (OHCHR) to investigate the responsibilities of TNCs and related business enterprises for human rights, and submit a report to the Commission.

The OHCHR reported that opinion on the Sub-Commission's norms was deeply divided, and that the human-rights obligations of business remained unclear. The Commission requested the UN Secretary-General to appoint a special representative on human rights and TNCs and OBEs. The Secretary-General appointed Professor John Ruggie to clarify the responsibilities of governments, TNCs and OBEs for human rights and business.

Ruggie estimated that there were about 80,000 TNCs with about 800,000 subsidiaries and millions of suppliers. Human-rights violations by some companies had led to demands, some from corporations, for greater corporate responsibility. Unregulated markets were destabilizing and human rights must be central to regulation. The problems of business and human rights varied by sector and type of government. Many of the world's largest companies had, however, adopted human-rights policies and practices. The effects of various initiatives on business and human rights were limited geographically and in the human rights covered. The worst offenders were untouched.

The Sub-Commission's norms incorrectly assumed that international law imposed binding human-rights obligations on companies. Most human-rights obligations were obligations of states. Only the norms specifying the worst human-rights crimes applied directly to corporations. The human-rights obligations of states and corporations should take account of their different social roles. The concept of 'sphere of influence' lacked legal definition and failed to make clear who was responsible for what. The Sub-Commission had been divisive rather than constructive (United Nations Commission on Human Rights 2006; United Nations Human Rights Council 2010).

Generally, states were not fulfilling their obligations to protect human rights by regulating corporations, although corporations might be liable under national laws for some violations (United Nations Human Rights Council 2007b). Ruggie proposed a 'protect, respect, remedy' framework: states should protect everyone against violations by business;

corporations should respect human rights; victims should have access to remedies. The concept of 'sphere of influence' was problematic: corporations do not have obligations to prevent violations by all those over whom they have influence, but to exercise due diligence for the *impact* of their activities. They should carry out human-rights impact assessments when planning ventures with human-rights risks. Access to remedies is least where it is most needed (United Nations Human Rights Council 2007a, 2008a, 2008b).

Some NGOs have criticized Ruggie for not investigating the causes of corporate violations and for not recommending complaint procedures or binding international standards. Ruggie holds that international adjudication of alleged corporate violations would face intractable problems of evidence gathering and due process. His framework is supported by some NGOs, business and the Human Rights Council. Some governments and corporations have begun to implement it.

International financial institutions

In 1944 the Allies met at Bretton Woods, New Hampshire, and established the World Bank and the International Monetary Fund (IMF) to redevelop Europe and restore global economic stability. These international financial institutions (IFIs) are considered to be UN agencies with mandates to act independently on economic, not political, grounds subject only to the Security Council. They have interpreted this to mean that they have no human-rights obligations, although they claim that they take human rights into account and that their work promotes human rights. They take little note, however, of international human-rights law or UN human-rights bodies. The IFIs have sometimes taken decisions on political or human-rights grounds but they have also used the 'non-political' principle to justify financing some of the world's worst human-rights violators. Human-rights NGOs neglected this until recently (Boisson de Chazournes 2007).

The World Bank is the world's most important lending institution for development, while the IMF is primarily concerned with financial stability. The two institutions began to converge in the 1980s on 'structural adjustment loans' (SALs) for development with strict conditions. By the mid-1990s almost 120 countries had 'structural adjustment programmes' (SAPs). Critics claimed that although some 'structural adjustment' might be necessary, SAPs have often been ineffectual, are undemocratic, violate economic and social rights, provoke instability and serve the interests of Western capital at the expense of the global poor (Stiglitz 2002; Sachs 2005; McBeth 2006; Abouharb and Cingranelli 2007: 3–4, 7, 24, 50, 77). Abouharb and Cingranelli, in a study of all countries undergoing structural adjustment from 1981 to 2003, found that, on average, SAPs led to less respect for most types of human rights. This held true when account was taken of the fact that countries seeking IFI help often had poor human-rights records before the IFI intervened (Abouharb and Cingranelli 2007). SAPs were often poorly implemented because of lack of governmental capacity, political opposition and failure of lenders to enforce them (Riddell 2007).

The IMF has been defended on the ground that the crises it addresses threaten human rights; its conditions are necessary to sustain the financial viability of its assistance; it does not always cut social expenditures; it is not competent to make human-rights judgements; financial help to countries where human-rights violations occur is better than refusal to help; and SAPs may improve human rights in the long term (Leite 2001: 2–6; McBeth 2006). In the 1990s the Bank and the Fund included safety nets and compensation in their SAPs.

Between 1968 and 1981 the Bank became concerned with poverty alleviation, accepted the 'basic needs' approach to development, and began to fund health, education, agriculture and housing, and then take up environmental, gender, governance and participation issues. In 1989 the Bank included human rights in its 'good governance' criteria. Both the Bank and IMF have accepted the Millennium Development Goals (Boisson de Chazournes 2007; Riddell 2007). The Bank has thus become more open to human rights, though in a limited way. In 1993 it established an Inspection Panel to hear complaints. The Panel can hear only complaints that Bank projects violate Bank policy, not complaints of human-rights violations as such. Borrowing countries resist the influence of NGOs with the Panel, and it has had limited effects (Fox 2002). The IMF has irregular contacts with UN human-rights bodies and informal discussions with NGOs. The IFIs advocate transparency and popular participation for client-states, but have been criticized for not practising these themselves. Popular participation is, however, not necessarily compatible with human rights or development. Some see the Bank as having had a positive effect on a wide range of human rights, especially relating to women and indigenous peoples. However, it has no human-rights policy, and considers human rights only if it thinks them relevant to its mandate. The Bank's encouragement of participation raises the question of protecting the civil and political rights of those who participate. If the IFIs refuse to make loans on human-rights grounds, the would-be borrowers may turn to other sources, even less concerned with human rights. NGOs may influence the Bank through its member governments, especially the USA. The influence of the USA with the IFIs has been criticized for being anti-poor, but it is not always anti-human rights.

In 1996 the Bank and the Fund introduced their Heavily Indebted Poor Countries Initiative (HIPCI). To qualify for HIPCI debt reduction, a government must formulate a Poverty Reduction Strategy Paper (PRSP). PRSPs include human-rights elements and the participation of civil society is required. PRSPs are subject to approval by the IFIs (Tostensen 2007: 186, 197–200, 210). Nearly all poor, highly indebted countries have produced PRSPs. Critics maintain that the power of the IFIs means that PRSPs are not very different from SAPs; civil-society participation is inadequate; insufficient debt relief has been provided to insufficient countries; and consequently they have done little for human rights (Darrow 2003; Stewart and Wang 2005). The World Bank has admitted that NGOs played a major role in its debt reduction programme. Debt reduction has, however, represented a very small proportion of the most heavily indebted countries' debt.

The IFIs are not parties to human-rights treaties, but the states that own them are. The IFIs emphasize their legal obligations to maintain financial soundness and believe that this constrains their commitment to human rights. The main causes of their limited commitment to human rights, however, are the interests of the rich states that dominate them and their economic theories. The IFIs' reluctance to acknowledge systematically that 'development' includes human rights is incompatible with UN development thinking and their own rhetoric.

Climate change

The idea that fossil-fuel combustion might increase concentrations of carbon dioxide (CO_2) in the atmosphere and cause climate warming originated in the nineteenth century. However, it was not until 1979 that the science of 'global warming' entered the political arena when the US National Academy of Sciences warned that increasing CO_2 might substantially increase global average temperatures. In 1988 the UN Environment Programme and the World Meteorological Organization created the Intergovernmental Panel on Climate Change (IPCC). In 1992 the UN Conference on the Environment and Development in Rio adopted the UN Framework Convention on Climate Change (FCCC). In 1995 the IPCC Second Assessment Report said that human activities were having a 'discernible' impact on the climate. In 2001 the IPCC's Third Assessment Report announced new evidence that most recent global warming was attributable to human activities and this was set to continue. The Kyoto Protocol to the UNFCCC was adopted in 1997. It provided for emission reductions by developed countries but none by developing countries. Kyoto would make little impact on climate change, especially since the USA failed to ratify it.

The IPCC predicts that the global temperature will rise by 1.4–5.8°C and global average sea level by 0.11–0.77 metres by 2100. Such rises would cause storms, floods and droughts, damage food production and cause massive loss of life, livelihoods and property damage. This in turn would produce millions of refugees, with potential for increased conflict. These predictions do not take account of certain climate catastrophes that the IPCC considers improbable but possible. Climate change will benefit some regions in the short term, but those most vulnerable will be those living on low-lying islands or coastal regions and in arid or semi-arid agricultural land. The poor are most vulnerable to climate change and least able to adapt to it. Although climate science is uncertain, Stern thinks that we should base policy on it because 1) it is the best knowledge we have, and 2) the risks of ignoring it are enormous. Climate-change and development policy are indivisible because neglecting climate change will harm development. Yet the international community has not included climate-change costs in calculating the costs of development (Stern 2009).

Who should pay the cost of adapting to, and mitigating, climate change? The favourite principle is probably that 'the polluter pays': the developed countries caused and have benefited from greenhouse gas emissions, so they should pay to rectify the damage. They also have the ability to pay and perhaps an obligation under international human-rights law to assist developing countries to mitigate climate harm. Three counter-arguments are that until recently no one knew that economic activity caused climate change; developing countries have benefited from that activity; and those now alive are not responsible for past emissions. Contrary arguments are that developed countries have done little to mitigate global warming since the science became clear; the global poor have benefited little from climate-damaging progress; and present generations have benefited from past emissions and are responsible for current emissions. It is nevertheless difficult to identify causal links between particular economic activities and particular natural disasters (Paterson 2001: 121–3; Baer 2006).

The developed countries do not accept responsibility for past emissions: the Kyoto Protocol assumes that obligations start now. Recent negotiations recognize that developing countries are increasing emissions and should bear part of the cost. There has been much discussion, but little agreement, on the allocation of 'the right to emit'. Some economists support the right to emit and 'emissions trading' on the ground that a market in this right will allocate it efficiently. Critics argue that emissions trading will favour the economically powerful and that trading 'the right to emit' will not necessarily reconcile optimal climate policy with human rights (Hayward 2007: 431–47). There is no agreement on allocating the costs of climate change, and the poor countries not only are likely to suffer most but also have least capacity to shape international agreements. There is a fund to help poor countries adapt to climate change, but it is small and as of 30 April 2010 no funds had actually been distributed (Mace 2006; Baer 2006; Adaptation Fund 2010).

Climate science is uncertain, which raises the question of how much we should spend now to prevent uncertain harm in future. Some economists believe that we should invest now in economic growth and increase expenditure on climate change slowly as the science becomes more certain and we become richer (Nordhaus 2008). Others believe that this would leave us vulnerable to catastrophic and irreversible change in future which could overwhelm our increased wealth; although current science tells us this is unlikely, it is not impossible (Stern 2009). Economists tend to seek the best-value climate policy *for the world*. They ignore the *distribution* of the costs, and especially the cost to the human rights of the most vulnerable (Gardiner 2004).

Some climate theorists distinguish between survival and luxury emissions: a human-rights approach would prioritize survival emissions. Human rights entail that climate policy respect the human rights of all. Climate change poses challenges to human-rights supporters, however, for human-rights activists and scholars are used to thinking about *violations*, not *probabilities*, of future harm: causal responsibility for climate harm may be more complex than for familiar violations. It is also difficult to attribute human rights to non-existent persons of distant future generations who may be harmed by climate change (Page 2006; International Council on Human Rights Policy 2008). Caney argues that we must assume that the interests and rights of future generations will probably be similar to ours. Contributing to climate change without due regard to its effect on the human rights of future generations is a grave human-rights violation. Yet the IPCC and the negotiations held under the FCCC have largely ignored human rights (Caney 2006; International Council on Human Rights Policy 2008).

At the FCCC Copenhagen conference in December 2009, five countries – the USA, China, India, Brazil and South Africa – set a goal of limiting global warming to 2°C accompanied by emission-reduction commitments across the world, and promised increased adaptation assistance. The EU has endorsed this agreement, but it is not legally binding and has no enforcement mechanism. The future of the FCCC is uncertain. The best hope is that the main emitting countries will reach an agreement that will limit emissions and aid the most vulnerable. The track record of the FCCC provides little ground for optimism.

Global justice

The theory of human rights says that a government is legitimate only if it respects the human rights of its citizens. Pogge argues that the global economic order is imposed on the world's people and is therefore legitimate only if it respects their human rights. The fact that many people prosper under this order does not make it just if the human rights of many are violated, even if the distribution of poverty depends on local factors. The massive non-fulfilment of economic and social human rights means that the global order falls short of the minimum conditions of global justice (Pogge 2002a: 117, 175, 199; 2007: 23–5, 44–5).

The continuing imposition of the global institutional order constitutes a massive violation of the human right to basic necessities, for which the governments and electorates of the more powerful countries bear primary responsibility. The rich countries have contributed to contemporary global poverty historically and benefit from it (Pogge 2007: 53). The moral value of this order should be judged not by *the rate of decline* of serious human-rights violations but by comparing *the current rate* with the rate that might be achieved by a *feasible* alternative order. Participation in a system in which avoidable human-rights violations occur is itself a massive human-rights violation. Abolishing poverty as defined by the World Bank would cost 1.21 per cent of the gross national incomes of the rich countries (Pogge 2002a: 92, 99, 230 n. 122; 2005c: 60; 2007: 30).

Pogge has been criticized on the ground that he shows neither how much poverty the global order causes nor how much his favoured alternative order would eliminate (Patten 2005: 21–4). His claim that the *electorates* of powerful countries bear *primary* responsibility for massive human-rights violations by the global order has also been questioned (Satz 2005: 50–1; Bleisch 2009: 157–65). Pogge replies that the global order harms the poor through the arms trade, by the borrowing privilege that permits dictators to impose international debts on their people, and the resource privilege which enables rich countries to buy resources that dictators have corruptly obtained. In these ways rich states and international institutions not only collaborate with bad institutions in developing countries but also make bad institutions more likely by increasing their incentives and durability. No global institutional order could prevent all human-rights violations but most severe poverty could be avoided if the global order were just. There is considerable empirical uncertainty about the causes of global poverty, but mobilization for a poverty-avoidance design of the global institutional order could eradicate most severe poverty within a few years (Pogge 2005c; 2007: 39–41, 46–53).

Others have emphasized various ways in which the global order harms the poor. For example, the cost to poor countries of rich-country subsidies, tariffs and quotas may be more than rich-country aid. Aid can save lives, and additional aid might have public support (Stiglitz 2002: xii–xv, 61, 269; Riddell 2007). The IFIs have collaborated with violating regimes (Darrow 2003: 95–6). The World Bank estimates that the West has received $500–800 billion in illegal transfers from poor countries since 1990, about ten times all aid (Baker and Joly 2009: 62).

Risse maintains that the global order not only does not harm the poor but has massively improved human well-being over the past 200 years. The global order is therefore not fundamentally unjust but incompletely just. Pogge assumes that the global order causes oppression and poverty, but oppression and poverty pre-existed this order, and it is hard to say whether that order has made them worse (Risse 2005a: 9–17). Empirical research suggests that the quality of national institutions is the primary explanation of developmental success or failure and that integration into the global economy plays little independent role. Pogge does not prove that the global order causes poverty: he implies that the global order causes poverty because the ideal world would cause none (Risse 2005b).

This argument is flawed. The empirical evidence upon which Risse relies does not show that the global order does not cause poverty but, rather, that national institutions are more important than international trade in explaining development. It does not refute Pogge's claim that international institutions cause some of the defects of national institutions. Pogge does not condemn the global order for not being ideal but for not being just. *Minimal justice* requires that human rights be fulfilled as far as possible. He claims that global rules *avoidably* deny many people enjoyment of their human rights. The cost of abolishing world poverty is affordable (Pogge 2005b: 1–5). The weakness of Pogge's argument is that it depends on an incomplete theory of the causes of global poverty.

Conclusion

The implementation of human rights depends on various economic factors. Human-rights activists and scholars have largely ignored economics, although this is beginning to change. Economists have largely ignored human rights. The concept of human rights emphasizes the rights of individuals with little concern for the costs of implementing rights or deciding priorities when resources are scarce. Human-rights policy should be based on sound economics while economic policy should be constrained by respect for human rights as far as possible.

9

Human Rights in the Twenty-first Century

Learning from history

The concept of human rights is now so familiar that we need to remember how new it is. It is true that, according to some scholars, the concept of 'rights' was implicit in ancient cultures: the commandment 'thou shalt not steal', for example, they say, implies the right to property. Other scholars, however, maintain that legal disputes in classical Greece were decided by reference to the common good rather than to the rights of the parties. Miller has nevertheless made a strong case that the concept of *citizens' rights* is found in the political philosophy of Aristotle (Miller, F. 1995). The Stoic philosophers had the concept of universal natural law, but not of natural rights. It was not until the Middle Ages that, within the framework of Christian theology, the concept of universal natural rights could emerge.

There is another way of thinking about the history of the concept of human rights in different cultures. At the core of *our* concept of human rights is the idea of protecting individuals (and perhaps groups) from *the abuse of power*. All human societies have power structures, and many of them have throughout history had some conception of the abuse of power. The concepts of *natural rights* and *human rights* are particular ways of expressing this concern about the abuse of power.

Some say that the concept of human rights derives from the political struggles and the property interests of the bourgeoisie in seventeenth-century England (Donnelly 1989: 89, 104–5). Recent research has, however, shown that there was lively debate, if little systematic theory, about natural rights among late-medieval Christian philosophers and theologians centuries earlier (Tierney 1997). Medieval debates about rights were concerned with property, but not only with property. The Magna Carta of 1215 provided for the right to a fair trial. Medieval Christian natural-rights theory was concerned with, among other things, the right to *subsistence*. In the sixteenth century Las Casas and Vitoria used a Christian conception of natural rights to condemn Spanish imperialism in America. Medieval debates were conducted in Latin, and in Latin the concept of 'property' refers to what is one's own, and that may include one's life and liberty. We see this late-medieval conception of rights in the political philosophy of Locke, who was the first modern natural-rights thinker, but influenced by medieval conceptions of natural rights. This more complex history of the origins of modern rights theory is relevant to human-rights debates today, because it shows that talk of 'three generations' of rights is unhistorical, and that the distinction between civil and political rights, on the one hand, and economic and social rights, on the other, cannot be derived from the history of the concept, which was concerned first with the right to subsistence and other (economic) property rights, and then with civil and political rights, because these were thought to be necessary to secure the basic rights to survival and property.

The concept of natural rights in the seventeenth and eighteenth centuries was associated with 1) opposition to absolute monarchy; 2) emergent capitalism; and 3) dissident Protestantism or secularized political thought. These themes burst onto the stage of world history in the English Revolution of 1642–49, and the American and French Revolutions of the late eighteenth century.

The violent disorder of the French Revolution provoked a strong *philosophical* reaction that targeted the concept of natural rights as a) subversive, and b) unscientific. The concept of natural rights derived the natural rights of individuals from the supposed will of God and the belief that *reason* could tell us what was right and wrong. The scientific philosophy of the eighteenth and nineteenth centuries undermined the concept of the natural rights of individuals and replaced it with that of the science of society (sociology). Saint-Simon, Comte, Marx, Weber and Durkheim were the leaders of this development. Rights were no longer fundamental moral ideas to regulate political life, but *ideological* products of social struggle. The social sciences marginalized the concept of rights. When the United Nations, after the Second World War, revived the eighteenth-century concept of the Rights of Man as *human rights* in order to express its liberal-democratic opposition to Fascism, it ignored this social-scientific tradition. Both the concept of human rights and the social sciences have flourished since 1945, but for the most part independently of each other. Recently, the increasing influence of the concept of human rights in international and national politics, especially since the end of the Cold War, has made some social scientists aware of the fact that they have ignored a major social development of the past 50 years. At last, they are applying their distinctive concepts, theories and methods to the real world of human rights and their violation. I have, in this book, offered a review, both sympathetic and critical, of the new social science of human rights in the hope that it will advance the reconciliation of ethical idealism and scientific realism that the academic study of human rights requires.

After the adoption of the Universal Declaration of Human Rights by the UN General Assembly in 1948, the slow process of standard-setting (international human-rights law) and institution-building began. The Cold War blocked progress for human rights, however, as Communist regimes perpetrated gross violations of civil and political rights, and the West was implicated in massive violations, either directly or through support of anti-Communist dictatorships. Worldwide decolonization brought many new states to the UN. At first anti-colonial elites found the concept of human rights helpful to their cause, but, after independence post-colonial state leaders gave priority to economic development, self-determination and anti-racism, but resisted human-rights criticism from the West and domestic oppositions. Many post-colonial states had terrible records in the violation of civil and political rights, and few were successful in protecting economic and social rights. Nevertheless, the international campaign against apartheid in South Africa established the principle that human-rights violations within one nation-state were properly the object of condemnation and sanctions by the international community.

The progress of human rights since 1948 has a number of significant landmarks: the foundation of Amnesty International (1961); the two UN covenants of 1966; the Helsinki Accord of 1975; the human-rights foreign policy of President Jimmy Carter in the 1970s; the democratization of various Latin American and European countries from the mid-1980s; the Vienna Conference 1993. The end of the Cold War at the end of the 1980s produced contradictory results: liberalization in many former Communist societies, but violent ethno-nationalist conflict in many others. By the end of the twentieth century the concept of human rights had become a 'hegemonic ideology'; there had been a tremendous expansion of human-rights law and institutions; there had been great real advances in many countries; and there were many unsolved political problems in the world that still gave rise to grave human-rights violations. Only six years before the century ended, more than half a million citizens of Rwanda were murdered by their government in a state-sponsored genocide. The battle for human rights was far from won.

Human rights may seem like an idea whose time has come, but this proposition must be treated with caution. We should not accept the extreme Idealist view that the concept of human rights is very powerful in international politics: states still resist human-rights pressures from within and outside their societies when they think that their interests are threatened. We should not, however, take the extreme Realist view that the concept makes no significant difference to international politics. Communist human-rights violations may have been brought to an end because the West won the Cold War, but the concept of human rights played a role in that war. The social sciences can clarify the respective roles of ideas and material interests in the politics of human rights, although isolating causal connections in international politics is difficult, and there is still much we do not know about the 'power' of human rights.

Some critics believe that the concept of human rights is too *individualistic* and *legalistic*, so that the *structural* causes of human-rights violations, especially of economic and social rights, are ignored. This view almost certainly underestimates the achievements of the human-rights movement based on human-rights law. The structural approach is nevertheless useful in emphasizing the role played by inequalities of political power and the dynamics of the global economy in the causation of human-rights violations. It is limited by the difficulty of identifying alternative structures that would better protect human rights and are attainable. States, international institutions and transnational corporations are the principal players in international politics. NGOs have played an increasingly important role, but their resources and power are relatively weak. The UN is seriously under-funded. Its weakness can be explained by *the principle of limited sacrifice*. We are human and decent, and so we say that everyone ought to enjoy their human rights. However, human-rights declarations are cheap, whereas human-rights implementation is rather expensive. We are unwilling to pay the bill. We are disappointed by the gap between human-rights ideals and human-rights realities, but we are unwilling to recognize our fault in creating that gap, and find it easier to blame economic structures or supposedly ineffective institutions such as the UN. The weakness of the structural approach is that it fails to locate sources of possible change. The strength of the activist approach is that it emphasizes that we are responsible for the structures that we support. Human-rights activists have, however, begun to tackle the structural sources of human-rights violations, and so the idealist and structuralist approaches may be converging.

The history of the concept of human rights supports the contemporary thesis that human rights are 'indivisible' in that basic human material interests are closely connected with political freedom. This history shows, too, that the concept reaches for the fundamental conditions of human well-being while evolving in response to changing social conditions. The social constructivist theory of human rights advocated by Donnelly emphasizes the changing nature of human rights (Donnelly 1985a: 87). The social sciences can explain these changes, although their achievements in doing so have so far been disappointing. Social constructivism, however, gives us no standard for *evaluating* these changes. The legacy of the history of the concept of human rights is confusion about how ethical, analytical and explanatory approaches are related to each other. Historically, social science attempted but failed to replace the ethical approach to human rights. Reconciling the ethics and social science of human rights is a principal challenge of the future.

Objections to human rights

The history of human rights teaches us not only *that* the concept of human rights is controversial, but also rather precisely *why* it is. The principal criticisms that were made in the late eighteenth and early nineteenth centuries of the Rights of Man still bite today. Burke said that the concept ignored the value of national traditions. Bentham argued that it ignored the social nature of moral and legal concepts. Marx complained that it concealed and legitimated exploitative and oppressive social structures. Such arguments are still made today. There is a danger that the success of the concept can induce complacency and dogmatism. In the face of relativist objections to human-rights universalism for being 'imperialistic', human-rights advocates would do well to recall the origin of the concept in the revulsion against Nazism. They would do well to remember the victims of genocide in Cambodia and Rwanda. It is reasonable and salutary to subject the concept of human rights to philosophical and practical criticism. The contemporary appeal and influence of the concept provide reasons to subject it to critical scrutiny. The rhetoric of human rights is universal; the scope of human rights is not: there is a human right to food, but millions starve. In this book I have tried to show both the moral power of the concept, and the difficult theoretical and practical problems that it raises.

Beyond human-rights law

We cannot know the future of human rights, but the social sciences can throw some light on the darkness ahead. Risse et al., for example, have argued that human-rights advances are brought about by a combination of external and internal pressures on rights-violating states (Risse, Ropp and Sikkink 1999). The Vienna Conference of 1993 reinforced the commitment of the international community in principle to universal human rights. Most governments are formally committed to human rights, and the number and effectiveness of human-rights NGOs have greatly increased in recent years. Unashamed human-rights violating states are now much rarer than they were 20 years ago. Yet serious violations continue, especially against vulnerable groups such as women, children, indigenous peoples, minorities, migrant workers and asylum seekers. Here the limits of law and the need for social science are clear. Human-rights scholars have begun to recognize that the global economy and the global climate may have massive implications for human rights. This takes us beyond law to a number of technical disciplines that have until recently not appeared on the human-rights radar. The state-individual model of human rights, which international human-rights law inherited from Locke, must be expanded to tackle the contemporary and probable future threats to human rights.

The socialist critique of capitalism has been replaced by a more diffuse concern with 'globalization'. We saw in chapter eight that the concept of human rights has a complex relation with globalization, for it claims global validity while criticizing several powerful global institutions. Donnelly emphasizes the persistence of state sovereignty as a barrier to human-rights advance (Donnelly 1998: 152–3). This is true, but not the whole truth in at least two important respects. The first is that states are not the only abusers of human rights: transnational corporations and international financial institutions that are partly independent of states can be human-rights violators. The second is that states do what certain human agents decide that they should do, and the relation between sovereignty and human rights can be changed in the future, as it has been changed in the past.

State sovereignty obstructs the implementation of human rights partly because state leaders have an interest in violating human rights, and partly because ordinary people have a limited willingness to make sacrifices to defend the human rights of others. However, even if we can summon the will to defend human rights, it may be very difficult to do so. In 1994 the international community stood by while genocide was committed in Rwanda. In response, the doctrine of the 'responsibility to protect' was developed to affirm that sovereignty entailed the obligation to protect human rights and that if a state failed to fulfil this responsibility the international community might intervene. In 1999 NATO intervened by bombing Serbia to halt the ethnic cleansing of Albanians from Kosovo without the authority of the UN Security Council, and thus apparently illegally. After 9/11, 2001, the USA led an international intervention in Afghanistan to topple the government of the Taliban and then, in 2003, an invasion of Iraq. All these interventions removed rights-violating regimes; all killed innocent civilians; all left human rights changed but facing an uncertain future. The international community expressed concern about gross human-rights violations in Darfur, Sudan – some even calling them 'genocide' – but 'intervened' only with inadequate humanitarian aid and peace-keeping operations. The 'responsibility to protect' was failing to protect millions whose human rights were being flagrantly violated. The legal conception of human rights is inadequate for understanding this political complexity. It helps to identify the problem, but says rather little about the solution.

There is much talk in academic and political circles about the need for 'early warning' of human-rights disasters. This raises another difficult problem. We now have fairly good social-scientific knowledge about the early-warning signs of human-rights disasters. Relatively small-scale but persistent and systematic human-rights violations are often the precursors of much greater ones. The Nazi genocide of the Jews was preceded by several years of *relatively* minor human-rights violations, such as discrimination in employment. Although effective human-rights pressure from governments and NGOs, and skilful conflict-resolution diplomacy, may both improve the human-rights situation and reduce the risk of disaster, this may leave a difficult question of *when* to intervene. The problem is that the concept of 'early warning' suggests early intervention, but early intervention may easily be disproportionate and counter-productive. The international human-rights movement may help to prevent human-rights violations from becoming human-rights catastrophes, but the concept of 'early warning' does not resolve all the dilemmas of intervention.

Concluding remarks

Since the end of the Cold War, Western policy-makers have presented human rights, democracy and market economies as a package. The relations between markets and human rights are, however, complex, problematic and not fully understood. The relations between democracy and human rights are also problematic, because, although democracies generally respect human rights better than authoritarian regimes do, democracies can violate human rights, and the protection of human rights may require limitations on democracy. In practice, the Western powers have interpreted 'democracy' to mean free and fair elections, and, desirable though these are, they are not only not sufficient conditions for the protection of human rights, but sometimes accompany, and perhaps even cause, the deterioration of human rights. In many recent cases, this has been because elected governments have pursued market-based economic policies that have not only worsened the protection of economic and social rights for the most vulnerable sections of society (especially women and children), but also provoked disorder that has led to restrictions on civil and political rights. We must also distinguish between *democracy* and *democratization*, the process of political change that has a problematic relation to human rights for somewhat different reasons. The transition from authoritarianism to democracy may be a change from imposed order to regulated conflict. Where there is little or no tradition of democratic politics, and also economic hardship and/or ethnic divisions, the restraints that democracy places on conflict may break down. The results may resemble the human-rights catastrophes of Rwanda or Yugoslavia, in both of which countries the processes of democratization were involved in the ensuing human-rights tragedies.

The twenty-first century began with the future of human rights uncertain. Great advances have been made since 1945 not only in 'standard-setting' (international and national laws) and 'institution-building' (human-rights commissions, committees, courts etc.), but also in freedom and well-being for many people in many countries. There are still many countries in which civil and political rights are trampled on. Progress towards the recognition of economic and social rights has been slow, and largely rhetorical. Worse, neo-liberal economic policies reduced the protection of these rights for millions of people around the world who enjoy them least, although there has been some recognition (again, perhaps more rhetorical than practical) that liberal economics should be accompanied by 'safety nets' for the most vulnerable.

Human-rights academics tend to devote excessive attention to the UN system of commissions and committees. These may be important, but they are certainly not the only important institutions that affect human rights in the world, and they are probably not the most important. The concept of human rights is centrally concerned with the misuse of *power*. The social-scientific study of human rights should give priority to the primary centres of power and to the possible sources of resistance. This entails that human-rights studies should attend more to the G8, the G20, IFIs, the WTO and the foreign policy of the USA. The study of human rights should be integrated with political economy, development economics, conflict studies and the politics of democratic transition. The political theory of human rights has, since Locke, accorded to the rule of law a central place in the protection of human rights. This is correct. Nevertheless, both the theory and practice of human rights have suffered from being excessively legalistic. The kind of economics practised by Amartya Sen and the kind of applied moral philosophy developed by Martha Nussbaum may have more to contribute to the advance of human-rights knowledge than refined legal analysis of human-rights texts (Nussbaum and Sen 1993).

Donnelly has said that the struggle for human rights will be won or lost at the national level (Donnelly 1994: 117). This is only a partial truth. It is true that, notwithstanding globalization, the nation-state is still an important field of power. It is also true that for many people the single most important power that affects their human rights is their state and its institutions, especially its legal and law-enforcement agencies. It is also true, however, that for many others the structures and processes of the global economy and of global politics are more important. We should recall that many private corporations are richer and more powerful than many states. Risse and his colleagues rightly argue that a complex and finely judged mix of states and NGOs, of internal and external actors, provides the best hope for human rights in the coming years. We have seen that human-rights NGOs have increased greatly in number in recent years, not least in poor countries. Important distinctions are emerging between *international* NGOs, *national* NGOs and *grassroots* or *community-based* NGOs. Observers have noted tensions among these different types of NGO, especially between those from the rich North and the poor South. I have suggested that these tensions may be healthy because they entail *the democratization of the human-rights movement*, that is, the bridging of the gap between the discourse and practices of UN diplomats and human-rights lawyers, on the one hand, and, on the other, the ordinary people of the world, to protect whose dignity, freedom and well-being the Universal Declaration of Human Rights was adopted. Anthropology may have a special contribution to make to understanding this aspect of human rights, for it can link the concept of human rights to the cultural understandings of real people in real situations. In addition, a kind of applied human-rights anthropology is being carried out by various projects of human-rights education, formal and informal, around the world (Andreopoulos and Claude 1997; Mihr and Schmitz 2007). The social sciences have, after too long a delay, begun to take human rights seriously. We should hope that this welcome development will be accompanied by human-rights activists taking social science seriously.

References

Aaronson, S. A. 2007: Seeping in slowly: how human rights concerns are penetrating the WTO. *World Trade Review*, 6 (3), 413–49.

Abouharb, M. R. and Cingranelli, D. 2007: *Human Rights and Structural Adjustment.* New York, NY: Cambridge University Press.

Adaptation Fund 2010: *Financial Status of the Adaptation Fund, Trust Fund and the Administrative Trust Fund (as at 30 April 2010) prepared by the World Bank as Trustee for the Adaptation Fund.* Adaptation Fund Board Ethics and Finance Committee, First Meeting, Bonn, 14 June, Agenda item 11 a), AFB/EFC.1/5, 20 May.

Alston, P. 1992: The Commission on Human Rights. In P. Alston (ed.), *The United Nations and Human Rights: a critical appraisal.* Oxford: Clarendon Press, 126–210.

Alston, P. 1994: The UN's human rights record: from San Francisco to Vienna and beyond. *Human Rights Quarterly*, 16 (2), 375–90.

Alston, P. and Crawford, J. (eds.) 2000: *The Future of UN Human Rights Treaty Monitoring.* Cambridge: Cambridge University Press.

American Anthropological Association Executive Board 1947: Statement on human rights submitted to the Commission on Human Rights, United Nations. *American Anthropologist*, New Series, 49 (4), 539–43.

Amnesty International 1993: *Getting Away With Murder: political killings and 'disappearances' in the 1990s.* London: Amnesty International Publications.

Amnesty International 2001: *Crimes of Hate, Conspiracy of Silence: torture and ill-treatment based on sexual identity*, http://web. amnesty.org/library/pdf/ACT400162001ENGLISH/$File/ ACT4001601.pdf.

Andersson, H. 2010: Afghans 'abused at secret prison' at Bagram air base. BBC News Channel, 15 April, http://news.bbc.co.uk/1/ hi/world/south_asia/8621973.stm.

Andreopoulos, G. J. and Claude, R. P. (eds.) 1997: *Human Rights Education for the Twenty-First Century*. Philadelphia, PA: University of Pennsylvania Press.

An-Na'im, A. A. 1992: Toward a cross-cultural approach to defining international standards of human rights: the meaning of cruel, inhuman, or degrading treatment or punishment. In A. A. An-Na'im (ed.), *Human Rights in Cross-Cultural Perspectives: a quest for consensus*. Philadelphia, PA: University of Pennsylvania Press, 19–43.

Ashcraft, R. 1986: *Revolutionary Politics and Locke's Two Treatises of Government*. Princeton, NJ: Princeton University Press.

Ashford, E. 2006: The inadequacy of our traditional conception of the duties imposed by human rights. *Canadian Journal of Law and Jurisprudence*, 19 (2), 217–35.

Avalon Project at Yale Law School, *Documents in Law, History and Diplomacy*, The Atlantic Charter, 14 August 1941, http:// www.yale.edu/lawweb/avalon/wwii/atlantic.htm.

Baderin, M. A. 2007: Islam and the realization of human rights in the Muslim world: a reflection on two essential approaches and two divergent perspectives. *The Muslim World Journal of Human Rights*, 4 (1), 1–25, http://www.bepress.com/mwjhr/vol4/iss1/ art6.

Baehr P. R. 1999: *Human Rights: universality in practice*. Basingstoke: Macmillan.

Baer, P. 2006: Adaptation: Who pays whom? In W. N. Adger, J. Paavola, S. Huq and M. J. Mace (eds.), *Fairness in Adaptation to Climate Change*. Cambridge, MA: MIT Press, 131–53.

Bailyn, B. 1992: *The Ideological Origins of the American Revolution*. Cambridge, MA: Harvard University Press, enlarged edition.

Baker, K. M. 1994: The idea of a declaration of rights. In D. Van Kley (ed.), *The French Idea of Freedom: the Old Regime and the Declaration of Rights of 1789*. Stanford, CA: Stanford University Press, 154–96.

Baker, R. and Joly, E. 2009: Illicit money: can it be stopped? *New York Review of Books*, LVI (19), 3–16 December, 61–4.

Barnett, C. R. 1988: Is there a scientific basis in anthropology for the ethics of human rights? In T. E. Downing and G. Kushner (eds.), *Human Rights and Anthropology*. Cambridge, MA: Cultural Survival, 21–6.

Barnett, H. G. 1948: On science and human rights. *American Anthropologist*, New Series, 50 (2), 352–5.

Barratt, B. 2004: Aiding or abetting: British foreign aid decisions and recipient country human rights. In S. C. Carey and S. C. Poe (eds.), *Understanding Human Rights Violations: New Systematic Studies*. Aldershot: Ashgate, 43–62.

Barria, L. A. and Roper, S. D. 2005: How effective are international criminal tribunals? An analysis of the ICTY and the ICTR. *International Journal of Human Rights*, 9 (3), 349–68.

Barry, B. M. 2001: *Culture and Equality: an egalitarian critique of multiculturalism*. Cambridge: Polity Press.

Becker, C. 1966: *The Declaration of Independence: a study in the history of political ideas*. New York, NY: Alfred A. Knopf.

Bellah, R. N. 1983: The ethical aims of social inquiry. In N. Haan, R. N. Bellah, P. Rabinow and W. M. Sullivan (eds.), *Social Science as Moral Inquiry*. New York, NY: Columbia University Press, 360–81.

Benedek, W. 2007: The World Trade Organization and human rights. In W. Benedek, K. De Feyter and F. Marrella (eds.), *Economic Globalisation and Human Rights*. Cambridge: Cambridge University Press, 137–69.

Beran, H. 1984: A liberal theory of secession. *Political Studies*, 32 (1), 21–31.

Beran, H. 1988: More theory of secession: a response to Birch. *Political Studies*, 36 (2), 316–23.

Besley, T. and Burgess, R. 2003: Halving global poverty. *Journal of Economic Perspectives*, 17 (3), 3–22.

Binion, G. 1995: Human rights: a feminist perspective. *Human Rights Quarterly*, 17 (3), 509–26.

Birch, A. H. 1984: Another liberal theory of secession. *Political Studies*, 32 (4), 596–602.

Blasi, G. J. and Cingranelli, D. L. 1996: Do constitutions and institutions help protect human rights? In D. L. Cingranelli (ed.), *Human Rights and Developing Countries*. Greenwich, CT: JAI Press, vol. 4, 223–37.

Bleisch, B. 2009: Complicity in harmful action: contributing to world poverty and duties of care. In E. Mack, M. Schramm, S. Klasen and T. Pogge (eds.), *Absolute Poverty and Global Justice: empirical data – moral theories – initiatives*. Farnham: Ashgate, 157–66.

Bob, C. 2002: Merchants of morality. *Foreign Policy*, March/April, 36–45.

Boisson de Chazournes, L. 2007: The Bretton Woods institutions and human rights: converging tendencies. In W. Benedek, K. De Feyter and F. Marrella (eds.), *Economic Globalisation and Human Rights*. Cambridge: Cambridge University Press, 210–42.

Breay, C. 2002: *Magna Carta: manuscripts and myths*. London: The British Library.

Breen, C. 2005: Rationalising the work of UN human rights bodies or reducing the input of NGOs? The changing role of human rights NGOs at the United Nations. *Non-State Actors and International Law*, 5 (2), 101–26.

Brett, A. S. 2003: *Liberty, Right and Nature*. Cambridge: Cambridge University Press.

Brett, R. 1995: The role and limits of human rights NGOs at the United Nations. *Political Studies*, 43, special issue 'Politics and Human Rights', 96–110.

Brown, G. W. 2006: Kantian cosmopolitan law and the idea of a cosmopolitan constitution. *History of Political Thought*, 27 (4), 661–84.

Brysk, A. 2000: *From Tribal Village to Global Village: Indian rights and international relations in Latin America*. Stanford, CA: Stanford University Press.

Buchanan, A. 2004: *Justice, Legitimacy, and Self-determination: moral foundations for international law*. Oxford: Oxford University Press.

Bueno De Mesquita, B., Downs, G. W., Smith, A. and Cherif, F. M. 2005: Thinking inside the box: a closer look at democracy and human rights. *International Studies Quarterly*, 49 (3), 439–57.

Burgerman, S. D. 1998: Mobilising principles; the role of transnational activists in promoting human rights principles. *Human Rights Quarterly*, 20 (4), 905–23.

Campbell, D. and Norton-Taylor, R. 2008: US accused of holding terror suspects on prison ships. *Guardian*, 2 June, 1, 9.

Caney, S. 1992: Liberalism and communitarianism: a misconceived debate. *Political Studies*, 40 (2), 273–89.

Caney, S. 2006: Cosmopolitan justice, rights and global climate change. *Canadian Journal of Law and Jurisprudence*, 19 (2), 255–78.

Cardenas, S. 2009. Mainstreaming human rights: publishing trends in political science. *PS: Political Science & Politics*, 42, 161–6.

Carey, S. C. and Poe, S. C. 2004: Human rights research and the quest for human dignity. In S. C. Carey and S. C. Poe (eds.), *Understanding Human Rights Violations: new systematic studies*. Aldershot: Ashgate, 3–15.

Carozza, P. G. 2003: From conquest to constitutions: retrieving a Latin American tradition of the idea of human rights. *Human Rights Quarterly*, 25 (2), 281–313.

Carr, E. H. 1949: The Rights of Man. In UNESCO (ed.), *Human Rights: comments and interpretations*. Westport, CT: Greenwood Press, 19–23.

Cassese, A. 1992: The General Assembly: historical perspective 1945–1989. In P. Alston (ed.), *The United Nations and Human Rights: a critical appraisal*. Oxford: Clarendon Press, 25–54.

Cassese A. 1995: *Self-determination of Peoples: a legal reappraisal*. New York: Cambridge University Press.

Chan, J. 1999: A Confucian perspective on human rights for contemporary China. In J. A. Bauer and D. A. Bell (eds.), *The East Asian Challenge for Human Rights*. Cambridge: Cambridge University Press, 212–37.

Chaplin, J. 1993: How much cultural and religious pluralism can liberalism tolerate? In J. Horton (ed.), *Multiculturalism and Toleration*. Basingstoke: Macmillan, 39–46.

Charnovitz, S. 1996–7: Two centuries of participation: NGOs and international governance. *Michigan Journal of International Law*, 18, 183–286.

Chase, A. 2006: The tail and the dog: constructing Islam and human rights in political context. In A. Chase and A. Hamzawy (eds.), *Human Rights in the Arab World*. Philadelphia, PA: University of Pennsylvania Press, 21–36.

Chase, A. 2007: The transnational Muslim world, the foundations and origins of human rights, and their ongoing intersections. *The Muslim World Journal of Human Rights*, 4 (1), 1–14.

Cingranelli, D. L. and Richards, D. L. 1999: Respect for human rights after the end of the Cold War. *Journal of Peace Research*, 36 (5), 511–34.

Clark, D. A. 2005: The capability approach: its development, critiques and recent advances. ESRC Global Policy Research Group Working Paper No. 32. Oxford: Economic and Social Research Council, Global Policy Research Group.

Claude, R. P. 1976: The classical model of human rights development. In R. P. Claude (ed.), *Comparative Human Rights*. Baltimore, MD: Johns Hopkins University Press, 6–50.

Claude, R. P. 2002a: *Science in the Service of Human Rights*. Philadelphia: University of Pennsylvania Press.

Claude, R. P. 2002b: Personal communication.

Clemens, M. A. and Moss, T. J. 2005: Ghost of 0.7%: origins and relevance of the international aid target. Center for Global Development, Working Paper Number 68, September.

Clemens, M. A., Kenny, C. J. and Moss, T. J. 2004: The trouble with the MDGs: confronting expectations of aid and development success. *Working Paper for the Center for Global Development.* Washington, DC.

Cole, D. and Lobel, J. 2007: *Less Safe, Less Free: why we are losing the War on Terror.* New York, NY: New Press.

Coleman, J. 1993: Medieval discussions of human rights, in W. Schmale (ed.), *Human Rights and Cultural Diversity.* Goldbach, Germany: Keip Publishing, 103–20.

Collier, P. 2007: *The Bottom Billion: why the poorest countries are failing and what can be done about it.* Oxford: Oxford University Press.

Compa, L. and Hinchliffe-Darricarrère, T. 1995: Enforcing international rights through corporate codes of conduct. *Columbia Journal of Transnational Law,* 33, 663–89.

Cottier, T., Pauwelyn, J. and Bürgi, E. 2005: Introduction: linking trade regulation and human rights in international law: an overview. In T. Cottier, J. Pauwelyn and E. B. Bonanomi (eds.), *Human Rights and International Trade.* Oxford: Oxford University Press, 1–26.

Cranston, M. 1973: *What are Human Rights?* London: The Bodley Head.

Dagger, R. 1989: Rights. In T. Ball, J. Farr and R. L. Hanson (eds.), *Political Innovation and Conceptual Change.* Cambridge: Cambridge University Press, 292–308.

Dahl, R. 1989: *Democracy and its Critics.* New Haven, CT: Yale University Press.

Darrow, M. 2003: *Between Light and Shadow: the World Bank, the International Monetary Fund and international human rights law.* Oxford: Hart.

Davenport, C. 2007: *State Repression and the Domestic Democratic Peace.* Cambridge: Cambridge University Press.

Davenport, C. and Armstrong, D. A. II 2004: Democracy and the violation of human rights: a statistical analysis from 1976 to 1996. *American Journal of Political Science,* 48 (3), 538–54.

Desai, M. 1999: From Vienna to Beijing: women's human rights activism and the human rights community. In P. Van Ness (ed.), *Debating Human Rights: critical essays from the United States and Asia.* London: Routledge, 184–96.

De Waal, A. 2008: Why Darfur intervention is a mistake. http://news.bbc.co.uk/1/hi/world/africa/7411087.stm, 21 May.

Dickinson, H. T. 1977: *Political Ideology in Eighteenth-Century Britain.* London: Methuen.

Dine, J. and Fagan, A. (eds.) 2006: *Human Rights and Capitalism: a multidisciplinary perspective on globalisation.* Cheltenham: Edward Elgar.

Donnelly, J. 1982: Human rights as natural rights. *Human Rights Quarterly,* 4 (3), 391–405.

Donnelly, J. 1985a: *The Concept of Human Rights.* London: Croom Helm.

Donnelly, J. 1985b: In search of the unicorn: the jurisprudence and politics of the right to development. *California Western International Law Journal,* 15 (3), 473–509.

Donnelly, J. 1989: *Universal Human Rights in Theory and Practice.* Ithaca, NY: Cornell University Press.

Donnelly, J. 1993: Third generation rights. In C. Brölmann, R. Lefeber and M. Zieck (eds.), *Peoples and Minorities in International Law.* Dordrecht: Martinus Nijhoff, 119–50.

Donnelly, J. 1994: Post-Cold War reflections on the study of international human rights. *Ethics and International Affairs,* 8, 97–117.

Donnelly, J. 1998: *International Human Rights.* Boulder, CO: Westview Press, second edition.

Donnelly, J. 1999: The social construction of international human rights. In T. Dunne and N. J. Wheeler (eds.), *Human Rights in Global Politics.* Cambridge: Cambridge University Press, 71–102.

Donnelly, J. 2003: *Universal Human Rights in Theory and Practice.* Ithaca, NY: Cornell University Press, second edition.

Donnelly, J. 2007a: *International Human Rights.* Boulder, CO: Westview Press, third edition.

Donnelly, J. 2007b: The West and economic rights. In S. Hertel and L. Minkler (eds.), *Economic Rights: conceptual, measurement, and policy issues.* New York: Cambridge University Press, 37–55.

Doughty, P. L. 1988: Crossroads for anthropology: human rights in Latin America. In T. E. Downing and G. Kushner (eds.), *Human Rights and Anthropology.* Cambridge, MA: Cultural Survival, 43–71.

Downing, T. E. 1988: Human rights research: the challenge for anthropologists. In T. E. Downing and G. Kushner (eds.), *Human Rights and Anthropology.* Cambridge, MA: Cultural Survival, 9–19.

Downing, T. E. and Kushner, G. 1988: Introduction. In T. E. Downing and G. Kushner (eds.), *Human Rights and Anthropology.* Cambridge, MA: Cultural Survival, 1–8.

Dworkin, R. 1978: *Taking Rights Seriously.* London: Duckworth, second, corrected impression.

Dworkin, R. 1996: *Freedom's Law: the moral reading of the American Constitution.* Cambridge, MA: Harvard University Press.

Easterly, W. R. 2007: *The White Man's Burden: why the West's efforts to aid the Rest have done so much ill and so little good.* Oxford: Oxford University Press.

Eide, A. 1992: The Sub-commission on Prevention of Discrimination and Protection of Minorities. In P. Alston (ed.), *The United Nations and Human Rights: a critical appraisal*. Oxford: Clarendon Press, 211–64.

Ellis, E. 2005: *Kant's Politics: provisional theory for an uncertain world*. New Haven: Yale University Press.

Evans, M. D. 2006: International law and human rights in a pre-emptive era. In M. Buckley and R. Singh (eds.), *The Bush Doctrine and the War on Terrorism: global responses, global consequences*. London: Routledge, 189–99.

Falk, R. 1992: Cultural foundations for the international protection of human rights. In A. A. An-Na'im (ed.), *Human Rights in Cross-Cultural Perspectives: a quest for consensus*. Philadelphia, PA: University of Pennsylvania Press, 44–64.

Fein, H. 1995: More murder in the middle: life-integrity violations and democracy in the world, 1987. *Human Rights Quarterly*, 17 (1), 170–91.

Fellmeth, A. X. 2000: Feminism and international law: theory, methodology, and substantive reform. *Human Rights Quarterly*, 22 (3), 658–733.

Finnis, J. 1980: *Natural Law and Natural Rights*. Oxford: Clarendon Press.

Flint, J. and de Waal, A. 2008: This prosecution will endanger the people we wish to defend in Sudan. *Observer*, 13 July, 41.

Foot, R. 2005: Human rights and counterterrorism in global governance: reputation and resistance. *Global Governance*, 11 (3), 291–310.

Forsythe, D. P. 1983: *Human Rights and World Politics*. Lincoln, NE: University of Nebraska Press.

Forsythe, D. P. 1989: *Human Rights and World Politics*. Lincoln, NE: University of Nebraska Press, second edition.

Forsythe, D. P. 1995: The UN and human rights at fifty: an incremental but incomplete revolution. *Global Governance*, 1, 297–318.

Forsythe, D. P. 2000: *Human Rights in International Relations*. Cambridge: Cambridge University Press.

Forsythe, D. P. 2006: *Human Rights in International Relations*. Cambridge: Cambridge University Press, second edition.

Fottrell, D. 2000: One step forward or two steps sideways? Assessing the first decade of the United Nations Convention on the Rights of the Child. In D. Fottrell (ed.), *Revisiting Children's Rights: 10 years of the UN Convention on the Rights of the Child*. The Hague: Kluwer Law International.

Foweraker, J. and Landman, T. 1997: *Citizenship Rights and Social Movements: a comparative and statistical analysis*. Oxford: Oxford University Press.

Fox, J. 2002: Transnational civil society campaigns and the World Bank Inspection Panel. In A. Brysk (ed.), *Globalisation and Human Rights*. Berkeley, CA: University of California Press, 171–200.

Franklin D. Roosevelt Presidential Library and Museum, Annual Message to Congress, 6 January 1941, 'The "Four Freedoms" speech', http://www.fdrlibrary.marist.edu/4free.html.

Freeman, M. A. 1980: *Edmund Burke and the Critique of Political Radicalism*. Oxford: Basil Blackwell.

Freeman, M. D. A. 1997: *The Moral Status of Children: essays on the rights of the child*. The Hague: Martinus Nijhoff.

Frey, B. A. 1997: The legal and ethical responsibilities of transnational corporations in the protection of international human rights. *Minnesota Journal of Global Trade*, 6, 153–88.

Fukuda-Parr, S. 2007: International obligations for economic and social rights: the case of the Millennium Development Goal Eight. In S. Hertel and L. Minkler (eds.), *Economic Rights: conceptual, measurement, and policy issues*. New York: Cambridge University Press, 284–309.

Futamura, M. 2008: *War Crimes Tribunals and Transitional Justice: The Tokyo Trial and the Nuremberg Legacy*. London: Routledge.

Gaer, F. D. 2001: Mainstreaming a concern for the human rights of women. In M. Agosín (ed.), *Women, Gender and Human Rights: a global perspective*. New Brunswick, NJ: Rutgers University Press, 98–122.

Gandhi, M. 1949: A letter addressed to the Director-General of UNESCO. In UNESCO (ed.), *Human Rights: comments and interpretations*. Westport, CT: Greenwood Press, 18.

Gardiner, S. M. 2004: Ethics and global climate change. *Ethics*, 114, 555–600.

Gewirth, A. 1981: The basis and content of human rights. In J. R. Pennock and J. W. Chapman (eds.), *Human Rights*. New York, NY: New York University Press, 121–47.

Gewirth, A. 1982: *Human Rights: essays on justification and applications*. Chicago, IL: University of Chicago Press.

Gewirth, A. 1996: *The Community of Rights*. Chicago, IL: University of Chicago Press.

Gilbert, J. 2007: Nomadic territories: a human rights approach to nomadic peoples' land rights. *Human Rights Law Review*, 7 (4), 681–716.

Glover, J. 1999: *Humanity: a moral history of the twentieth century.* London: Jonathan Cape.

Goodale, M. 2006a: Introduction to 'Anthropology and Human Rights in a New Key'. *American Anthropologist,* 108 (1), 1–8.

Goodale, M. 2006b: Ethical theory as social practice. *American Anthropologist,* 108 (1), 25–37.

Goodman, R. and Jinks, D. 2003: Measuring the effects of human rights treaties. *European Journal of International Law,* 14 (1), 171–83.

Gordon, N. 2008: Human rights, social space and power: why do some NGOs exert more influence than others? *International Journal of Human Rights,* 12 (1), 23–39.

Griffin, J. 2008: *On Human Rights.* Oxford: Oxford University Press.

Gurr, T. R. 1986: The political origins of state violence and terror: a theoretical analysis. In M. Stohl and G. A. Lopez (eds.), *Government Violence and Repression: an agenda for research.* New York, NY: Greenwood Press, 45–71.

Hafner-Burton, E. 2005: Right or robust? The sensitive nature of government repression in an era of globalization. *Journal of Peace Research,* 42 (6), 679–98.

Hafner-Burton, E. M. 2009: *Forced to be Good: why trade agreements boost human rights.* Ithaca, NY: Cornell University Press.

Hafner-Burton, E. M. and Tsutsui, K. 2007: Justice lost! The failure of international law to matter where needed most. *Journal of Peace Research,* 44 (4), 407–25.

Hannum, H. 1990: *Autonomy, Sovereignty and Self-determination: the accommodation of conflicting rights.* Philadelphia, PA: University of Pennsylvania Press.

Hathaway, O. A. 2002: Do human rights treaties make a difference? *Yale Law Journal,* 111, 1935–2042.

Hawkins, D. G. 2002: *International Human Rights and Authoritarian Rule in Chile.* Lincoln, NE: University of Nebraska Press.

Hayner, P. B. 2002: *Unspeakable Truths: facing the challenge of truth commissions.* New York, NY: Routledge.

Hayward, T. 2007: Human rights versus emissions rights: climate justice and the equitable distribution of ecological space. *Ethics & International Affairs,* 21 (4), 431–50.

Healy, P. 2006: Human rights and intercultural relations: a hermeneutico-dialogical approach. *Philosophy and Social Criticism,* 32 (4), 513–41.

Henderson, C. W. 1991: Conditions affecting the use of political repression. *Journal of Conflict Resolution,* 35 (1), 120–42.

Hirschman, A. O. 1983: Morality and the social sciences: a durable tension. In N. Haan, R. N. Bellah, P. Rabinow and W. M. Sullivan (eds.), *Social Science as Moral Inquiry*. New York, NY: Columbia University Press, 21–32.

Holt, J. C. 1965: *Magna Carta*. Cambridge: Cambridge University Press.

Howard, R. E. 1986: *Human Rights in Commonwealth Africa*. Totawa, NJ: Rowman and Littlefield.

Howard-Hassmann, R. E. 2010: *Can Globalization Promote Human Rights?* Philadelphia, PA: Pennsylvania State University Press.

Hunt, P. 2004: *Report of the Special Rapporteur on the Right to Health*. United Nations Commission on Human Rights, 16 February, E/CN.4/2004/49.

Hunter, I. 2001: *Rival Enlightenments: civil and metaphysical philosophy in early modern Germany*. Cambridge: Cambridge University Press.

International Council on Human Rights Policy 2000: *Performance and Legitimacy: national human rights institutions*. Versoix, Switzerland: International Council on Human Rights Policy.

International Council on Human Rights Policy 2008: *Climate Change and Human Rights: a rough guide*. Versoix, Switzerland: International Council on Human Rights Policy.

International Service for Human Rights 2010: The Democratic People's Republic of Korea accepts none of UPR's 167 recommendations, 22 March.

Jacobson, R. 1992: The Committee on the Elimination of Discrimination against Women. In P. Alston (ed.), *The United Nations and Human Rights: a critical appraisal*. Oxford: Clarendon Press, 444–72.

Joachim, J. 2003: Framing issues and seizing opportunities: the UN, NGOs, and women's rights. *International Studies Quarterly*, 47 (2), 247–74.

Johnson, D. 1992: Cultural and regional pluralism in the drafting of the UN Convention on the Rights of the Child. In M. Freeman and P. Veerman (eds.), *The Ideologies of Children's Rights*. Dordrecht: Martinus Nijhoff, 95–114.

Jones, P. 1994: *Rights*. Basingstoke: Macmillan.

Keal, P. 2003: *European Conquest and the Rights of Indigenous Peoples: the moral backwardness of international society*, Cambridge: Cambridge University Press.

Keck, M. E. and Sikkink, K. 1998: *Activists Beyond Borders: advocacy networks in international politics*, Ithaca, NY: Cornell University Press.

Keith L. C. 1999: The United Nations International Covenant on Civil and Political Rights: does it make a difference in human rights behaviour? *Journal of Peace Research*, 36, 95–118.

Keith, L. C. 2002: Constitutional provisions for individual human rights (1977–1996): are they more than mere 'window dressing'? *Political Research Quarterly*, 55 (1), 111–43.

Khan, I. 2009: *The Unheard Truth: poverty and human rights.* New York, NY: W. W. Norton.

King, M. 2004: Children's rights as communication: reflections on autopoietic theory and the United Nations Convention. In M. D. A. Freeman (ed.), *Children's Rights.* Aldershot: Dartmouth, 311–27.

Korey, W. 1998: *NGOs and the Universal Declaration of Human Rights: 'a curious grapevine'.* Basingstoke: Macmillan.

Kristof, N. D. 2006: Genocide in slow motion. *New York Review of Books*, 53 (2), 9 February, http://www.nybooks.com/articles/archives/2006/feb/09/genocide-in-slow-motion.

Kuper, J. 2000: Children and armed conflict: some issues of law and policy. In D. Fottrell (ed.), *Revisiting Children's Rights: 10 years of the UN Convention on the Rights of the Child.* The Hague: Kluwer Law International, 101–13.

Kymlicka, W. 1989: *Liberalism, Community and Culture.* Oxford: Clarendon Press.

Kymlicka, W. 1995: *Multicultural Citizenship: a liberal theory of group rights.* Oxford: Clarendon Press.

Kymlicka, W. 2001: Human rights and ethnocultural justice. In W. Kymlicka, *Politics in the Vernacular: nationalism, multiculturalism and citizenship.* Oxford: Oxford University Press, 69–90.

Kymlicka, W. 2007: *Multicultural Odysseys: navigating the new international politics of diversity.* Oxford: Oxford University Press.

Landman, T. 2002: Comparative politics and human rights. *Human Rights Quarterly*, 24 (4), 890–923.

Landman, T. 2005a: *Protecting Human Rights: a comparative study.* Washington, DC: Georgetown University Press.

Landman, T. 2005b: Review article: the political science of human rights. *British Journal of Political Science*, 35 (3), 549–72.

Landman, T. 2006: *Studying Human Rights.* London: Routledge.

Langford, M. 2008: The justiciability of social rights: from practice to theory. In M. Langford (ed.), *Social Rights Jurisprudence: emerging trends in international and comparative law.* Cambridge: Cambridge University Press, 3–45.

Lauren, P. G. 2007: 'To preserve and build on its achievements and to redress its shortcomings': the journey from the Commission on Human Rights to the Human Rights Council. *Human Rights Quarterly*, 29 (2), 307–45.

Leary, V. A. 1992: Lessons from the experience of the International Labour Organization. In P. Alston (ed.), *The United Nations and Human Rights: a critical appraisal*. Oxford: Clarendon Press, 580–619.

LeBor, A. 2006: '*Complicity with Evil*': the United Nations in the age of modern genocide. New Haven, CT: Yale University Press.

Leite, S. P. 2001: Human rights and the IMF. *Finance and Development*, 38 (4), http://www.imf.org/external/pubs/ft/fandd/2001/12/leite.htm.

Locke, J. [1689] 1970: *Two Treatises of Government*. Cambridge: Cambridge University Press.

McBeth, A. 2006: Breaching the vacuum: a consideration of the role of international human rights law in the operations of international financial institutions. *International Journal of Human Rights*, 10 (4), 385–404.

Macdonald, M. 1963: Natural rights. In P. Laslett (ed.), *Philosophy, Politics and Society*. Oxford: Basil Blackwell, 35–55.

McDonnell, T. M. 1999: Introduction. In *Human Rights and Non-state Actors. Pace International Law Review*, 11 (1), 205–7.

Mace, M. J. 2006: Adaptation under the UN Framework Convention on Climate Change: the international legal framework. In W. N. Adger, J. Paavola, S. Huq and M. J. Mace (eds.), *Fairness in Adaptation to Climate Change*. Cambridge, MA: MIT Press, 53–76.

McGrade, A. S. 1974: *The Political Thought of William of Ockham: personal and institutional principles*. Cambridge: Cambridge University Press.

MacIntyre, A. 1981: *After Virtue*. Notre Dame, IN: University of Notre Dame Press.

McNally, D. 1989: Locke, Levellers and liberty: property and democracy in the thought of the first Whigs. *History of Political Thought*, 10 (1), 17–40.

Macpherson, C. B. 1962: *The Political Theory of Possessive Individualism*. Oxford: Clarendon Press.

Margalit, A. and Raz, J. 1990: National self-determination. *Journal of Philosophy*, 87 (9), 439–61.

Maritain, J. 1949: Introduction. In UNESCO (ed.), *Human Rights: comments and interpretations*. Westport, CT: Greenwood Press, 9–17.

Mayer, A. E. 2007: *Islam and Human Rights: tradition and politics*. Boulder, CO: Westview Press, fourth edition.

Méndez, J. E. 1997: Accountability for past abuses. *Human Rights Quarterly*, 19 (2), 255–82.

Merry, S. E. 2006: *Human Rights and Gender Violence: translating international law into local justice*. Chicago, IL: University of Chicago Press.

Mertus, J. 2005: *The United Nations and Human Rights*. London: Routledge.

Messer, E. 1993: Anthropology and human rights. *Annual Review of Anthropology*, 22, 221–49.

Meyer, W. H. 1996: Human rights and MNCs: theory versus quantitative analysis. *Human Rights Quarterly*, 18 (2), 368–97.

Mihr, A. and Schmitz, H. P. 2007: Human rights education (HRE) and transnational activism. *Human Rights Quarterly*, 29 (4), 973–93.

Milgram, S. 1974: *Obedience to Authority: an experimental view*. New York, NY: Harper & Row.

Miller, A. M. 2009: *Sexuality and Human Rights*. Versoix, Switzerland: International Council on Human Rights Policy.

Miller D. 1995: *On Nationality*. Oxford: Clarendon Press.

Miller, F. Jr 1995: *Nature, Justice, and Rights in Aristotle's Politics*. Oxford: Clarendon Press.

Milner, W. T. 2002: Economic globalization and rights: an empirical analysis. In A. Brysk (ed.), *Globalisation and Human Rights*. Berkeley, CA: University of California Press, 77–97.

Milner, W. T., Poe, S. C. and Leblang, D. 1999: Security rights, subsistence rights and liberties: a theoretical survey of the empirical landscape. *Human Rights Quarterly*, 21 (2), 403–43.

Mitchell, N. J. and McCormick, J. M. 1988: Economic and political explanations of human rights violations. *World Politics*, 40 (4), 476–98.

Mitsis, P. 1999: The Stoic origin of natural rights. In K. Ierodiakonou (ed.), *Topics in Stoic Philosophy*. Oxford: Clarendon Press, 153–77.

Modirzadeh, N. K. 2006: Taking Islamic law seriously: INGOs and the battle for Muslim hearts and minds. *Harvard Human Rights Journal*, 19, 191–233.

Moravcsik, A. 1995: Explaining international human rights regimes: liberal theory and Western Europe. *European Journal of International Relations*, 1 (2), 157–89.

Morsink, J. 1999: *The Universal Declaration of Human Rights: origins, drafting, and intent*. Philadelphia, PA: University of Pennsylvania Press.

Mulhall, S. and Swift, A. 1996: *Liberals and Communitarians*. Oxford: Blackwell, second edition.

Murphy, S. D. 2004–5: Taking multinational corporate codes of conduct to the next level. *Columbia Journal of Transnational Law*, 43 (2), 389–433.

Mutua, M. 2001: Human rights international NGOs: a critical evaluation. In C. E. Welch, Jr (ed.), *NGOs and Human Rights: promise and performance.* Philadelphia, PA: University of Pennsylvania Press, 151–63.

Neuman, G. L. 2002–3: Human rights and constitutional rights: harmony and dissonance. *Stanford Law Review*, 55, 1863–1900.

Neumayer, E. 2005: Do international treaties improve respect for human rights? *Journal of Conflict Resolution*, 49 (6), 925–53.

Newman, F. and Weissbrodt, D. 1996: *International Human Rights: law, policy, and process.* Cincinnati, Ohio: Anderson Publishing Co., second edition.

Nickel, J. W. 1987: *Making Sense of Human Rights: philosophical reflections on the Universal Declaration of Human Rights.* Berkeley, CA: University of California Press.

Nickel, J. W. 2007: *Making Sense of Human Rights.* Malden, MA: Blackwell, second edition.

Nordhaus, W. D. 2008: *A Question of Balance: weighing the options on global warming policies.* New Haven, CT: Yale University Press.

Nussbaum, M. C. 1993: Commentary on Onora O'Neill: Justice, gender, and international boundaries. In M. Nussbaum and A. Sen (eds.), *The Quality of Life.* Oxford: Clarendon Press, 324–35.

Nussbaum, M. C. 1997: Capabilities and human rights. *Fordham Law Review*, 66 (2), 273–300.

Nussbaum, M. C. and Sen, A. (eds.) 1993: *The Quality of Life.* Oxford: Clarendon Press.

Oliner S. P. and Oliner P. M. 1988: *The Altruistic Personality: rescuers of Jews in Nazi Europe.* New York, NY: The Free Press.

O'Neill, O. 1993: Justice, gender, and international boundaries. In M. Nussbaum and A. Sen (eds.), *The Quality of Life.* Oxford: Clarendon Press, 303–23.

O'Neill, O. 2005: Agents of justice. In A. Kuper (ed.), *Global Responsibilities: who must deliver on human rights?* New York: Routledge, 37–52.

Opsahl, T. 1992: The Human Rights Committee. In P. Alston (ed.), *The United Nations and Human Rights: a critical appraisal.* Oxford: Clarendon Press, 369–443.

Othman, N. 1999: Grounding human rights arguments in non-Western culture: *Shari'a* and the citizenship rights of women in a modern Islamic state. In J. A. Bauer and D. A. Bell (eds.), *The East Asian Challenge for Human Rights.* Cambridge: Cambridge University Press, 169–92.

Otto, D. 1996: Non-governmental organizations in the United Nations system: the emerging role of international civil society. *Human Rights Quarterly*, 18 (1), 107–41.

Pagden, A. 1982: *The Fall of Natural Man: the American Indian and the origins of comparative ethnology*. Cambridge: Cambridge University Press.

Page, E. A. 2006: *Climate Change, Justice and Future Generations*. Cheltenham: Edward Elgar.

Paine, T. 1988: *The Rights of Man*. London: Penguin Books.

Paterson, M. 2001: Principles of justice in the context of global climate change. In U. Luterbacher and D. F. Sprinz (eds.), *International Relations and Global Climate Change*. Cambridge, MA: The MIT Press, 119–26.

Patten, A. 2005: Should we stop thinking about poverty in terms of helping the poor? *Ethics and International Affairs*, 19 (1), 19–27.

Paul, J. A. 2001: A short history of the NGO Working Group on the Security Council. Global Policy Forum, http://www.globalpolicy.org/security/ngowkgrp/history.htm.

Pauwelyn, J. 2005: Human rights in WTO dispute settlement. In T. Cottier, J. Pauwelyn and E. B. Bonanomi (eds.), *Human Rights and International Trade*. Oxford: Oxford University Press, 205–31.

Pavković, A. and Radan, P. 2007: *Creating New States: theory and practice of secession*. Aldershot: Ashgate.

Philp, M. 1989: *Paine*. Oxford: Oxford University Press.

Poe, S. C. 2004: The decision to repress: an integrative theoretical approach to the research on human rights and repression. In S. C. Carey and S. C. Poe (eds.), *Understanding Human Rights Violations: new systematic studies*. Aldershot: Ashgate, 16–38.

Poe, S. C. and Tate, C. N. 1994: Repression of human rights to personal integrity in the 1980s: a global analysis. *American Political Science Review*, 88 (4), 853–72.

Pogge, T. W. 2002a: *World Poverty and Human Rights: cosmopolitan responsibilities and reforms*. Cambridge: Polity Press.

Pogge, T. W. 2002b: Can the capability approach be justified? *Philosophical Topics*, 30 (2), 167–228.

Pogge, T. W. 2005a: Human rights and human responsibilities. In A. Kuper (ed.), *Global Responsibilities: who must deliver on human rights?* New York: Routledge, 3–35.

Pogge, T. W. 2005b: World poverty and human rights. *Ethics and International Affairs*, 19 (1), 1–7.

Pogge, T. W. 2005c: Severe poverty as a violation of negative duties: reply to the critics. *Ethics and International Affairs*, 19 (1), 55–83.

Pogge, T. W. 2007: Severe poverty as a human rights violation. In T. W. Pogge (ed.), *Freedom from Poverty as a Human Right: who owes what to the very poor?* Oxford: UNESCO and Oxford University Press, 11–53.

Pogge, T. W. 2008: *World Poverty and Human Rights.* Cambridge: Polity Press, second edition.

Pogge, T. W. 2009: Shue on rights and duties. In C. R. Beitz and R. E. Goodin (eds.), *Global Basic Rights.* Oxford: Oxford University Press, 113–30.

Pogge, T. W. 2010: *Politics as Usual: what lies behind the pro-poor rhetoric.* Cambridge: Polity Press.

Pritchard, K. 1989: Political science and the teaching of human rights. *Human Rights Quarterly*, 11 (3), 459–75.

Ratner, S. R. 2001–2: Corporations and human rights: a theory of legal responsibility. *Yale Law Journal*, 111, 443–546.

Rawls, J. 1999: *The Law of Peoples.* Cambridge, MA: Harvard University Press.

Raz, J. 1986: *The Morality of Freedom.* Oxford: Clarendon Press.

Reanda, L. 1992: The Commission on the Status of Women. In P. Alston (ed.), *The United Nations and Human Rights: a critical appraisal.* Oxford: Clarendon Press, 265–303.

Reeves, E. 2006: Quantifying genocide in Darfur (Part I), 28 April, http://www.sudanreeves.org/Article102.html.

Reeves, E. 2008: Darfur: millions of vulnerable civilians sliding closer to starvation: the international community fail to heed warning signs or hold Khartoum accountable. H-GENOCIDE@H-NET.MSU.EDU, 15 June.

Richards, D. L., Gelleny R. D. and Sacko, D. H. 2001: Money with a mean streak? Foreign economic penetration and government respect for human rights in developing countries. *International Studies Quarterly*, 45 (2), 219–39.

Riddell, R. C. 2007: *Does Foreign Aid Really Work?* Oxford: Oxford University Press.

Risse, M. 2005a: Do we owe the global poor assistance or rectification? *Ethics and International Affairs*, 19 (1), 9–18.

Risse, M. 2005b: How does the global order harm the poor? *Philosophy & Public Affairs*, 33 (4), 349–76.

Risse, T. and Ropp, S. C. 1999. International human rights norms and domestic change: conclusion. In T. Risse, S. C. Ropp, and K. Sikkink (eds.), *The Power of Human Rights: international norms and domestic change.* Cambridge: Cambridge University Press, 234–78.

Risse, T. and Sikkink, K. 1999: The socialization of international human rights norms into domestic practices: introduction. In T. Risse, S. C. Ropp and K. Sikkink (eds.), *The Power of Human*

Rights: international norms and domestic change. Cambridge: Cambridge University Press, 1–38.

Risse, T., Ropp S. C. and Sikkink K. (eds.) 1999: *The Power of Human Rights: international norms and domestic change*. Cambridge: Cambridge University Press.

Robertson, A. H. and Merrills, J. G. 1996: *Human Rights in the World: an introduction to the study of the international protection of human rights*. Manchester: Manchester University Press.

Rodman, K. 2008: Darfur and the limits of legal deterrence. *Human Rights Quarterly*, 30 (3), 529–60.

Rodrik, D., Subrahamian, A. and Trebbi, F. 2004: Institutions rule: the primacy of institutions over geography and integration in economic development. *Journal of Economic Growth*, 9, 131–65.

Ron, J., Ramos H. and Rodgers, K. 2005: Transnational information politics: NGO human rights reporting, 1985–2000. *International Studies Quarterly*, 49 (3), 557–87.

Rorty, R. 1993: Human rights, rationality, and sentimentality. In S. Shute and S. Hurley (eds.), *On Human Rights: the Oxford Amnesty Lectures 1993*. New York, NY: Basic Books, 111–34.

Roshwald, R. 1959: The concept of human rights. *Philosophy and Phenomenological Research*, 19, 354–79.

Rousseau, J.-J. 1968: *The Social Contract*. Harmondsworth: Penguin Books.

Rudolph, C. 2001: Constructing an atrocities regime: the politics of war crimes tribunals. *International Organization*, 55 (3), 655–91.

Rummel, R. J. 1994: *Death by Government*. New Brunswick, NJ: Transaction Publishers.

Sachs, J. 2005: *The End of Poverty: how we can make it happen in our lifetime*. London: Penguin Books.

Salomon, M. E. 2007: *Global Responsibility for Human Rights: world poverty and the development of international law*. Oxford: Oxford University Press.

Satz, D. 2005: What do we owe the global poor? *Ethics and International Affairs*, 19 (1), 47–54.

Saurette, P. 2005: *The Kantian Imperative: humiliation, common sense, politics*. Toronto: University of Toronto Press.

Schirmer, J. 1997: Universal and sustainable human rights? Special tribunals in Guatemala. In R. A. Wilson (ed.), *Human Rights, Culture and Context: anthropological perspectives*. London: Pluto Press, 161–86.

Sengupta, A. 2002: The theory and practice of the right to development. *Human Rights Quarterly*, 24 (4), 837–89.

Shachar, A. 1999: The paradox of multicultural vulnerability: individual rights, identity groups, and the states. In C. Joppke and S. Lukes (eds.), *Multicultural Questions*. Oxford: Oxford University Press, 87–111.

Shehadi, K. S. 1993: *Ethnic Self-determination and the Break-up of States*. London: Brassey's.

Shue, H. 1996: *Basic Rights: subsistence, affluence, and U.S. foreign policy*. Princeton, NJ: Princeton University Press, second edition.

Sikkink, K. and Walling, C. B. 2007: The impact of human rights trials in Latin America. *Journal of Peace Research*, 44 (4), 427–45.

Simmons, B. A. 2009: *Mobilizing for Human Rights: international law in domestic politics*. New York, NY: Cambridge University Press.

Slim, H. 2002: *By What Authority? The legitimacy and accountability of non-governmental organisations*. Geneva: International Council on Human Rights Policy.

Smith, J., Bolyard, M. and Ippolito, A. 1999: Human rights and the global economy: a response to Meyer. *Human Rights Quarterly*, 21 (1), 207–19.

Smith, J., Pagnucco, T. and Lopez, G. A. 1998: Globalizing human rights: the work of transnational human rights NGOs in the 1990s. *Human Rights Quarterly*, 20 (2), 379–412.

Snyder, J. and Vinjamuri, L. 2003–4: Trials and errors: principle and pragmatism in strategies of international justice. *International Security*, 28 (3), 5–44.

Sorabji, R. 1993: *Animal Minds and Human Morals: the origins of the Western debate*. London: Duckworth.

Sorell, T. and Landman, T. 2006: Justifying human rights: the roles of domain, audience, and constituency. *Journal of Human Rights*, 5 (4), 383–400.

Spar, D. L. 1998: The spotlight and the bottom line: how multinationals export human rights. *Foreign Affairs*, 77 (2), 7–12 .

Speed, S. and Collier, J. F. 2000: Limiting indigenous autonomy in Chiapas, Mexico: the state government's use of human rights. *Human Rights Quarterly*, 22 (4), 877–905.

Stammers, N. 1999: Social movements and the social construction of human rights. *Human Rights Quarterly*, 21 (4), 980–1008.

Steiner, H. 1994: *An Essay on Rights*. Oxford: Blackwell.

Stern, N. 2009: *The Global Deal: climate change and the creation of a new era of progress and prosperity*. New York, NY: Public Affairs.

Stewart, F. and Wang, M. 2005: Poverty reduction strategy papers within the human rights perspective. In P. Alston and M.

Robinson (eds.), *Human Rights and Development: Towards Mutual Reinforcement*. Oxford: Oxford University Press, 447–74.

Stiglitz, J. E. 2002: *Globalization and Its Discontents*. London: Penguin Books.

Stoll, D. 1997: To whom should we listen? Human rights activism in two Guatemalan land disputes. In R. A. Wilson (ed.), *Human Rights, Culture and Context: anthropological perspectives*. London: Pluto Press, 187–215.

Strouse, J. C. and Claude, R. P. 1976: Empirical comparative rights research: some preliminary tests of development hypotheses. In R. P. Claude (ed.), *Comparative Human Rights*. Baltimore, MD: Johns Hopkins University Press, 51–67.

Talbott, W. J. 2005: *Which Rights Should Be Universal?* New York: Oxford University Press.

Thompson, J. 2002: *Taking Responsibility for the Past: reparation and historical justice*. Cambridge: Polity Press.

Thornberry, P. 1991: *International Law and the Rights of Minorities*. Oxford: Clarendon Press.

Thornberry, P. 2002: *Indigenous Peoples and Human Rights*. Manchester: Manchester University Press.

Tierney, B. 1988: Villey, Ockham and the origin of individual rights. In J. Witte, Jr. and F. S. Alexander (eds.), *The Weightier Matters of Law: essays on law and religion. A tribute to Harold J. Berman*. Studies in Religion 51, 1–31. Atlanta, GA.

Tierney, B. 1989: Origins of natural rights language: texts and contexts, 1150–1250. *History of Political Thought*, 10 (4), 615–46.

Tierney, B. 1992: Natural rights in the thirteenth century: a *quaestio* of Henry of Ghent. *Speculum*, 67 (1), 58–68.

Tierney, B. 1997: *The Idea of Natural Rights: studies on natural rights, natural law and church law 1150–1625*. Atlanta, GA: Scholars Press.

Todres, J. 2004: Emerging limitations on the rights of the child: the U.N. Convention on the Rights of the Child and its early case law. In M. D. A. Freeman (ed.), *Children's Rights*. Aldershot: Ashgate Dartmouth, volume II, 139–80.

Tostensen, A. 2007: The Bretton Woods institutions: human rights and the PRSPs. In M. E. Salomon, A. Tostensen and W. Vandenhole (eds.), *Casting the Net Wider: human rights, development and new duty-bearers*. Antwerp: Intersentia, 185–210.

Tuck, R. 1979: *Natural Rights Theories: their origin and development*. Cambridge: Cambridge University Press.

Tully, J. 1980: *A Discourse on Property: John Locke and his adversaries.* Cambridge: Cambridge University Press.

Tully, J. 1993: *An Approach to Political Philosophy: Locke in contexts.* Cambridge: Cambridge University Press.

Tully, J. 1995: *Strange Multiplicity: constitutionalism in an age of diversity.* Cambridge: Cambridge University Press.

Turner, B. S. 1993: Outline of a theory of human rights. *Sociology,* 27 (3), 489–512.

United Nations Commission on Human Rights 2006: *Interim Report of the Special Representative of the Secretary-General on the Issue of Human Rights and Transnational Corporations and Other Business Enterprises,* 22 February, E/CN.4/2006/97.

United Nations Development Programme 2005: *Human Development Report 2005: international co-operation at a crossroads – aid, trade and security in an unequal world.* New York, NY: United Nations Development Programme.

United Nations Human Rights Council 2007a: Human rights impact assessments – resolving key methodological questions. *Report of the Special Representative of the Secretary-General on the Issue of Human Rights and Transnational Corporations and Other Business Enterprises.* A/HRC/4/74, 5 February.

United Nations Human Rights Council 2007b: Business and Human Rights: mapping international standards of responsibility and accountability for corporate Acts. *Report of the Special Representative of the Secretary-General on the Issue of Human Rights and Transnational Corporations and Other Business Enterprises, John Ruggie.* A/HRC/4/035, 9 February.

United Nations Human Rights Council 2008a: Protect, respect and remedy: a framework for business and human rights. *Report of the Special Representative of the Secretary-General on the Issue of Human Rights and Transnational Corporations and Other Business Enterprises, John Ruggie.* A/HRC/8/5, 7 April.

United Nations Human Rights Council 2008b: Clarifying the concepts of 'sphere of 'influence' and 'complicity'. *Report of the Special Representative of the Secretary-General on the Issue of Human Rights and Transnational Corporations and Other Business Enterprises, John Ruggie.* A/HRC/8/16, 15 May.

United Nations Human Rights Council 2009: Business and Human Rights: towards operationalizing the 'Protect, Respect and Remedy' framework. *Report of the Special Representative of the Secretary-General on the Issue of Human Rights and Transnational Corporations and Other Business Enterprises, John Ruggie,* 22 April, A/HRC/11/13.

United Nations Human Rights Council 2010: Business and human rights: further steps toward the operationalization of the 'protect, respect and remedy' framework. *Report of the Special Representative of the Secretary-General on the Issue of Human Rights and Transnational Corporations and Other Business Enterprises, John Ruggie.* A/HRC/14/27, 9 April.

Vincent, R. J. 1986: *Human Rights and International Relations.* Cambridge: Cambridge University Press.

Wade, R. H. 2004: On the causes of increasing world poverty and inequality, or why the Matthew Effect prevails. *New Political Economy,* 9 (2), 163–88.

Waldron, J. (ed.) 1987: *'Nonsense Upon Stilts': Bentham, Burke and Marx on the Rights of Man.* London: Methuen.

Waldron, J. 1988: *The Right to Private Property.* Oxford: Clarendon Press.

Waldron, J. 1992: Superseding historic injustice. *Ethics,* 103, 4–28.

Waldron, J. 1993: A rights-based critique of constitutional rights. *Oxford Journal of Legal Studies,* 13 (1), 18–51.

Waltz, S. 2001: Universalizing human rights: the role of small states in the construction of the Universal Declaration of Human Rights. *Human Rights Quarterly,* 23 (1), 44–72.

Waltz, S. 2004: Universal human rights: the contribution of Muslim states. *Human Rights Quarterly,* 26 (4), 799–844.

Washburn, W. E. 1987: Cultural relativism, human rights, and the AAA. *American Anthropologist,* 89 (4), 939–43.

Waters, M. 1996: Human rights and the universalisation of interests: towards a social constructionist approach. *Sociology,* 30 (3), 593–600.

Weeramantry, C. G. 1997: *Justice Without Frontiers: furthering human rights.* The Hague: Kluwer Law International, volume 1.

Weiss, T. G. 2004: The sunset of humanitarian intervention? The responsibility to protect in a unipolar era. *Security Dialogue,* 35 (2), 135–53.

Welch, C. B. 1984: *Liberty and Utility: The French idéologues and the transformation of liberalism.* New York, NY: Columbia University Press.

Wilson, R. A. 1997a: Human rights, culture and context: an introduction. In R. A. Wilson (ed.), *Human Rights, Culture and Context: anthropological perspectives.* London: Pluto Press, 1–27.

Wilson, R. A. 1997b: Representing human rights violations: social contexts and subjectivities. In R. A. Wilson (ed.), *Human Rights, Culture and Context: anthropological perspectives.* London: Pluto Press, 134–60.

Wilson, R. A. 2005: Judging history: the historical record of the International Criminal Tribunal for the Former Yugoslavia. *Human Rights Quarterly,* 27 (3), 908–42.

Wilson, R. A. and Mitchell, J. P. (eds.) 2003: *Human Rights in Global Perspective: anthropological studies of rights, claims and entitlements*. London: Routledge.

Wiseberg, L. S. 1992: Human rights non-governmental organizations. In R. P. Claude and B. H. Weston (eds.), *Human Rights in the World Community: issues and action*. Philadelphia, PA: University of Pennsylvania Press, second edition, 372–83.

Wiseberg, L. 2003: The role of non-governmental organizations (NGOs) for the protection and enforcement of human rights. In J. Symonides (ed.), *Human Rights: Protection, Monitoring, Enforcement*. Paris: UNESCO, 347–72.

Woodiwiss, A. 1998: *Globalisation, Human Rights and Labour Law in Pacific Asia*. Cambridge: Cambridge University Press.

Woodiwiss, A. 2005: *Human Rights*. London: Routledge.

Yogyakarta Principles 2006: *The Yogyakarta Principles: the application of international human rights law in relation to sexual orientation and gender identity*, http://yogyakartaprinciples.org.

Young, K. G. 2008: The minimum core of economic and social rights: a concept in search of content. *Yale Journal of International Law*, 33, 113–75.

Zanger, S. C. 2000: A global analysis of the effect of political regime changes on life integrity violations, 1977–93. *Journal of Peace Research*, 37 (2), 213–33.

Index